# The Golden Door Cookbook

# The Golden Door Cookbook

200 DELICIOUS AND
HEALTHFUL RECIPES
FROM THE WORLD'S
MOST LUXURIOUS SPA

*Michel Stroot*

INTRODUCTION BY

*Deborah Szekely*

BROADWAY BOOKS

NEW YORK

Broadway Books titles may be purchased for business or promotional use or for special sales. For information, please write to: Special Markets Department, Bantam Doubleday Dell Publishing Group, Inc., 1540 Broadway, New York, NY 10036.

BROADWAY BOOKS and its logo, a letter B bisected on the diagonal, are trademarks of Broadway Books, a division of Bantam Doubleday Dell Publishing Group, Inc.

Library of Congress Cataloging-in-Publication Data
Stroot, Michel.
The Golden Door cookbook : 200 delicious and healthful recipes from the world's most
    luxurious spa / Michel Stroot ; introduction by Deborah Szekely.
        p.    cm.
    Includes index.
    ISBN 0-553-06186-0
    1. Cookery (Natural foods)    2. Low-calorie diet—Recipes.
    I. Title.
    TX741.S77  1997
    641.5′63—dc21                                                          97-1654
                                                                              CIP

FIRST EDITION

Designed by Vertigo Design NYC

97 98 99 00 01 10 9 8 7 6 5 4 3 2 1

# Contents

# Acknowledgments

My great thanks go to

Deborah Szekely, founder of the Golden Door, for whom I have worked for the past twenty years. Her encouragement, fair judgment, and insight into what is possible in a first-class health resort taught me that there are no limitations—only a vast horizon of possibilities.

Alex Szekely, Deborah's son and our president, who has always been there for me with thoughtful and kind encouragement.

Rachel Caldwell, the general manager, my friend, and interlocutor, who has given me the gift of her patience. She has fostered my triumphs and minimized my errors.

Martha Shissler, our dining room supervisor, always at hand with her generous manner and humor.

Bill Wavrin, executive chef at Rancho La Puerta, opened my eyes to the simple artistry and nuances of Mexican cuisine during my stint there. And Ignacio Cerda Leon taught me their baking techniques.

Rebecca Kissler, a graduate of the Scottsdale Culinary Institute, has been a tremendous help, giving form to the many recipes. Our combined efforts have made the kitchen at the Golden Door more efficient and productive.

Peter Jensen, Mary-Elizabeth Gifford, and Anne Bernstein helped me put into words what I am more accustomed to putting on a plate.

Mary Goodbody, who adapted my recipes for the home kitchen, brought her considerable experience and consummate sensitivity to these pages.

My wife Irma, with whom I share the joys of healthy eating, has been my greatest ally during the many hours of writing, testing, and editing.

Finally, my gratitude to the guests at the Golden Door. Without their urging and constant prodding, this book would not have been written. They have been both my severest critics and strongest supporters. Their feedback is immediate; I would hear instantly which dishes were fabulous and which needed improving. The Golden Door guests, gourmet connoisseurs all, have challenged me to exceed my own expectations. To them I give my deepest thanks.

# Introduction

NOTHING STIRS THE MEMORY and emotions as much as good food. Only hours ago I ate a simple fruit salad at the Golden Door that was ambrosial—so many different miracles of tree and vine, each at perfect ripeness, crisp or silken, sweet or tart. While healthful eating is often this simple, it doesn't mean turning one's back on inspired cuisine. You can enjoy splendidly prepared foods while reaping incalculable benefits. We know this because it happens every day at the Golden Door.

At the Golden Door our cooking, even our snacks, astonish first-time visitors with their freshness, taste, presentation, and healthfulness. Thirty-nine guests each week feel positively indulgent, feasting on what's good and good for them. They eat with zest and without guilt knowing that each dish turned out by Michel Stroot, our remarkable chef, will delight the eye, the palate, and the soul.

The ambience of the Golden Door is the perfect setting for these revelations. Our Japanese gardens, with their meandering stone paths that make each step an act of contemplation, embody a peace and gentle passage of time that many guests haven't felt in years. Powerful in the worlds of entertainment, finance, and government, they expect the finest and receive it. While they discover our food, they rediscover their own wellsprings of fitness and energy. The Door is not a passive place: days are filled with hikes on a mountain fragrant with sages, stretching, exercises, massage, cooking classes, beauty treatments, long soaks in steaming waters, and provocative evening programs.

But ahh, the food. Here, in these pages, are the simple secrets of the Golden Door's cooking, which have served us so well for forty years. All of our guests' favorite dishes are here, as well as some of our most recent culinary creations. Our food is one of the many things that make the Golden Door unique, and the way we prepare and present it can change the way you eat forever.

To begin, keep in mind that the food we eat for nourishment also presents us with a pleasurable ritual. We seem to have forgotten what our parents and grandparents knew: the twilight hours can mark a true transition, an unwinding, from work to home. When our fathers and grandfathers got off the streetcar or train they strolled a few blocks to the house and sat awhile on the front porch sipping or nibbling something. Only then, at ease, did they dine with the family—the ultimate satisfaction of communal nourishment.

Racing today from car to office to gym to home, we forget that our bodies are the temples of our souls. We need to slow down to ask ourselves not only *what* we are eating, but *which* type of meal serves us best: a light one enjoyed in pleasant surroundings, or a hamburger and fries gulped down in five minutes? What builds lasting good health and provides continuous delight?

My passion for fresh fruits and vegetables, and how they are prepared, has been a central theme of my life since 1926. When I was four years old my mother, who was then vice president of the New York Vegetarian Society, encountered fruitarianism. One afternoon she emptied the icebox, gave away everything in the kitchen, including the bread box, and said, "From now on, we will eat nothing but raw, fresh foods!" I was too young to protest, but I do remember my father's and older brother's howls of dismay.

I remember the evening in 1931 when Father returned to our Brooklyn home from his usual day at work. Mother waved four steamship tickets to Tahiti at him. She announced that we were moving to this island paradise of fresh fruits and vegetables, and she'd never again have to attempt to ripen great clumps of bananas in our Brooklyn basement. And so Tahiti became our home for five years.

In the early 1930s, Tahiti was the proverbial land of milk and honey. Papayas, mangos, coconuts, and oranges virtually dropped from trees into our laps, and fish leapt into our pirogue. Except for the bread we bought from the baker, all foods on the island were grown locally. Refrigeration didn't exist, but it didn't matter; we simply ate what was in season. Early on I was exposed to this natural cycle of looking forward to certain fruits, watching with anticipation as they ripened, enjoying them fresh, and then moving on to something else.

Although I never became the extremist my mother was, my vocation and avocation began in Tahiti. The island's clime and geographic isolation made it a veritable Garden of Eden. I learned to trust the wholeness of natural foods. Although I could count my ribs, I felt the great reserves of energy I had as I bicycled miles each day to and from school, or paddled out with my brother to check our fish traps. In short, I learned to be guided in my eating by the wisdom of the body.

The next leap in my relationship with healthful eating occurred when my husband, Professor Edmond Szekely, and I founded the world's first health camp, which ultimately led to the founding of the Golden Door. Located in Tecate, Baja California, in a lovely vineyard in rural Mexico, Rancho La Puerta opened in 1940 to several dozen guests, mostly friends from Hollywood and Los Angeles. The minimal fee ($17.50 a week, bring your own tent!) was a standing joke, but people came. Originally called the Essene School of Life, the professor and I hoped to emulate the simple monastic life of the Essenes, who lived at the time of Christ and practiced the philosophy of Hippocrates, who wrote about the essential difference between living to eat and eating to live.

At Rancho La Puerta we consciously ate to enhance happiness, clarity, and vitality. We kept goats for milk and cheese. We grew organic wheat and vegetables. To supplement our menu, we bought beans, lentils, and chickpeas from local farmers. A photograph from those days shows an earthenware plate with homegrown sliced tomatoes, our own goat cheese, and a freshly baked sprouted wheat bun. That was dinner. We encouraged guests to find a quiet spot for eating and to acknowledge the wonder of their food before beginning. We urged them to visualize and admire the incredibly complex process of digestion, and marvel at the body's ingenious manner of utilizing food to sustain itself and build toward the future. Each savored, flavorful bite became a metaphor for a simple, vital life.

I feel enormous gratitude to those few spa guests who refused to go home that first winter. To accommodate them, we rented an adobe house and divided it into six monastic cells. There was no electricity or running water. My summer garden was dormant and, operating on a shoestring, I had to figure out how to feed everyone. Soups and vegetable stews, which I kept simmering on our wood-burning stove, became the backbone of our diet. We built a root cellar beneath our one-room house and stocked it with pickles, sauerkraut, and jars of home-canned tomatoes and fruit. We germinated wheat and baked bread in a traditional outdoor oven. I was gardener, cook, and bottle washer, and I had only one abiding concern, the health and satisfaction of our spa guests.

After a year I hired my first kitchen helper, Marguerita, who later became our cook. She stayed with us for more than thirty years. I taught her the elements of healthful cooking, and she introduced me to cooking with herbs, spices, and condiments, which I soon realized was the key to flavorful cooking. In the experimental years that followed, I became an aficionado of fresh herbs and spices from around the world, which are integral to the recipes in this book.

By the time the Golden Door welcomed its first guests in 1958, I had been feeding people both in body and spirit for eighteen years. Situated among citrus groves in southern California, the Golden Door attracted an ever greater variety of clientele. Hollywood producers, movie stars, and socialites came to the Golden Door to exercise, lose weight, rest, and renew. But serving them healthful meals in an atmosphere of serenity was not enough—we had to match up with the finest gourmet establishments. Although many experts had their own chefs and supped with royalty, I was not intimidated. What I had learned at Rancho La Puerta served me well, and the cuisine I instructed my early chefs to prepare for these guests did not disappoint. Like its sister spa, the Golden Door grows 75 percent of its food in summer and spring. From day one, the food we set before our Golden Door guests was organically grown, garden-fresh, delicious, nutritionally balanced, and elegantly presented.

Back then, portion control was a radical concept. Our low-fat, low-calorie servings were usually larger than their "sinful" equivalents, but how could I help guests realize they weren't "denying" themselves? You can't lecture about this concept, you have to show it! Each week we created our "100 Calorie Table." It was a chance to see *exactly* what a 100-calorie portion of an individual food looked like. We set out a wide selection. Here might be a platter of healthy, fresh cucumbers from our garden. The portion looked mountainous next to a bowl of six to ten lonely peanuts. A 100-calorie feast of spiced, unbuttered popcorn looked positively grand next to a two-inch square morsel of steak, or a portion of fish the size of (and almost as thin as) a playing card. Once our guests saw these incredible differences side by side, we knew they'd begin making healthier choices when they returned home.

I feel a profound pride when I think of the wonderful effect the Golden Door has had on our guests. We change their lives. Guests continue to shed pounds long after their visit. Over and over they tell me how they have adopted the Golden Door nutrition plan as their way of life. For breakfast they have fruit, a whole grain cereal (usually hot) topped with 1 percent low-fat milk, and a hot beverage. Lunch and dinner are, of course, interdependent and complementary. When a big dinner is slated, lunch might be salad with grilled seafood or chicken. Inversely, if there will be a low-calorie dinner, lunch might be pasta or soup and a light sandwich. We can create the best cookbook in the world, we can cook and eat the finest foods imaginable, but until we learn to routinely balance the relationship between each day's activities and the foods we eat, we're bound to run into trouble. Our spa guests soon learn to murmur to themselves as they peruse any menu, "Life enhancing or life diminishing?", and consider a day without exercise incomplete.

The good news for us is that medicine, science, and technology have joined forces to double and triple our life spans. At the turn of the nineteenth century, the average man lived to be forty-two, a woman forty-six, while today we are pushing ninety. The bad news is that we will now live long enough to suffer the cumulative effects of the preservatives, chemicals, pesticides, and contaminants increasingly present in our foods. If our bonus years are to be bountiful, we must keep a close eye on the quality of air, earth, water, and food we ingest and surround ourselves with because they will determine not only the length of our life but the quality of that life as well.

Although our nutritional needs have remained much the same over the years, the nature of how and what we eat has changed enormously—from a time when hunter-gatherers devoted the whole of each day to staving off hunger to the advent of the general store with its bulk staples to the supermarket and the mass availability of fast food. But additives, packaging, and advertising do *nothing* for our health. If we aren't mindful, mass marketing will take over the food we eat, further diluting much of its inherent virtue.

Being hooked on food itself—rather than on the way it is sold to you—is great fun. Soon you find that your kitchen isn't an archeological site full of half-used foodstuffs, stacks of heavy cans, and ancient herbs. You no longer ask "Isn't there anything to eat?" with hundreds of dollars' worth of food stockpiled in freezer and pantry, and depart for the nearest restaurant or takeout. You learn how to cook healthfully and creatively with the best foods nature has to offer. The recipes in this book will set you on that path.

Prepare a few of Michel Stroot's Golden Door recipes and you will quickly acquire a taste for the simplicity embedded in the preparation of the most delicious, whole and wholesome foods. The pearls of gourmet wisdom will then be yours. Any standard recipe can be made more healthful and delicious through conscious attention to the ingredients. Michel has mastered the art of cooking with pans that require only the slightest wisp of oil, if any. Michel always selects foodstuffs that are whole, low in fat, and seasonal (making them far tastier, more nutritional, and more affordable). He prepares them with love and awareness. We hope that *The Golden Door Cookbook* will awaken your appreciation of healthful foods and expand your imagination in a way that will go on serving you, in increased pleasure and vitality, forever.

There are, I have been told, one hundred billion stars in our galaxy. The universe inside us is every bit as vast and complicated; there are as many cells in the human brain as stars in the greatest galaxy. As long as they are supplied with fresh food, air, and water, these cells continue to grow, die, and replace themselves throughout life. Every instant of our lives we are building and rebuilding. We emerged from the oceans, and the liquid balance within our bodies reiterates that of the sea by bathing, lubricating, protecting us. Reverence toward the foods we prepare and take into our bodies is our way of participating in the mystery of life.

Deborah Szekely
*Founder, the Golden Door*

# Inside the
# Golden Door Kitchen

WELCOME TO THE GOLDEN DOOR. As you prepare the recipes in this book, I hope you feel as though you have visited me in my kitchen and I have guided you every step of the way. I want you to enjoy preparing these dishes as much as I do. At the Golden Door, we are extremely proud of our food and believe it epitomizes the best of spa cuisine.

Spa cuisine is about fresh, wonderful flavors and foods that are cooked carefully, but simply—never manipulated beyond recognition or drenched in obliterating sauces. It's about selecting the freshest and best fruits and vegetables you can, cooking ocean-fresh fish and free-range poultry. It's also about eating sensibly and healthfully in keeping with the Golden Door philosophy of balance in all things. It's about the pure enjoyment of life.

When guests gather for a revitalizing week of healthful living at our spa, enjoying the food prepared in our kitchen is only one of many pleasures. They also hike, exercise, meditate, relax with daily massages and facials, and socialize in a stress-free environment, surrounded by serene Japanese gardens, gently flowing waterfalls, and quiet ponds. The food, however, is always a highlight as guests look forward to their meals, juice breaks, and snacks. Because so many guests have asked for recipes to take home, I have compiled notebooks full of typewritten versions for copying, but until now have not codified them in a book. The more than two hundred recipes included here do not represent every dish ever served at the Door—but they are some of the best and certainly speak of the overall spirit of the food.

## THE ORIGIN OF THE RECIPES

Many of the recipes included in this book began as typed handouts for guests. Although I may have taught them at a weekly cooking class— which is among the best-attended events at the spa—guests have assured me that even recipes that had not been taught in class but that had appeared as handouts were accurate and easy to prepare in a home kitchen.

If you have been a guest at the spa, you will find some familiar favorite recipes here, such as Eggplant Caviar with Pita Chips, Fruit "Club Sandwich," Blueberry Bran Muffins, Stir-Fried Tamarind Chicken and Shiitake Mushrooms, and Turkey Patties on Garlic-Rosemary Buns. I have not neglected the vegetarian main courses: there are more than twenty, including our much-admired and requested Twice-Baked Potatoes, Caramelized Red Onion Pizza, and Wonton Ravioli. And when it comes to dessert, indulge in Phyllo-Dough Apple Strudel, Orange-Carrot Cake, Gingersnap Cookies, and fresh fruit sorbets. All wonderful, all much loved by our regular guests.

Even if you have never been our guest, these and the many other recipes will intrigue you and inspire you to try your hand at cooking healthfully and elegantly. At the spa, the swinging door to our kitchen is always open to guests who want to visit. I hope this book will be as welcoming and inviting to the home cook.

## THE SPA KITCHEN

Many first-time guests are surprised when they encounter my airy, bright kitchen. There are no shelves bulging with bottles of oils, boxes of spices, or packages of pasta and rice. Instead, there are bowls and small bins of grains, potatoes, and legumes on the countertops, and recently picked fruit, squash, and tomatoes from our gardens line the windowsills. A large walk-in refrigerator is piled with baskets of greens, mushrooms, beans, and berries. Because I cook food at its freshest, I do not stockpile large amounts. I rarely rely on packaged food.

A short walk from the kitchen door is an expansive organic garden, with the fruit orchards just beyond. It's not unusual to find me or one of my assistants stooped in the garden a few hours before dinner picking herbs, edible flowers, and lettuces to use that evening. Without question, my kitchen and gardens are a chef's dream of culinary heaven, and I am well aware of how fortunate I am to work in such ideal surroundings. But this does not mean you cannot create your own spa kitchen—on a smaller, more practical scale. And I've tried, with some of my recipes, to give an alternative to a fresh ingredient if you live where the winters are long.

Begin by reading through the recipes, the advice boxes, and the recipe notes. Do not be put off by the long lists of ingredients in some recipes. Each touch of spice and sprig of herb adds immensely to the flavor of the food, so I have not simplified these recipes at all. On the contrary, I have included every ingredient I use at the Golden Door. Do, however, rely on your common sense. If you cannot find a sprig of fresh rosemary or thyme, prepare the dish anyway. The same is true of techniques. If you choose not to fire up the grill to make grill marks on a chicken breast or tuna steak, omit the step, but do not omit the recipe from your repertoire.

Stock your pantry with a good variety of spices, vinegars, vegetable oil sprays, olive oils, chili sauces, dried beans, dried fruits, grains, and pastas, and, very soon, the more complex recipes will seem far less overwhelming. Additionally, shop seasonally and buy the freshest food you can find, and you will be well on your way to successful spa cooking. Get into the habit of making stock whenever you have a spare hour or two (vegetable stock in particular) and freeze it in small quantities so that you always have it on hand. It's essential to spa cooking.

## CALORIES, FAT GRAMS, AND A SENSIBLE DIET

Long ago, the Golden Door menu was dedicated almost exclusively to weight loss. Happily, those days are long gone and I now concentrate on preparing healthful, low-fat dishes that taste and look deliciously appealing without having to count every calorie and fat gram. This is the right approach to spa cooking, which, after all, is nothing more than interesting healthful cooking. Don't spend hours with calculators and thick books that list every gram and calorie for specific foods. Instead, concentrate on eating sensibly and seasonally, choosing foods that you know are good for you and eating a wide variety of them. These include vegetables, fruits, legumes, fish, seafood, poultry, grains, and whole-grain breads. They do not include rich cheeses, fried foods, red meat, cream sauces, and over-the-top desserts.

Guests at the Golden Door can opt for a low-fat, low-calorie menu designed for weight loss, which offers approximately 700 well-balanced calories and 20 grams of fat a day. Otherwise, the daily fat intake will be around 30 grams. While we do not count calories as diligently as we once did, the daily amount is in the 1200 range. (When we host men's week, the calorie and fat gram counts rise to meet the larger appetites.)

Every recipe in this book is accompanied by a nutritional breakdown so that you can easily calculate how much total fat, saturated fat, protein, carbohydrates, fiber, and sodium are involved. You also can determine the calories and cholesterol. The analysis for each recipe is per serving, and the amount of fat, carbohydrates, and protein is rounded off, which explains why you will sometimes see 0 grams registering as a percentage of total calories. If the number of grams is less than 0.45 grams, the amount will be stated as 0, but the trace amount still registers as a percentage of total calories. You will also find that the total percentages do not always add up to 100 percent. When calculating the percentage of calories from fat, carbohydrates, and protein, the number, or grams, is used in its actual decimal form, not the rounded off number. Use these as a guide, not an unyielding yoke. If you consume more than 30 or 40 grams of fat one day, cut back the next day. The goal is to feel satisfied, to eat healthfully, and to enjoy cooking and eating. For so many of us, this contributes greatly to our overall enjoyment of life.

# Breakfast and Brunch

WE ARE WELL KNOWN for our predawn mountain hikes at the
Golden Door, timed so that guests return to their rooms shortly after
the sun rises, more than ready for breakfast. This is served on a tray
in the room to give everyone a little quiet time before plunging into
the day's activities. Breakfast is simple: fresh fruit, a slice of bread or a
muffin, or a bowl of muesli or oatmeal. The juice is just-squeezed, the
coffee freshly brewed, and the entire meal designed to provide
optimum energy and clean, fresh flavors.

## THE BRAN TRICK AT BREAKFAST

The importance of fiber in the daily diet is now well known. Despite this, few people get enough of it unless they have a diet rich in vegetables, fruits, and grains.

Fiber is present in abundance in a daily Golden Door series of meals, of course, but at breakfast we're rather straightforward about being sure you get a good start on the day. We place a small egg-size cup containing a few generous tablespoons of bran on the breakfast tray, along with a very small tumbler of apple juice. It's a simple matter to pour the bran *into* the juice, stir with your spoon, and eat. Delicious, really. Add a teaspoonful of currants or chopped fruit as an added treat.

# Baked Apples with Kashi and Raisins

**T**HESE BAKED APPLES can be prepared a day ahead and reheated for breakfast in a microwave oven, which makes them great for busy families.

PER SERVING:

*168 calories*

*1 g total fat (4% of calories)*

*0 g saturated fat*

*0 mg cholesterol*

*1 g protein (2% of calories)*

*40 g carbohydrates*

*(94% of calories)*

*2 g fiber*

*4 mg sodium*

MAKES 6 SERVINGS

*NOTE: Kashi Breakfast Pilaf, a prepared grain mixture, is sold in many health food stores and some supermarkets. Do not confuse it with Kashi Puffed Grain Cereal.*

*If you make the apples the day before serving, cool them completely, cover, and refrigerate. When ready to heat, cover the dish with plastic wrap and microwave at High (100 percent) power for 2 to 3 minutes.*

½ cup Kashi Breakfast Pilaf (see Note)

¼ cup raisins or currants

1 teaspoon ground cinnamon

6 large Golden Delicious apples (2½ pounds)

1 cup unsweetened apple juice

2 to 3 tablespoons honey

*In a small saucepan,* combine the Kashi, raisins, and cinnamon with 1¼ cups of water. Bring to a boil over high heat, reduce the heat to low, and simmer, covered, for 40 minutes. Remove from the heat and set aside.

*Preheat the oven* to 375°F.

*Core the apples* and slice ¼ inch of apple from stem end. Holding a small sharp knife at a 45-degree angle, cut a shallow cone-shaped wedge out of the top of each apple to hold the filling.

*Spoon the cooked Kashi* into the apple cavities, mounding any excess filling up onto the tops of the apples. Arrange the apples in a baking dish just large enough to hold them upright. Pour the apple juice into the dish and drizzle the honey over the Kashi. Erect a tent of aluminum foil over the apples to prevent the Kashi from drying out.

*Bake* for about 45 minutes, until the apples are tender when pierced with a sharp knife. Cool slightly before serving.

# Oatmeal

VICTORIA REYNOSO, who is in charge of breakfast at the Golden Door, revealed her secret for delicious oatmeal. Patience and a very low flame are their own reward. For the best flavor and texture, serve the oatmeal as soon as it thickens.

PER SERVING:

176 calories

1 g total fat (7% of calories)

0 g saturated fat

0 mg cholesterol

4 g protein (8% of calories)

37 g carbohydrates

(84% of calories)

1 g fiber

3 mg sodium

MAKES 4 SERVINGS

1 cup old-fashioned rolled oats

¼ teaspoon kosher salt (optional)

¼ teaspoon ground cinnamon

1 red or green apple, unpeeled, cored, and grated (4 ounces)

8 teaspoons honey

¼ cup raisins or currants

*In a medium-sized saucepan,* bring 2 cups of water to a boil over high heat. Add the oats, the salt, if desired, and cinnamon. Stir once, reduce the heat to low, and simmer, uncovered, for 5 minutes, without stirring.

*Add the grated apple* and simmer for 5 to 7 minutes longer, stirring only once or twice, until the oatmeal is quite thick. Remove from the heat, cover, and let stand for 10 minutes, until very thick.

*Spoon into warmed bowls,* drizzle with the honey, and top each serving with a sprinkling of the raisins.

# Muesli

MUESLI ORIGINATED AT THE FAMED BIRCHER-BRENNER CLINIC in Switzerland and now is a worldwide favorite, often referred to as granola. While there are numerous blends of grains and dried fruit, I particularly like this one. It makes a hearty and satisfying breakfast, and it is thought that the soluble fiber may help lower serum cholesterol in some people.

PER SERVING:

*156 calories*

*4 g total fat (24% of calories)*

*1 g saturated fat*

*1 mg cholesterol*

*6 g protein (15% of calories)*

*24 g carbohydrates*

*(61% of calories)*

*1 g fiber*

*35 mg sodium*

**MAKES 6 SERVINGS
(ABOUT 2¹/₂ CUPS)**

1 cup old-fashioned rolled oats

¹/₄ cup sliced almonds

2 tablespoons honey

¹/₂ cup grated red or green apple, unpeeled

2 tablespoons diced dried figs, preferably Mission

¹/₂ teaspoon ground cinnamon

1 tablespoon grated orange zest (optional)

1 cup plus 2 tablespoons nonfat plain yogurt

1¹/₂ cups mixed chopped fruit, such as apples, pears, peaches, plums, and/or berries

*Preheat the oven* to 350°F.

*Toast the oats* for 15 minutes on a rimmed baking sheet. Remove from the oven and add the almonds. Using a metal spatula, stir the mixture well. Return to the oven for about 5 minutes longer, or until the almonds begin to turn golden.

*Drizzle with the honey,* stir well, and bake for about 5 minutes longer, until the mixture is fragrant and golden. Transfer to a large bowl and cool.

*Add the grated apple,* figs, cinnamon, and the orange zest, if using, tossing to combine. Store, covered, in the refrigerator for up to 5 days.

*To serve,* spoon into bowls and top with the yogurt and fresh fruit.

# Bulgur-Cinnamon Breakfast

**M**OST PEOPLE THINK ONLY OF OATMEAL when they consider hot cereal, but hot, cooked bulgur mixed with dried cranberries and sweetened with a little honey welcomes the morning just as happily. Our guests love the idea of pouring apple juice over hot cereal instead of the more expected milk—although both are very good.

PER SERVING:

215 calories

1 g total fat (4% of calories)

0 g saturated fat

2 mg cholesterol

9 g protein (16% of calories)

43 g carbohydrates

(80% of calories)

1 g fiber

70 mg sodium

**MAKES 4 SERVINGS**

1 cup medium-grind bulgur

3 tablespoons sweetened dried cranberries

$^1$/$_2$ teaspoon ground cinnamon

2 cups skim milk or unsweetened apple juice

4 teaspoons honey

*In a saucepan,* bring 1$^1$/$_2$ cups of salted water to a boil over high heat. Stir in the bulgur, cranberries, and cinnamon. Reduce the heat and simmer, partially covered, for about 10 minutes, until the bulgur softens. Add 1 cup of hot water and continue simmering for 5 minutes, or until all the water is absorbed.

*Serve in heated bowls* with the milk and drizzle with the honey.

# California Frittata

**T**HE MEXICAN-STYLE SALSA, crisp jicama, and tortillas contribute as much to the California flavor of this frittata as does the medley of fresh vegetables.

PER SERVING:

263 calories

7 g total fat (26% of calories)

1 g saturated fat

106 mg cholesterol

11 g protein (17% of calories)

38 g carbohydrates

(57% of calories)

3 g fiber

142 mg sodium

**MAKES 4 SERVINGS**

2 to 3 small red potatoes (6½ ounces)

1 tablespoon olive oil

1½ cups thinly sliced onions (4 ounces)

1 zucchini, thinly sliced (6 ounces)

1 cup thinly sliced cremini mushrooms (1¾ ounces)

2 plum tomatoes, cored, halved, and thinly sliced (6½ ounces)

½ teaspoon kosher salt (optional)

½ teaspoon freshly ground black pepper

1 cup shredded spinach or Swiss chard (1 ounce)

1 tablespoon slivered fresh basil (optional)

2 large eggs

3 large egg whites

3 tablespoons crumbled feta cheese (optional)

2 tablespoons chopped fresh flat-leaf parsley

¾ cup Salsa Mexicana (page 287) or other salsa

Four 6-inch corn tortillas

½ jicama, peeled and cut into ¼-inch-thick matchsticks (8 ounces)

2 teaspoons fresh lime juice

*Preheat the oven* to 350°F.

*In a saucepan,* combine the potatoes with enough water to cover and bring to a boil over high heat. Reduce the heat and simmer for 15 to 20 minutes, until fork-tender. Drain and cool. Cut into ¼-inch-thick slices.

*In a medium-sized bowl,* whisk together the eggs and egg whites.

*In a nonstick ovenproof sauté pan,* heat the oil over medium heat. Add the onions and sauté for 5 minutes. Add the potatoes, zucchini, mushrooms, and tomatoes and sauté for 2 to 3 minutes. Season with the salt, if using, and pepper. Add the spinach and basil, if using, and sauté for 1 to 2 minutes.

*Using a spatula,* pour the eggs into the pan. Transfer the pan to the oven and bake for 3 to 5 minutes, until the eggs are set.

*Sprinkle with the feta cheese* and parsley. Cut the frittata into 4 pieces and serve with the salsa, tortillas, and jicama, sprinkled with the lime juice.

# Spanakopita

**T**HIS GREEK FAVORITE, made at the Door with plenty of sautéed spinach mixed with eggs and low-fat cheeses, is a filling and tasty breakfast or brunch dish. You may also choose to serve it for lunch or even a light supper. Whatever your preference, take care to keep the phyllo dough under a damp, well-wrung dish towel when not working with it so that it does not dry out. This is particularly important in spa cooking because the phyllo is not drenched with melted butter, as it is in traditional recipes for spanakopita.

PER SERVING:

120 calories

3 g total fat (21% of calories)

1 g saturated fat

42 mg cholesterol

11 g protein (37% of calories)

13 g carbohydrates

(42% of calories)

1 g fiber

384 mg sodium

MAKES 6 SERVINGS

12 cups loosely packed spinach leaves (10 ounces)

½ cup diced onions (2 ounces)

1 large egg

1 large egg white

1½ cups 1% low-fat cottage cheese

¼ cup crumbled feta cheese (1¼ ounces)

1 tablespoon minced fresh basil or 2 teaspoons dried basil

1 teaspoon chopped fresh oregano

¼ teaspoon freshly grated nutmeg

Five 11-by-17-inch sheets phyllo dough (2⅔ ounces)

1 teaspoon poppy seeds

*In a large nonstick sauté pan,* sauté the spinach over medium-high heat for 1 to 2 minutes, until wilted. Cool, squeeze out the excess moisture, and finely chop. Set aside.

*In a small nonstick saucepan* sprayed with vegetable oil spray, sauté the onions for about 5 minutes, until translucent. Set aside to cool.

*In a small bowl,* whisk together the egg and egg white. Add the spinach, onions, cottage cheese, feta cheese, basil, oregano, and nutmeg.

*Preheat the oven* to 350°F. Spray an 8-by-8-inch baking pan with vegetable oil spray.

*Cut the sheets of phyllo* crosswise in half. Cover half of the sheets with a damp dish towel while you work with the other half. Lay 1 sheet in the baking pan and spray with vegetable oil spray. (The phyllo sheet will outsize the pan, but let it climb the sides of the pan.) Continue stacking 4 more phyllo sheets, spraying each one.

*Spread the spinach mixture* over the phyllo. Stack the remaining 5 sheets of phyllo over the spinach, spraying each sheet with vegetable oil spray. Tuck the edges of the phyllo into the pan. Sprinkle with the poppy seeds. Bake for 1 hour and 15 minutes, or until the top is golden brown. Serve hot or at room temperature, cut into squares.

## A LONGER BREAKFAST HIKE

As a week progresses, many guests enjoy being challenged by one of the Door's longer morning hikes. For these, each hiker carries a small, light knapsack containing a breakfast that she has requested the night before. We keep these trail meals very simple, knowing that the body is running at full steam and needs only something light, flavorful, and easy-to-digest: an orange, an apple, or a banana; a low-fat muffin; a hard-cooked egg, and perhaps a tiny piece of light cheese for those who request it; a small serving of nonfat yogurt; and bottled water.

# Appetizers

AT THE GOLDEN DOOR, we believe in eating well and eating
frequently. Throughout the day, we provide our guests with fresh fruit
and vegetables for munching, and we pay close attention to our
carefully prepared and beautifully presented meals. Perhaps no meal
is more important than dinner, when our guests feel refreshed and
relaxed after a full day of exercising both their bodies and spirits.
Appetizers and hors d'oeuvres begin the meal, and I take great care
that they appeal intensely to the senses of taste, sight, and smell.
Following this small indulgence, our guests enter the dining room for
dinner with their appetites pleasantly piqued, but not ravenously
hungry.

# Potato Skins with Ricotta–Sundried Tomato Dip

WHILE WORKING IN MEXICO, I noticed that the cooks snipped rosemary from the garden to use as a bed for baking potatoes or potato skins. Since then, I have made this a practice. The potatoes pick up some of the flavor of the rosemary—and the aroma that fills the kitchen is incredible!

*Dip*

2 tablespoons sliced soaked dry-packed sundried tomatoes (see Note)

1 tablespoon reserved tomato soaking water (see Note)

¾ cup low-fat ricotta cheese

1 tablespoon minced shallots

1 tablespoon balsamic vinegar

1 teaspoon dried basil

¼ teaspoon freshly ground black pepper

*Potato skins*

About 20 sprigs fresh rosemary

2 teaspoons dried salt-free seasoned parsley flakes (see Note)

1 teaspoon chili powder

1 teaspoon ground cumin

1 teaspoon paprika

½ teaspoon celery salt

4 russet potatoes, scrubbed (2¾ pounds)

*To make the dip,* in a food processor, combine the tomatoes, reserved soaking water, ricotta, shallots, vinegar, basil, and pepper and process until smooth. Transfer to a bowl, cover, and refrigerate until ready to serve. Let come to room temperature before serving.

*To prepare the potato skins,* preheat the oven to 375°F. Spread the rosemary sprigs on a rimmed baking sheet.

*In a small bowl,* combine the parsley, chili powder, cumin, paprika, and celery salt. Set aside.

*Using a small sharp knife,* slice off a ¼-inch-thick slice from all four sides of each potato. (Save the peeled potatoes for another use.) Blot the cut sides of the potato skins dry with paper towels and arrange them, skin sides down, on the rosemary. Sprinkle the cut sides evenly with the spice mixture. Spray with vegetable oil spray.

*Bake* for about 20 minutes, remove from the oven, and spray with vegetable oil spray again. Return to the oven and continue baking for 10 to 15 minutes, or until the potatoes are golden brown and beginning to puff. Serve with the dip.

NOTE: *To rehydrate dry-packed sundried tomatoes, soak them in warm water to cover for 15 to 20 minutes. Drain and slice. Be sure to reserve 1 tablespoon of the soaking water for this recipe.*

*Dried seasoned parsley flakes are sold commercially as Parsley Patch Seasoning.*

# Gravlax with Cucumber Salad and Mustard Sauce

G RAVLAX REQUIRES TWO DAYS to marinate. Then we slice it paper-thin and serve it with a small salad of cucumbers in a mint-yogurt dressing. The success of this first course depends on using impeccably fresh ocean, not farm, salmon.

PER SERVING:

142 calories

5 g total fat (33% of calories)

1 g saturated fat

38 mg cholesterol

16 g protein (45% of calories)

7 g carbohydrates

(20% of calories)

1 g fiber

1015 mg sodium

**MAKES 8 SERVINGS**

NOTE: *European cucumbers, sometimes called English cucumbers, are long and slender and essentially seedless. If you cannot find them, substitute garden-variety cucumbers, choosing specimens on the small side, which should have small, unobtrusive seeds.*

*Gravlax*

1 pound salmon fillet in one piece with skin (remove any scales, bones)

2 teaspoons crushed whole allspice berries

2 teaspoons kosher salt

1 tablespoon coarsely ground black pepper

2 tablespoons sake (rice wine) or aquavit

2 tablespoons chopped scallions (white parts only)

2 tablespoons chopped fresh cilantro

*Cucumber salad*

1 seedless European cucumber (14 ounces; see Note)

1 teaspoon kosher salt

1 tablespoon fresh lemon juice

1 cup nonfat plain yogurt

3 tablespoons chopped fresh mint

Pinch of cayenne pepper

*Sauce*

3/4 cup nonfat plain yogurt

1/4 cup low-fat 1% cottage cheese

1 teaspoon fresh lemon juice or cider vinegar

1 1/2 tablespoons grainy mustard

Pinch of cayenne pepper

*To make the gravlax,* place the salmon skin side down in a shallow glass dish. In a small bowl, combine the allspice, salt, and pepper. Rub the spice mixture evenly over the top of the fish and sprinkle with about half the sake. Scatter the scallions and cilantro over the fish and sprinkle with the remaining sake. Wrap the fish in two sheets of plastic wrap and return to the dish.

*Lay another dish or pan on top* of the wrapped salmon and fill it with heavy cans or other suitable weights to weigh down the salmon. Refrigerate for 2 days.

*To prepare the salad,* peel the cucumber, leaving a few thin decorative strips of peel. Using a vegetable slicer or a mandoline, cut into very thin slices. Combine in a bowl with the salt, tossing to coat. Cover and refrigerate for 1 hour.

*Drain the cucumber* in a strainer, pressing out any excess liquid. Rinse and drain again, to rid the cucumber of excess salt. Transfer to a bowl and stir in the lemon juice, yogurt, mint, and cayenne. Cover and refrigerate until ready to serve.

*To make the sauce,* combine the yogurt, cottage cheese, and lemon juice in a blender or food processor and process until smooth. Add the mustard and cayenne and pulse briefly to blend.

*To serve,* unwrap the gravlax and cut the fish into paper-thin diagonal slices. Serve with the salad and sauce on the side.

# Cucumber Filled with Smoked Salmon and Ricotta

**R**ATHER THAN RELYING ON CRACKERS, I spoon this full-bodied filling into hollowed-out cucumber slices.

PER SERVING:

*61 calories*

*3 g total fat (38% of calories)*

*1 g saturated fat*

*10 mg cholesterol*

*5 g protein (30% of calories)*

*5 g carbohydrates*

*(33% of calories)*

*1 g fiber*

*119 mg sodium*

**MAKES 4 SERVINGS**

1 English cucumber
(1 pound)

½ cup low-fat ricotta cheese
(4 ounces)

½ ounce smoked salmon,
finely chopped

½ teaspoon prepared
horseradish

½ teaspoon fresh lemon juice

1 teaspoon drained capers

Sprigs of fresh dill

*Trim the ends* of the cucumber and, using a spoon or dull knife, cut shallow channels along the length of the cucumber about 1 inch apart. Cut the cucumber into ¾-inch-thick slices. Using a melon baller, hollow out the slices to make a bowl, taking care to leave a sturdy shell.

*In a food processor,* combine the ricotta, salmon, horseradish, and lemon juice and process until smooth.

*Spoon the cheese filling* into a pastry bag and generously fill each scooped-out cucumber slice with filling. Garnish each with capers and dill.

# Salmon-Asparagus Log

**T**HIS DISH PARTICULARLY EXEMPLIFIES OUR PHILOSOPHY of presenting gorgeous food that, of course, tastes good too. The pale pink salmon contrasts beautifully with the spring green of the asparagus, and the Two-Pepper Coulis adds another splash of color. This is good served with a crudités platter.

PER SERVING:

*46 calories*

*2 g total fat (35% of calories)*

*0 g saturated fat*

*13 mg cholesterol*

*6 g protein (50% of calories)*

*1 g carbohydrates*

*(11% of calories)*

*0 g fiber*

*118 mg sodium*

**MAKES 12 SERVINGS**

NOTE: *Hot chili sauce is a familiar table condiment in Southeast Asia. It's a bottled mixture of vinegar, salt, and chilies—often sweetened with a little sugar. Asian markets carry an array of these sauces. Try them to determine which you like best. Some are hotter or sweeter than others.*

1 roasted red bell pepper (see page 99; 5 ounces)

Five 4-inch asparagus tips (1 ounce)

3 large egg whites, lightly beaten

8 ounces skinless salmon fillet, cut into 1-inch pieces

2 ounces smoked salmon

1 tablespoon minced shallots (¼ ounce)

2 tablespoons dry white wine

1 tablespoon fresh lemon juice

Pinch of cayenne pepper or dash of hot chili sauce (see Note)

2 tablespoons minced fresh flat-leaf parsley

2 tablespoons minced fresh dill

1 teaspoon minced fresh tarragon

Two-Pepper Coulis (page 285)

*Cut one half of the pepper* into strips. Put the strips in a bowl. Set aside the other half of pepper.

*Bring a saucepan of water to a boil* and cook the asparagus tips for 1 to 2 minutes, until fork-tender. Cool under cold running water, drain, and transfer to the bowl with the pepper strips. Add 1 tablespoon of the egg whites and toss to coat.

*In a food processor,* combine the salmon fillet, smoked salmon, shallots, the reserved piece of red pepper, the wine, lemon juice, and cayenne and process until nearly smooth. Add the remaining egg whites, the parsley, dill, and tarragon and process just until combined.

*Lay a 20-inch-long piece of plastic wrap* on a work surface and spoon the salmon mixture down the middle to make a 12-inch-long mound. Press asparagus tips and red pepper strips into the middle of the salmon mixture. Fold the plastic over the salmon log and twist the ends, forming the mixture into a log that it is about 2½ inches in diameter.

*Lay the log in a large steaming basket* set over boiling water and steam, covered, for about 15 minutes, or until firm. Remove the steamer from the heat and set aside, covered, for 10 minutes. Remove the steaming basket and let the log cool in the basket. Remove the plastic, slice into 12 slices, and serve with the coulis.

## MOVEABLE FEASTS

A tray is a marvelous thing. It allows a meal to go wherever we want it to: into the garden, by the pool, or onto the small table beside each room's private *engawa* and garden view. At home, it liberates you to enjoy your own deck, garden patio, or other sunny spots, indoors or out.

In the early days of the Golden Door's sister spa, Rancho La Puerta in Baja California, Mexico, founder Deborah Szekely and her husband, Professor Edmond Szekely, asked guests to simply choose their tray and take it to a quiet place in the garden. Eating was a time of contemplation and giving thanks for good health and whole foods. There was no dining room! An almost ideal climate (and plenty of comfortable rocks) made it possible.

Changing the *place* you eat lunch, especially, is a revitalizing tradition. Whether it be a break from the office in a nearby park or a special place to eat outdoors at home, we believe in lunch as a time to celebrate light, fresh air—and friendship. Today at the Door lunch is served at the umbrella-shaded tables near the pool. Our climate makes this possible year-round.

Sometimes guests ask for a tray to be delivered to a special corner of the gardens. We happily oblige.

# Vegetarian Wontons with Plum Sauce

**G**UESTS LOVE THESE when we serve them at the predinner cocktail gathering. They are among our most popular appetizers and are a good choice for home entertaining, since they can be assembled ahead of time and stored, covered, in the refrigerator. It's hard to believe these are not deep-fried.

*Plum sauce*

⅓ cup packed light brown sugar

¼ cup rice vinegar

¼ cup mirin (sweet rice wine)

1 teaspoon low-sodium tamari or soy sauce

1 whole star anise

½ cinnamon stick

2 whole cloves

1 cardamom pod, cracked

1 bay leaf

1 teaspoon garam masala (optional; see Note)

¼ cup water

1 pound Santa Rosa plums, pitted and quartered

*Wontons*

1 teaspoon canola oil

1½ teaspoons minced garlic

1 teaspoon minced fresh ginger

1 cup Chinese-cut zucchini (3 ounces; see Note)

⅔ cup Chinese-cut carrots (2 ounces; see Note)

⅔ cup Chinese-cut green bell peppers (1 ounce; see Note)

½ cup Chinese-cut celery (2 ounces; see Note)

2 shiitake mushrooms, cleaned, stemmed, and cut into ¼-inch slices (2 ounces)

½ cup Chinese-cut scallions (1 ounce; see Note)

⅔ cup shredded Napa cabbage (1 ounce)

⅔ cup mung bean sprouts

1 to 2 tablespoons low-sodium tamari or soy sauce

2 teaspoons arrowroot or cornstarch, dissolved in 2 tablespoons water

3 tablespoons Vegetable Broth (page 280) or water

About 8 ounces 3½-inch square wonton wrappers (32 wrappers)

1 large egg white, lightly beaten

*To make the plum sauce,* in a nonreactive saucepan, combine the brown sugar, vinegar, mirin, tamari, star anise, cinnamon stick, cloves, cardamom, bay leaf, the garam masala, if using, and water. Bring to a simmer over medium-high heat and immediately remove from the heat. Set aside for 10 minutes.

*NOTE: The plum sauce can be made up to 24 hours in advance and stored in a covered container in the refrigerator. Let it come to room temperature before serving. Garam masala is a blend of spices available in Indian and Pakistani markets as well as specialty stores and many supermarkets.*

*To Chinese-cut vegetables, trim and seed each vegetable as necessary and then slice into ¼-inch-thick slices or strips. Line up the slices and, holding the knife on the diagonal, cut the slices into ½-inch pieces.*

*Strain the syrup* through a fine sieve into a bowl, discard the spices, and return the syrup to the saucepan. Add the plums and bring to a simmer over medium heat. Cook, stirring occasionally, for about 25 minutes, until the mixture begins to thicken. Set aside to cool.

*Transfer the sauce* to a blender or food processor and puree until nearly smooth; some small pieces of plum should still be visible. Set aside.

*To make the wontons,* in a large nonstick skillet or wok, heat the oil over medium-high heat. In quick succession, add the garlic, ginger, zucchini, carrots, peppers, celery, and mushrooms and stir-fry, tossing, for 2 to 3 minutes, just until the vegetables start to soften. Add the scallions, cabbage, and sprouts and stir-fry for about 1 minute, until all the vegetables are well mixed. Add the tamari and toss briefly. Add the arrowroot mixture and broth and stir-fry for 2 to 3 minutes, until the mixture thickens. Transfer to a large plate and let cool.

*Preheat the oven* to 375°F. Lightly spray a baking sheet with vegetable oil spray.

*Lay 7 or 8 wonton wrappers on a work surface* and brush each one with egg white. Mound 1 tablespoon of the vegetables in the center of each and fold the wrapper diagonally over the vegetables to make a triangle. Press the edges together to seal and transfer to the baking sheet. Continue until you have 32 wontons.

*Generously spray the tops* of the wontons with vegetable oil spray. Bake for about 15 minutes, until crisp and lightly golden. Serve immediately with the plum sauce.

# California Rolls

CALLED CALIFORNIA ROLLS because they contain avocados, these Japanese-style rolls are a long-time favorite at the Golden Door, where we grow our own buttery avocados in our garden. The word *sushi* refers to vinegared rice—not to fish, as many believe. To make these rolls, you will need a sushi mat or a lightweight bamboo placemat.

PER SERVING:

*61 calories*

*1 g total fat (19% of calories)*

*0 g saturated fat*

*0 mg cholesterol*

*1 g protein (10% of calories)*

*11 g carbohydrates*

*(72% of calories)*

*0 g fiber*

*5 mg sodium*

MAKES 8 SERVINGS

NOTE: *Sushi rice is medium-grain rice usually imported from Asia. Nori are dark-colored (almost black) sheets of dried seaweed. Wasabi is hot green Japanese horseradish that is sold as a paste or a powder. The powder is mixed with an equal part of water to make a paste. All these ingredients are readily available in Asian markets.*

*Rice*

½ cup sushi rice, rinsed and drained (see Note)

2 tablespoons Japanese pickled ginger (*shoga*), minced

2 tablespoons black sesame seeds

¼ cup rice vinegar

1 tablespoon mirin

*Sushi rolls*

1 carrot, julienned

2 sheets toasted nori (see Note)

½ cup julienned cucumbers (2 ounces)

½ cup julienned roasted red bell peppers (see page 99)

½ avocado, peeled, pitted, and cut into thin slices

Reduced-sodium tamari or soy sauce (optional)

Wasabi (see Note; optional)

*To prepare the rice,* in a small saucepan, bring ¾ cup of water to a boil over high heat. Add the rice, reduce the heat to low, cover, and cook for about 15 minutes. Remove from the heat and let stand for 10 minutes.

*Transfer the rice to a bowl* and while it is still hot, add the pickled ginger and sesame seeds. Toss to combine.

*In a small bowl,* combine the vinegar and mirin. Sprinkle 2 tablespoons of the vinegar-mirin mixture over the rice and toss. (Reserve the remaining 2 tablespoons for making the sushi rolls.)

*To assemble the rolls,* blanch the carrot in a saucepan of boiling water for 2 minutes, or until crisp-tender. Drain and cool.

*Place a nori sheet,* smooth side down, on a sushi mat or bamboo placemat. Spread half of the rice mixture over the nori. Moisten your fingers with the reserved vinegar-mirin mixture and use your fingertips to press the rice evenly over the nori, leaving a 1-inch border at the top. Scatter half the vegetables over the rice. Use the sushi mat to help roll up the nori, and seal the seam. Press any loose ingredients back into the ends of the sushi roll. Repeat with the remaining nori, rice, and vegetables.

*Cut each sushi roll* into 8 slices. Serve with tamari and wasabi for dipping, if desired.

# Wild Mushroom Phyllo Strudel

**O**UR GUESTS LOVE MUSHROOMS, with their earthy, meaty flavor and subtle aroma. I like to serve them as often as I can, trying different varieties in various recipes. As well as being versatile, they're rich in potassium and niacin. Using phyllo dough for this makes it easy to execute—but it appears very elegant.

PER SERVING:

*146 calories*

*4 g total fat (25% of calories)*

*2 g saturated fat*

*14 mg cholesterol*

*9 g protein (24% of calories)*

*19 g carbohydrates*

*(51% of calories)*

*1 g fiber*

*337 mg sodium*

MAKES 8 SERVINGS

NOTE: *A package of phyllo dough contains more than five sheets. After removing the sheets needed for the recipe, rewrap the remaining phyllo securely in plastic wrap and refrigerate or freeze for another use.*

*Strudel*

10 cups loosely packed spinach leaves (8 ounces)

2 pounds mushrooms, such as shiitake, oak, cremini, and/or white mushrooms, cleaned and trimmed

1/4 cup sliced shallots

1 teaspoon chopped fresh thyme

1/8 teaspoon freshly grated nutmeg

1/2 teaspoon freshly ground black pepper

1 cup crumbled feta cheese (4 ounces)

1/4 cup chopped fresh flat-leaf parsley

1/2 cup fresh whole wheat bread crumbs

Five 12-by-17-inch sheets phyllo dough (2²/3 ounces)

*Mock sour cream*

2/3 cup 1% low-fat cottage cheese

1/3 cup nonfat plain yogurt

1 teaspoon fresh lemon juice

2 to 3 drops hot pepper sauce

*Heat a large nonstick* sauté pan over medium-high heat. Add the spinach and cook for about 3 minutes, stirring, until wilted. Transfer to a colander and press to extract the excess liquid. Transfer to a cutting board and chop. Set aside.

*Preheat the oven* to 350°F. Lightly coat a baking sheet with vegetable oil spray.

*In a food processor,* combine the mushrooms and shallots and pulse to chop coarsely.

*Heat a large nonstick sauté pan* over medium heat. Add the mushroom-shallot mixture, the thyme, nutmeg, and pepper, reduce the heat to medium-low, and cook for 15 to 20 minutes, stirring occasionally, until most of the moisture evaporates. Stir in the cheese and spinach and cook, stirring, until the cheese softens. Stir in the parsley and bread crumbs. Spread out onto a large platter or tray to cool.

*Lay 1 sheet of phyllo on a work surface* with a long side facing you and spray lightly with vegetable oil spray. Top with a second sheet and continue stacking and spraying all 5 sheets of phyllo. Spoon the cooled mushroom mixture lengthwise across the phyllo 1 to 2 inches from the bottom, making a long mound. Fold the bottom of the dough over the filling and roll up. Tuck the ends under and place, seam side down, on the baking sheet. Spray the top of the strudel with vegetable oil spray.

*Bake* for 35 to 40 minutes, until the pastry is a rich golden brown. Remove from the oven and let cool for 15 minutes before serving.

*To make the mock sour cream,* combine the cottage cheese, yogurt, lemon juice, and hot pepper sauce in a blender or food processor. Blend or pulse to a smooth consistency.

*Cut the warm strudel into slices* and serve with the mock sour cream on the side.

# Beet and Chili Quesadillas

**W**HILE VISITING NEW YORK CITY, I spent a grand evening at Mesa Grill, a restaurant known for its Southwestern and Mexican-inspired food. My adaptation of one of their quesadillas combines the sweet taste of beets, slightly hot Anaheim chilies, and a hint of salty feta cheese.

PER SERVING:

*206 calories*

*3 g total fat (12% of calories)*

*1 g saturated fat*

*7 mg cholesterol*

*9 g protein (18% of calories)*

*36 g carbohydrates*

*(70% of calories)*

*3 g fiber*

*433 mg sodium*

**MAKES 5 SERVINGS**

2 beets (12 ounces)

1 large red onion, halved and thinly sliced (6 ounces)

1 teaspoon dried oregano

½ cup 1% low-fat cottage cheese

¼ cup crumbled feta cheese (1¼ ounces)

1 teaspoon fresh lemon juice

½ teaspoon hot pepper sauce

Four 10-inch whole wheat tortillas (7 ounces)

1 large roasted Anaheim chili (see page 99), cut into ½-inch-wide strips (6 ounces)

*In a medium saucepan,* cover the beets with water and bring to a boil over high heat. Reduce the heat to low and simmer, covered, for 30 to 35 minutes. Drain and when cool, peel and slice into thin rounds. Set aside.

*In a large nonstick sauté pan* lightly sprayed with vegetable oil spray, cook the onion over medium-high heat for about 8 minutes, stirring frequently, until softened and lightly browned. Stir in the oregano and set aside.

*In a food processor,* combine the cottage cheese, feta, lemon juice, and hot pepper sauce and process until smooth. Set aside.

*Preheat the oven* to 375°F. Spray a baking sheet with vegetable oil spray and spray the bottom of a second baking sheet.

*To assemble the quesadillas,* heat a large sauté pan or griddle over medium-high heat. Briefly warm each tortilla for about 30 seconds on each side to soften. Arrange on a work surface and spread with the cheese mixture. Place 2 tortillas on the prepared baking sheet. Layer the beets, onion, and chili strips on them. Cover with the remaining tortillas, cheese side down, to form 2 sandwiches. Place the bottom-sprayed baking sheet on top of the quesadillas and press down gently.

*Bake* the quesadillas (with the baking sheet in place) for about 15 minutes. Remove the sheet and bake for 10 more minutes, until crisp and golden. Cut each quesadilla into wedges and serve hot.

# Black Bean Dip with Whole Wheat Tortilla Chips

**B**LACK BEANS ARE THE TRADITIONAL BEAN to use in this type of dip, but other dried beans, such as pinto or Anasazi, work well too. If you prefer, or if you are serving someone with a wheat intolerance, substitute high-quality corn tortillas for the wheat tortillas.

*Dip*

½ cup dried black beans, rinsed, or one 15-ounce can low-sodium black beans, drained and liquid reserved

1 teaspoon red pepper flakes, or to taste

½ teaspoon minced garlic

½ teaspoon ground cumin

Dash of hot chili sauce (see page 22), or to taste

*Tortilla chips*

Four 10-inch whole wheat tortillas (6½ ounces)

2 large egg whites, lightly beaten

1 tablespoon black sesame seeds

*To make the dip,* put the beans in a bowl and add enough cold water to cover by 2 inches. Set aside for at least 4 and up to 8 hours. Change the water once or twice during soaking. Drain and rinse the beans.

*Put the beans in a medium-sized saucepan* and add 3 cups of water and the pepper flakes. Bring to a boil over high heat. Reduce the heat and simmer for about 1½ hours, or until the beans are tender and the water just barely covers the beans. (Add more water if necessary while cooking the beans.) Drain, reserving the cooking liquid. Set aside to cool.

*Transfer the beans* and half the cooking liquid (or half the liquid from the can) to a food processor. Add the garlic, cumin, and chili sauce. Process until coarsely blended. Add more of the bean liquid if necessary to thin the dip. Transfer to a serving bowl and set aside.

*To make the chips,* preheat the oven to 350°F. Lightly spray a baking sheet with vegetable oil spray.

*Lay the tortillas on a work surface* and brush them on both sides with the egg whites. Cut the tortillas into 10 to 12 triangles each and lay the triangles on the baking sheet. Sprinkle the triangles with the sesame seeds. Bake for about 10 minutes, then remove from the oven. Use a metal spatula to loosen any chips that have stuck to the sheet, turn the chips over, and bake for a few more minutes, until golden brown. Lift from the baking sheet and serve warm or at room temperature with the dip.

# Eggplant Caviar with Pita Chips

**T**HIS FLAVORFUL SPREAD IS ELEGANT when served with crisp crudités.

*Eggplant caviar*

1 large eggplant (1 pound)

1/2 cup chopped fresh flat-leaf parsley

1 tablespoon drained capers, chopped

1 tablespoon balsamic vinegar

2 teaspoons olive oil

1 clove garlic, chopped

1 shallot, chopped

1/2 teaspoon ground cumin

1/2 teaspoon freshly ground black pepper

*Pita chips*

Two 6-inch whole wheat pita breads

2 large egg whites, lightly beaten

1 tablespoon sesame seeds

*To prepare the eggplant,* preheat the oven to 350°F. Pierce the eggplant in several places with a fork and place in a shallow baking dish. Roast, uncovered, for about 1 hour, or until very soft. Quarter the eggplant lengthwise and, when cool enough to handle, scrape out the pulp. (Leave the oven on.)

*In a blender* or food processor, pulse the eggplant pulp with the parsley, capers, vinegar, oil, garlic, shallot, cumin, and pepper until just chopped. Transfer to a serving bowl.

*To make the pita chips,* lightly spray a baking sheet with vegetable oil spray. Using kitchen scissors or a sharp knife, cut around the edges of the pita breads and gently separate each one into two rounds. Brush both sides of the pita rounds with the egg whites and cut each round into 10 or 12 triangles. Place on the prepared baking sheet and sprinkle with the sesame seeds.

*Bake* for 10 minutes. Using a metal spatula, loosen any chips that are sticking to the baking sheet, turn the chips over, and bake for about 5 minutes longer, or until the chips are crisp and golden.

*Arrange the chips* around the eggplant caviar and serve.

*Note: You can bake the pita chips 1 to 2 hours before serving, but be sure to store them in a dry place.*

# Hummus

**U**SE CANNED CHICKPEAS—they work just as well as dried and are one of my rare exceptions to a no-canned-foods ethic. This classic vegetarian dip goes well with raw vegetables, pita bread chips, or Whole Wheat Tortilla Chips (page 31).

PER TABLESPOON:

*31 calories*

*1 g total fat (32% of calories)*

*0 g saturated fat*

*0 mg cholesterol*

*1 g protein (13% of calories)*

*4 g carbohydrates*

*(55% of calories)*

*0 g fiber*

*53 mg sodium*

**MAKES ABOUT 1¹/₂ CUPS**

One 14¹/₂-ounce can chickpeas, drained and rinsed (1³/₄ cups)

1 tablespoon tahini

¹/₄ cup Vegetable Broth (page 280) or water

1 to 2 tablespoons extra-virgin olive oil

2 tablespoons fresh lemon juice

1 to 2 teaspoons minced garlic

1 teaspoon ground cumin, or to taste

Pinch of cayenne pepper, or to taste

*In a food processor* or blender, combine the chickpeas, tahini, broth, oil, and lemon juice and process until smooth and creamy, scraping down the bowl once or twice. (If using a blender, you may have to do this in batches.) Add the garlic, cumin, and cayenne and pulse briefly to blend.

*Adjust the seasonings* and transfer to a serving bowl, or cover and refrigerate until ready to serve.

# Tortilla Bites with Spa Guacamole and Turkey

**T**HESE TASTY BITES can be assembled a couple of hours before serving and sliced at the last minute, which makes them great for entertaining.

PER SERVING:

*279 calories*

*7 g total fat (21% of calories)*

*2 g saturated fat*

*36 mg cholesterol*

*19 g protein (28% of calories)*

*36 g carbohydrates*

*(51% of calories)*

*3 g fiber*

*372 mg sodium*

**MAKES 4 SERVINGS**

*Guacamole*

½ cup fresh peas (2½ ounces)

2 tablespoons chopped onion

1 small avocado, peeled and pitted (3¼ ounces)

½ cup nonfat plain yogurt

1 tablespoon fresh lime juice

1 to 3 drops hot pepper sauce, or to taste

*Tortillas*

1 cup diced seeded tomatoes (6 ounces)

2 tablespoons chopped fresh cilantro

5 ounces cooked turkey breast, julienned

1 tablespoon fresh lime juice

Four 10-inch whole wheat tortillas (6½ ounces)

2 cups shredded crisp lettuce (3½ ounces)

¼ cup crumbled feta cheese (1 ounce)

*To make the guacamole,* blanch the peas in a saucepan of boiling water for 2 to 3 minutes, until crisp-tender and bright green. Drain and cool.

*In a food processor,* combine the peas, onion, avocado, yogurt, lime juice, and hot pepper sauce. Process until smooth. Set aside.

*To assemble the tortillas,* combine the tomatoes and cilantro in a bowl and stir to mix. In another bowl, toss the turkey with the lime juice.

*Heat a large nonstick sauté pan* over medium-high heat. Place a tortilla in the skillet and heat for about 1 minute, turning once, until softened. Transfer to a work surface. Spread the tortilla with about 2 tablespoons of the guacamole and sprinkle with ½ cup of the lettuce, one quarter of the tomato-cilantro mixture, one quarter of the turkey, and 1 tablespoon of the cheese. Repeat with the remaining tortillas and fillings. Cut the uneven ends off the tortillas, wrap each one in a moist cloth or paper towel, and refrigerate until ready to serve, or up to 2 hours.

*Cut each chilled tortilla* into 6 slices and arrange cut sides down on a platter.

# Crostini with Tomato-Basil Topping

**S**OME MIGHT IDENTIFY these as tiny bruschetta, but regardless of what they are called, they taste fresh and delicious.

PER SERVING:

*174 calories*

*2 g total fat (10% of calories)*

*0 g saturated fat*

*1 mg cholesterol*

*6 g protein (13% of calories)*

*34 g carbohydrates*

*(77% of calories)*

*1 g fiber*

*286 mg sodium*

MAKES 6 SERVINGS

NOTE: *To rehydrate dry-packed sundried tomatoes, soak them in warm water to cover for 15 to 20 minutes. Drain and dice. For ¹/₂ cup, begin with 1¹/₄ ounces dried tomatoes.*

One 10-ounce whole wheat baguette, sliced diagonally into 18 thin slices

¹/₂ cup diced soaked sundried tomatoes (see Note)

3 plum tomatoes, cored and diced (10 ounces)

1 tablespoon minced shallots or scallions (white part only)

2 teaspoons minced garlic

3 tablespoons balsamic vinegar

1 tablespoon extra-virgin olive oil (optional)

¹/₄ cup thinly sliced basil

¹/₂ teaspoon freshly ground black pepper

*Preheat the oven* to 350°F. Lightly spray a baking sheet with olive oil spray.

*Arrange the bread slices* on the baking sheet and bake for 15 to 20 minutes, until crispy, turning once or twice. Let the slices cool on wire racks.

*In a bowl,* combine the sundried tomatoes, plum tomatoes, shallots, garlic, vinegar, the olive oil, if using, basil, and pepper. Toss gently and set aside for about 5 minutes to allow the flavors to blend.

*Spoon the tomato mixture* onto the bread slices and serve immediately.

# Spinach and Red Pepper Pâté

**T**HE FLAVORS OF spinach and red pepper are two that seem custom-made for each other. Here they come together to form a very pretty pâté that is excellent served with an endive salad or any other crisp raw vegetable garnish.

PER SERVING:

*64 calories*

*2 g total fat (32% of calories)*

*1 g saturated fat*

*1 mg cholesterol*

*6 g protein (36% of calories)*

*5 g carbohydrates*

*(32% of calories)*

*0 g fiber*

*150 mg sodium*

**MAKES 8 SERVINGS**

*Spinach layer*

6 cups loosely packed spinach leaves (5 ounces)

1/3 cup low-fat ricotta cheese

1 tablespoon chopped shallots

2 large egg whites

Pinch of freshly grated nutmeg

1/4 teaspoon kosher salt

Pinch of freshly ground black pepper

*Red pepper layer*

3 roasted red bell peppers (see page 99; 11 ounces)

1/2 cup low-fat ricotta cheese

2 large egg whites

1 1/2 teaspoons tomato puree

Pinch of cayenne pepper

*Preheat the oven* to 350°F. Lightly spray a mini loaf pan, approximately 4 by 2 inches, with vegetable oil spray. Cut a piece of parchment or waxed paper to fit the bottom of the pan. Spray the parchment paper with vegetable oil spray.

*To prepare the spinach layer,* in a saucepan of boiling water, blanch the spinach for about 1 minute until wilted. Drain and squeeze out the excess moisture. (You will have about 3/4 cup spinach.)

*In a food processor,* combine the spinach, cheese, shallots, egg whites, nutmeg, salt, and pepper and process until smooth. Spread the mixture in the loaf pan and tap the pan several times on the countertop to pop any air bubbles. Smooth the mixture with a spatula.

*To prepare the red pepper layer,* in the (clean) food processor, combine the peppers, cheese, egg whites, tomato puree, and cayenne and process until smooth. Spoon the mixture over the spinach layer and smooth it with a rubber spatula.

*Set the loaf pan in a larger baking pan* and add enough hot water to come halfway up the sides of the loaf pan. Bake for about 1 1/2 to 2 hours, or until set and a toothpick inserted in the center comes out clean. (Add more boiling water to the larger pan if necessary during baking.) Set the pan on a wire rack and let the pâté cool completely in the pan.

*To unmold the pâté,* run a kitchen knife around the edges of the pâté. Dip the pan in a bowl or sinkful of warm water, put a flat plate over the top of the pan, and invert the loaf pan and plate. Gently lift the pan off the pâté. Serve immediately, or cover and refrigerate.

*Using a sharp knife,* slice the pâté. Serve at room temperature or slightly chilled.

# Artichoke and Goat Cheese Pâté

**T**HE MILD YET DISTINCTIVE FLAVOR of artichokes calls out for the tang of goat cheese, and the two blend deliciously in this first-course vegetable loaf. The trickiest part of the entire recipe is preparing the artichokes. The rest is easy and can be done well ahead of time, which makes this great for parties.

12 artichokes

3 tablespoons fresh lemon juice

5 large egg whites

1 large egg

3$\frac{1}{2}$ ounces soft goat cheese, cut into small pieces

2 tablespoons chopped fresh flat-leaf parsley

1 tablespoon minced fresh tarragon

$\frac{3}{4}$ cup diced peeled red bell peppers

$\frac{1}{8}$ teaspoon freshly grated nutmeg

1 teaspoon freshly ground black pepper

*NOTE: Use a vegetable peeler or a sharp paring knife to peel the red pepper. Peeling the pepper removes any trace of bitterness.*

*To prepare the artichokes,* trim the stems and break off all of the tough outer leaves. Cut off the inner core of pale green leaves. Place the artichoke bottoms in a large nonreactive saucepan, add the lemon juice and enough water to cover, and bring to a boil. Reduce the heat to low and simmer for about 20 minutes, until the artichokes are tender. Drain and cool. Using a small spoon, scrape away the fuzzy chokes and discard. Dice the artichoke bottoms and set aside.

*Preheat the oven* to 375°F. Lightly spray a 7$\frac{1}{2}$-by-3$\frac{1}{2}$-inch loaf pan with vegetable oil spray and line the bottom of the pan with parchment paper. Spray the paper.

*In a bowl,* whisk together the egg whites, egg, and goat cheese until smooth. Stir in the parsley and tarragon. Add the artichoke bottoms, red peppers, nutmeg, and pepper and stir gently to combine.

*Pour the mixture* into the prepared loaf pan, place in a larger baking pan, and add enough hot water to come about halfway up the sides of the loaf pan. Bake for about 1 hour, until the pâté is set and a toothpick inserted in the center comes out clean. Set the pan on a wire rack and let the pâté cool completely in the pan.

*To unmold the pâté,* run a kitchen knife around the edges of the pâté. Warm the bottom of the pan in a bowl or sinkful of warm water, put a flat plate over the top of the pan, and invert the loaf pan and plate. Gently lift the pan off the pâté. Serve immediately, or cover and refrigerate.

*Using a sharp knife,* slice the pâté. Serve at room temperature or slightly chilled.

## SHOP WITH THE SEASONS

Our kitchen is located only steps from our garden, so we can literally plan a meal by walking outside. We enjoy being in touch with the seasons: watching the rhythms of the garden, soil, rainfall, and sun.

It's also true that we're very fortunate at the Golden Door to have a never-ending growing season. A temperate, marine-influenced southern California climate keeps winters quite warm, although in cooler weather we grow cauliflower, greens, cabbages, leeks, and other vegetables.

Wherever you live, you can stay in touch with the seasons by purchasing produce from local farmers at the farmers' markets springing up all over the country. We love the pride our gardeners—and farmers everywhere—take in what they grow: herbs so fragrant you want to grab a bouquet or two; crisp celery with its strong aroma; or plump tomatoes, bursting with juice. Fresh, whenever possible, is best.

# Soups

SINCE I WAS A CHILD IN BELGIUM, I have loved soup. In Europe, soup usually precedes the main course, but here it frequently *is* the meal. At the Golden Door, I serve it for lunch or offer it as a first course at dinner. Either way, our guests categorically love our soups. I rely on lots of vegetables and legumes when I develop my recipes, as well as on seafood, chicken, and fresh fruit. Whether cool and refreshing for the summer or hot and hearty for the winter, soups always satisfy.

# Creamy Corn Soup

GUESTS FREQUENTLY ASK IF I ADD CREAM to this Golden Door favorite. The answer is a definite "no." It's the corn itself that makes the soup creamy.

PER SERVING:

*112 calories*

*1 g total fat (9% of calories)*

*0 g saturated fat*

*23 mg cholesterol*

*3 g protein (10% of calories)*

*23 g carbohydrates*

*(73% of calories)*

*1 g fiber*

*6 mg sodium*

**MAKES 8 SERVINGS**

NOTE: *To remove the kernels from the cobs, stand the cobs upright in a shallow bowl and use a small sharp knife to cut off the kernels. This way, the kernels will fall into the bowl with any of the sweet corn "milk" that is released at the same time.*

1 teaspoon canola oil

½ cup diced onions (2 ounces)

1 small carrot, thinly sliced

1 bay leaf

1 teaspoon dried basil

6 cups fresh white corn kernels (from 5 ears; 30 ounces), with cobs reserved

5 cups Vegetable Broth (page 280) or water, plus more if necessary

½ teaspoon kosher salt (optional)

½ teaspoon freshly ground white pepper

Two-Pepper Coulis (page 285)

2 tablespoons finely sliced fresh chives

*In a large pot,* heat the oil over medium heat. Add the onions, carrot, bay leaf, basil, and corn cobs and sauté for 5 to 6 minutes, until the onions are translucent. Add the corn and cook, stirring, for 3 to 4 minutes. Remove the cobs after 10 to 15 minutes. Add the broth and salt and pepper, if using, bring to a boil, reduce the heat, and simmer, uncovered, for 35 to 40 minutes, or until the vegetables soften. Remove and discard the bay leaf and set the soup aside to cool.

*Transfer the soup* to a food processor or blender and process until smooth and creamy. (This may have to be done in batches.) Strain through a fine sieve and return to the pot. Adjust the consistency with more broth if necessary. Heat over medium heat until hot, stirring occasionally.

*Ladle into soup bowls* and drizzle with the pepper coulis and chives. Serve immediately.

# Curried Carrot Soup

**I** FREQUENTLY USE COMPLEX SPICE MIXTURES at the Golden Door to enhance and boost the flavors of dishes, and curry is one of my favorites. Use a high-quality curry powder. Here, I combine it with carrots to make a golden-colored soup that is always in demand with our guests.

PER SERVING:

*88 calories*

*2 g total fat (17% of calories)*

*0 g saturated fat*

*0 mg cholesterol*

*2 g protein (9% of calories)*

*16 g carbohydrates*

*(73% of calories)*

*2 g fiber*

*349 mg sodium*

**MAKES 4 SERVINGS**

1 teaspoon canola oil or olive oil

1 onion, chopped (4 ounces)

1 rib celery, chopped (2 ounces)

1 tablespoon curry powder

1 teaspoon dried tarragon

1 pound carrots, thinly sliced

4½ cups Vegetable Broth (page 280) or water, plus more if necessary

1 bay leaf

½ teaspoon kosher salt, or to taste

3 tablespoons chopped fresh flat-leaf parsley, plus 4 sprigs parsley

½ cup cooked rice (optional)

*In a large saucepan,* heat the oil over medium heat. Add the onion and celery and sauté until the onion is translucent, about 5 minutes. Add the curry powder and tarragon and cook, stirring, for 1 minute. Add the carrots, broth, bay leaf, and salt. Bring to a boil, reduce the heat, and cook, partially covered, for 30 to 45 minutes, until the carrots are fork-tender. Remove from the heat, remove the bay leaf, and cool for 10 minutes.

*In a blender* or food processor, process the soup until smooth. (This may have to be done in batches.) Return the soup to the saucepan and reheat gently, adjusting the consistency by adding more broth if necessary. Stir in the chopped parsley.

*To serve,* ladle the soup into heated bowls over rice, if using, and garnish each serving with a parsley sprig.

# Butternut Squash Soup

**T**HIS LOVELY AUTUMNAL SOUP is flavored with orange and garnished with apple slices.

PER SERVING:

*141 calories*

*2 g total fat (10% of calories)*

*0 g saturated fat*

*0 mg cholesterol*

*2 g protein (7% of calories)*

*29 g carbohydrates*

*(83% of calories)*

*3 g fiber*

*611 mg sodium*

**MAKES 8 SERVINGS**

2 teaspoons canola oil

2 cups 1-inch slices leeks (white part only; 2 leeks)

½ cup coarsely chopped onions (2 ounces)

2 carrots, sliced (8 ounces)

1 green apple, peeled, cored, and cut into 1-inch wedges (4 ounces)

1 butternut squash, peeled, seeded, and cut into 1-inch chunks (2 pounds)

1 sprig fresh thyme or ½ teaspoon dried

1 bay leaf

1 teaspoon ground allspice

1 teaspoon ground cinnamon

2 teaspoons kosher salt

7 cups Vegetable Broth (page 280) or Chicken Stock (page 282), plus more if necessary

¼ cup frozen orange juice concentrate, thawed

8 teaspoons nonfat plain yogurt

1 green or red apple, peeled, cored, and thinly sliced (4 ounces)

8 sprigs fresh chervil

*In a large pot,* heat the oil over medium heat. Add the leeks, onions, carrots, apple wedges, squash, thyme, bay leaf, allspice, cinnamon, and salt. Cook, stirring occasionally, for about 10 minutes, until the vegetables begin to soften. Add the broth. Bring to a boil over high heat, reduce the heat to medium-low, and simmer, partially covered, for about 45 minutes, or until the vegetables are tender. Remove the thyme sprig and bay leaf and let the soup cool for 15 minutes.

*In a blender* or food processor, process the soup to a smooth consistency. (This may have to be done in batches.) Return to the pot, stir in the orange juice concentrate, and reheat gently, adjusting the consistency by adding more broth if necessary.

*Ladle the soup* into heated soup bowls and garnish each with a teaspoon of yogurt, a couple of apple slices, and a sprig of chervil.

# Creamy Mushroom Soup

**I** USED TO THINK that any soup with the word "creamy" in the title meant you had to use cream. However, this soup—without a drop of cream—is richly delicious yet obviously more healthful than any mushroom soup containing heavy cream.

PER SERVING:

*68 calories*

*1 g total fat (14% of calories)*

*0 g saturated fat*

*0 mg cholesterol*

*3 g protein (16% of calories)*

*12 g carbohydrates*

*(70% of calories)*

*1 g fiber*

*299 mg sodium*

**MAKES 8 SERVINGS**

¹/₃ cup uncooked white rice

1 bay leaf

1 teaspoon kosher salt

1 teaspoon canola oil

¹/₂ cup chopped onions (2 ounces)

1¹/₂ pounds white or cremini mushrooms, cleaned, trimmed, and chopped

1 teaspoon fresh lemon juice

Sprig of fresh thyme

¹/₂ teaspoon freshly ground white pepper

5 cups Vegetable Broth (page 280) or water, plus more if necessary

2 ounces enoki or other mushrooms, cleaned, trimmed, and finely sliced

¹/₄ cup minced fresh flat-leaf parsley

*In a small saucepan,* combine the rice with 2¹/₂ cups of water, the bay leaf, and salt, and bring to a boil over high heat. Reduce the heat and simmer for about 30 minutes, until the rice is very tender. Discard the bay leaf.

*In a large saucepan,* heat the oil over medium heat. Add the onions and sauté for about 5 minutes, until translucent. Stir in the chopped mushrooms, lemon juice, thyme, and pepper. Add the broth and simmer for 20 minutes.

*Add the cooked rice* and simmer for about 10 minutes. Remove the thyme sprig and let the soup cool for 15 minutes.

*In a blender* or food processor, process the soup to a coarse puree. There should still be some texture from the mushrooms. (This may have to be done in batches.) Return the soup to the pan and reheat gently, adjusting the consistency by adding more broth if necessary.

*Ladle the soup* into heated bowls and garnish with the enoki mushrooms and parsley.

# Eggplant Soup with Brown Rice

WHEN THE GARDENERS FROM OUR SISTER SPA, Rancho La Puerta, supplied me with baskets full of shiny eggplants and juicy, ripe tomatoes, I let my imagination take flight and developed this full-bodied, nutritious soup. Use the bumper crop from your own late-summer garden or make a trip to the farmers' market.

PER SERVING:

136 calories

2 g total fat (14% of calories)

0 g saturated fat

0 mg cholesterol

3 g protein (10% of calories)

26 g carbohydrates

(77% of calories)

3 g fiber

177 mg sodium

MAKES 8 SERVINGS

2 eggplants (2 pounds)

2 teaspoons olive oil

1 green or red apple, quartered and cored (4 ounces)

1/2 cup diced onions (2 ounces)

3 cloves garlic, minced

2 tablespoons curry powder

1 teaspoon fennel seeds

3 tomatoes, cored and chopped (12 ounces)

1/2 cup tomato puree

10 1/4 cups Vegetable Broth (page 280) or Chicken Stock (page 282)

1/3 cup uncooked brown rice

1/2 teaspoon salt, or more to taste

2 carrots, diced (8 ounces)

1 rib celery, diced (2 ounces)

1 to 3 drops hot chili sauce (see page 22), or more to taste

1 red or green apple, peeled, cored, and thinly sliced

1/4 cup chopped fresh flat-leaf parsley

*Preheat the oven* to 350°F.

*Pierce the skin* of the eggplants in several places with a fork. Place in a shallow baking dish and bake, uncovered, for about 1 hour, until soft. Cool and when cool enough to handle, quarter the eggplants, scrape out the pulp, and discard the skin. Chop the pulp and set aside.

*In a large pot,* heat the oil over medium heat. Add the quartered apple, the onions, and garlic and cook for about 5 minutes, stirring occasionally, until softened. Stir in the curry powder and fennel seeds and cook, stirring, for 1 minute. Add the eggplant pulp, tomatoes, tomato puree, and 9 cups of the vegetable broth. Simmer, partially covered, over medium-low heat for about 45 minutes, stirring occasionally, until the flavors are well blended. Set aside to cool for about 15 minutes.

*Meanwhile,* in a small saucepan, combine the rice, the remaining 1¼ cups broth, and the salt and bring to a boil over high heat. Reduce the heat to low and simmer, uncovered, for about 35 minutes, until the rice is almost tender and liquid is absorbed. Remove from the heat and let stand for 10 minutes.

*In a blender* or food processor, process the soup until smooth. (This may have to be done in batches.) Return to the pot, add the carrots, celery, and chili sauce, and simmer, uncovered, for 10 to 15 minutes, until the carrots and celery are tender. Stir in the cooked rice. Taste and adjust the seasonings if necessary.

*Ladle the soup* into heated bowls and garnish with the apple slices and chopped parsley.

# Doris's Broccoli Soup

**A**T A SYMPOSIUM IN SAN FRANCISCO in 1994, I was on a panel with Jane Brody to discuss the cancer-fighting properties of cruciferous plants. This recipe is made with one of the stars of that group of vegetables: broccoli. Others are cauliflower, broccoli rabe, Brussels sprouts, and cabbage. With great pleasure I have named the soup for Doris Fisher, a sponsor of the symposium.

**PER SERVING:**

*52 calories*

*1 g total fat (17% of calories)*

*0 g saturated fat*

*0 mg cholesterol*

*4 g protein (27% of calories)*

*7 g carbohydrates*

*(56% of calories)*

*1 g fiber*

*325 mg sodium*

**MAKES 4 SERVINGS**

1 pound broccoli, separated into florets and stems

½ teaspoon canola oil or light olive oil

½ cup chopped onions (2 ounces)

4 cups Vegetable Broth (page 280) or water, plus more if necessary

2 tablespoons chopped fresh basil or flat-leaf parsley

½ teaspoon kosher salt, or to taste

¼ teaspoon freshly ground black pepper

*Peel the broccoli stems* and slice ¼ inch thick. Coarsely chop the florets.

*In a saucepan,* heat the oil over medium heat. Add the onions and cook for about 5 minutes, stirring occasionally, until translucent. Add the broccoli and vegetable broth, bring to a boil over high heat, reduce the heat to medium, and simmer, uncovered, for about 10 minutes, until the broccoli is fork-tender. Cool for 5 minutes.

*In a blender* or food processor, process the soup until fairly smooth, with only a few small broccoli "buds" remaining. (If using a blender, this may have to be done in batches.) Add the basil and pulse a few times. Return the soup to the pan and reheat gently, adjusting the consistency with more broth if necessary. Season with the salt and pepper.

*Ladle into* heated soup bowls.

# Hot-and-Sour Shrimp Soup

**T**HIS VIETNAMESE-INSPIRED SOUP always gets rave reviews at the Golden Door. A good shrimp stock enhances the flavors considerably, although it is very good indeed made with vegetable broth. Once you have all the ingredients prepared, cooking the soup takes only about ten minutes. For the best flavor, serve it immediately.

1 teaspoon sesame oil

6 large shrimp, peeled, deveined, and chopped (8 ounces before peeling)

2 cloves garlic, minced

1 teaspoon minced fresh ginger

5 cups Vegetable Broth (page 280) or shrimp stock (see Note)

1½ cups thinly sliced shiitake mushrooms (3 ounces)

1 cup diagonally sliced celery (3½ ounces)

1 to 2 tablespoons low-sodium tamari or soy sauce

2 tablespoons rice vinegar

2 tablespoons mirin (sweet rice wine)

2 tablespoons fresh lime juice

1 teaspoon hot chili sauce (see page 22)

4 teaspoons cornstarch or arrowroot, dissolved in ¼ cup water

½ cup diagonally sliced scallions (including green tops)

6 sprigs fresh cilantro

NOTE: *To make shrimp stock, add the shrimp shells and any other nonoily fish trimmings you may have on hand to the Vegetable Broth and simmer for about 20 minutes.*

*In a large saucepan,* heat the sesame oil over medium heat. Add the shrimp, garlic, and ginger and sauté, stirring, for 2 to 3 minutes until shrimp just turn pink. Add the broth, mushrooms, celery, and tamari. Simmer for 2 minutes, then add the vinegar, mirin, lime juice, and chili sauce.

*Bring the soup to a boil* over high heat. Whisk in the cornstarch mixture and simmer for 2 to 3 minutes, stirring, until the soup is slightly thickened.

*Ladle the soup* into heated bowls and garnish with the scallions and cilantro sprigs.

# Waterzooi

**W**ATERZOOI, *POULE AU POT*, *caldo de pollo*, Jewish chicken soup—all are the same good, basic chicken soup, but from different parts of the world. Regardless of the name or the origin, this is a comforting soup that warms both the heart and the soul, especially when the weather is inclement or you have a cold. Here is the version from my native Belgium, where it is prepared in every home kitchen, country inn, and restaurant. In this reduced-fat rendition of the traditional classic, fresh parsley and chervil add bright, fresh notes.

1 teaspoon canola oil

2 leeks (white parts only), cut into strips 2 inches long and ½ inch wide (6 ounces)

1 large onion, halved and cut into ½-inch lengthwise slices (6 ounces)

6 ribs celery, cut into slices 2 inches long and ½ inch thick (1 pound)

2 large turnips, peeled and cut into slices 2 inches long and ½ inch thick (10 ounces)

7 cups Chicken Stock (page 282) or Vegetable Broth (page 280)

1 whole chicken breast (1 pound)

1 bay leaf

1 teaspoon kosher salt (optional)

¼ teaspoon freshly ground black pepper, or to taste

3 red potatoes, halved and sliced ¼ inch thick (9 ounces)

2 tablespoons fresh lemon juice

¼ cup minced fresh flat-leaf parsley

¼ cup minced fresh chervil or scallions

6 lemon wedges

*In a large pot,* heat the oil over medium heat. Spread the leeks, onion, celery, and turnips evenly over the bottom of the pot. Cover, reduce the heat to medium low, and cook for 8 to 10 minutes, or until the vegetables begin to soften.

*Add 6 cups of the broth,* the chicken breast, bay leaf, the salt, if desired, and pepper. Bring to a boil, reduce the heat to medium-low, and simmer, partially covered, for 45 minutes, skimming off any fat that rises to the surface.

*Place the sliced potatoes in a strainer* or colander and rinse under cold water to remove excess starch. Add the potatoes and the remaining 1 cup of broth to the pot and simmer, uncovered, for 15 to 20 minutes, or until the potatoes are tender.

*Remove any fat* from the top of the soup by blotting with a paper towel. Discard the bay leaf. Remove the chicken breast, pull off and discard the skin and bones, and tear the meat into bite-sized pieces. Return the meat to the soup. Stir in the lemon juice and reheat if necessary.

*Ladle into heated soup bowls,* sprinkle with the parsley and chervil, and garnish each serving with a lemon wedge.

# Red Pepper Bisque with Plum Tomatoes and Saffron

**S**TRAINING THIS GORGEOUS DEEP RED BISQUE through a sieve after it is pureed guarantees its silken texture.

PER SERVING:

*73 calories*

*3 g total fat (33% of calories)*

*0 g saturated fat*

*74 mg cholesterol*

*2 g protein (9% of calories)*

*11 g carbohydrates*

*(58% of calories)*

*1 g fiber*

*8 mg sodium*

MAKES 6 SERVINGS

1 tablespoon olive oil

1 large onion, coarsely chopped (6 ounces)

1 clove garlic, minced

3 red bell peppers, cored, seeded, and coarsely chopped (1 pound)

8 to 10 plum tomatoes, cored and quartered (12 ounces)

4½ cups Vegetable Broth (page 280) or Chicken Stock (page 282)

1 bay leaf

1 teaspoon kosher salt (optional)

Pinch of saffron

2 tablespoons slivered fresh basil or 6 sprigs fresh chervil

*In a saucepan,* heat the oil over medium heat. Add the onion, garlic, and red peppers and sauté for about 5 minutes, until the vegetables begin to soften. Stir in the tomatoes and cook for about 5 minutes, until they soften. Add the broth, bay leaf, and the salt, if desired. Bring to a boil over high heat, reduce the heat to medium-low, and simmer for about 35 minutes, until all the vegetables are soft. Remove the bay leaf and let the soup cool for 15 minutes.

*In a blender* or food processor, process the soup until smooth. (This may have to be done in batches.) Strain through a fine sieve, pressing on any remaining solids to extract as much liquid as possible. Return to the pan, stir in the saffron, and simmer gently for 10 to 15 minutes.

*Ladle the soup* into heated bowls and garnish with the basil.

# Spicy Black Bean Soup

**W**HEN I MAKE THIS FULL-FLAVORED SOUP, I like to make enough so that I can set aside half to use another time. The soup keeps well for two or three days in the refrigerator.

2 cups dried black beans, rinsed (1 pound)

2 teaspoons olive oil

1 cup chopped onions (4 ounces)

3 ribs celery, chopped (8 ounces)

2 Anaheim chilies (4½ ounces) or 1 green bell pepper (4½ ounces), cored, seeded, and diced

1 tablespoon minced garlic

1 teaspoon red pepper flakes

2 teaspoons dried oregano

1 teaspoon chopped fresh rosemary

1 bay leaf

1½ teaspoons kosher salt

3 large tomatoes, cored and chopped (18 ounces)

12 cups Vegetable Broth (page 280) or water, plus more if necessary

½ cup tomato puree

2 carrots, cut into small dice (8 ounces)

1 cup fresh or frozen corn kernels (5 ounces)

½ cup thinly sliced scallions (2 ounces)

2 tablespoons chopped fresh cilantro

*Soak the beans in water* to cover for at least 4 hours, or overnight. Drain and rinse.

*In a large pot,* heat the olive oil over medium heat. Add the onions, celery, peppers, garlic, and red pepper flakes and cook for about 5 minutes, stirring occasionally, until the vegetables begin to soften. Stir in the oregano, rosemary, bay leaf, salt, tomatoes, drained beans, broth, and tomato puree. Bring to a boil over high heat, reduce the heat to medium-low, and simmer, partially covered, for 1 to 1½ hours, or until the beans are very tender. Remove from the heat and, using a potato masher, mash the beans so that some disintegrate to thicken the soup.

*Return the soup to the heat,* add the carrots and corn, and simmer for about 10 minutes, until tender. Adjust the consistency by adding more broth and correct the seasonings if necessary. Discard the bay leaf. Stir in the scallions.

*Ladle the soup* into heated bowls and garnish with the cilantro.

# White Bean Soup au Pistou

**P**ISTOU IS THE MIXTURE of crushed basil, garlic, and olive oil that is Provence's version of Italian pesto. Here we make a pistou using cooked white beans to enrich and thicken the soup.

**PER SERVING:**

*327 calories*

*3 g total fat (7% of calories)*

*1 g saturated fat*

*0 mg cholesterol*

*17 g protein (21% of calories)*

*59 g carbohydrates*

*(72% of calories)*

*5 g fiber*

*662 mg sodium*

**MAKES 8 SERVINGS**

2 cups dried navy beans or cannellini beans, rinsed (1 pound)

12 cups water

2 bay leaves

2 sprigs fresh thyme

2 teaspoons kosher salt

1 teaspoon freshly ground black pepper

1 onion, studded with 5 whole cloves (4 ounces)

½ cup tomato puree

2 teaspoons olive oil

2 leeks (white part only), thinly sliced (6 ounces)

4 ribs celery, diced (10 ounces)

2 turnips, peeled and diced (8 ounces)

4 tomatoes, cored and diced (18 ounces)

2 medium-sized zucchini, diced (14 to 16 ounces)

2 cups Vegetable Broth (page 280) or water, plus more if necessary

1 cup whole wheat elbow macaroni

1 cup torn fresh basil leaves

6 cloves garlic, crushed

*Soak the beans in water* to cover for at least 4 hours, or overnight. Drain and rinse.

*In a large pot,* combine the beans with the water, bay leaves, thyme, salt, pepper, onion, and tomato puree. Bring to a boil over high heat, reduce the heat, and simmer, partially covered, for about 1½ hours, or until the beans are tender and the cooking liquid looks milky. Remove the onion from the soup and discard the cloves. Coarsely chop the onion and return it to the pot. Remove from the heat.

*In a large saucepan,* heat the oil over medium heat. Add the leeks, celery, and turnips and sauté for about 8 minutes, stirring occasionally, until the vegetables begin to soften. Add the tomatoes, zucchini, and vegetable broth and add to the beans. Stir well. Bring to a boil over high heat, add the macaroni, reduce the heat, and simmer for about 15 minutes, until the pasta is al dente. Discard the bay leaves.

*Transfer 1 cup* of the soup to a blender or food processor and let it cool for about 10 minutes. Add the basil and garlic and process to a coarse consistency. Return to the soup and reheat gently, adjusting the consistency by adding more broth if necessary. Taste and correct the seasonings if necessary.

*Ladle into* heated soup bowls.

## A WALK TO THE GATE

How many of us eat a meal and then retire to a chair for the rest of the evening?

At the Golden Door, evenings are quiet as well—a time for provocative speakers, discussions, and some reading. However, we always begin each post-dinner activity with our lively tradition of a *promenade digestif* to the main entrance gate.

Literally a "walk to aid digestion," the twilight promenade is common to many cultures. At the Door we take a short walk, many of us continuing our dinner conversations, past the garden, across our bridge, through the golden entry doors, and up the curving drive to the main entry gate. It's over in ten minutes or less, but it reinvigorates body and mind—and is a very gentle reminder of our commitment to exercise. Guests always reach out and *touch* the large wooden gate. That's become part of the tradition, too!

At home this short promenade can take the form of walking the dog, touring the garden, strolling to the corner, or searching for the evening star.

# Creamy Chickpea Soup

T HIS SOUP IS PREPARED at our sister spa, Rancho La Puerta, in Mexico.

PER SERVING:

148 calories

2 g total fat (13% of calories)

0 g saturated fat

0 mg cholesterol

7 g protein (20% of calories)

25 g carbohydrates

(67% of calories)

2 g fiber

311 mg sodium

MAKES 10 SERVINGS

NOTE: White miso is a rice-and-soy paste that is available in Asian markets.

You can use 3 cups canned low-sodium chickpeas, drained and rinsed, instead of dried beans. Combine the onion, bay leaves, thyme, salt, and pepper with 7 cups of water and simmer for about 30 minutes. Add the beans and simmer for 30 to 45 minutes longer. Proceed to puree the soup and complete the recipe.

## Soup

1½ cups dried chickpeas

14 cups water

1 onion, studded with 5 whole cloves

2 bay leaves

1 sprig fresh thyme or 1 teaspoon dried

1 teaspoon kosher salt

2 teaspoons freshly ground white pepper

1 tablespoon white miso, or more to taste (see Note)

## Garnish

½ cup finely diced carrots (4 ounces)

1 small red bell pepper, cored, seeded, and finely diced (2½ ounces)

1 cup fresh or frozen peas (5 ounces)

½ cup thinly sliced green beans (2½ ounces)

½ cup thinly sliced scallions (2 ounces)

To prepare the chickpeas, cover them with cold water and set aside to soak for at least 4 hours, or overnight. Drain and rinse.

In a stockpot, combine the chickpeas with the water, onion, bay leaves, thyme, salt, and white pepper. Bring to a boil, reduce the heat to low, and simmer, covered, for about 2½ hours, until the chickpeas are tender; if necessary, add more water. When the chickpeas are done, there should be about half the original amount of cooking liquid remaining.

Remove from the heat and let cool. Remove the bay leaves, thyme, and onion. Remove the cloves from the onion; return the onion to the pot.

In a blender or food processor, puree the soup with the miso until smooth, adding additional miso if necessary. (This may have to be done in batches.) Return the soup to the pot and reheat gently.

Meanwhile, in a saucepan of boiling water, blanch the carrots, red pepper, peas, and green beans for about 1 minute, until crisp-tender.

Drain the vegetables and add them to the soup. Add more water if necessary. Ladle the soup into heated bowls and garnish with the scallions.

# Seven-Spice Bean Soup

**I**T WAS OUR FOUNDER Deborah's idea to package the beans and spices used in this soup with an accompanying recipe to raise money in the fight against poverty. Homeless women are given the opportunity to earn money by packaging the ingredients for distribution.

PER SERVING:

*188 calories*

*1 g total fat (4% of calories)*

*0 g saturated fat*

*0 mg cholesterol*

*9 g protein (20% of calories)*

*36 g carbohydrates*

*(76% of calories)*

*4 g fiber*

*210 mg sodium*

MAKES 6 SERVINGS

NOTE: *Adzuki beans are small red beans available in Asian markets and some supermarkets. Anasazi beans are speckled red and white beans, larger than adzukis, and are considered white beans. Substitute Navy beans or white kidney beans for anasazi beans. There is no substitute for adzuki beans.*

1 cup tomato puree or sauce (8 ounces)

½ cup cup dried adzuki beans rinsed

⅓ cup dried anasazi beans, rinsed

¼ cup medium-grain brown rice

2 tablespoons finely chopped dry-packed sun-dried tomatoes

2 teaspoons curry powder

2 teaspoons dried basil

1 teaspoon dried oregano

1 teaspoon cumin

½ teaspoon red pepper flakes

½ teaspoon fennel seeds

½ teaspoon dried rosemary

½ teaspoon salt, or to taste

1½ cups diced mixed vegetables such as carrots, celery, leeks, and scallions

1 apple, peeled, cored and thinly sliced (5 ounces)

1 tablespoon fresh lime juice

2 tablespoons chopped cilantro or flat-leaf parsely

*In a stockpot,* combine the tomato puree, beans, lentils, rice, sun-dried tomatoes, curry powder, basil, oregano, cumin, pepper flakes, fennel seeds, rosemary, and salt. Add 8 cups of water and bring to a boil over high heat. Reduce the heat and simmer, partially covered, for about 1½ hours, or until the beans are tender. Skim any foam that rises to the top of the soup during cooking.

*Add the vegetables* and simmer for about 20 minutes longer, or until the vegetables soften. Add more water if the soup is too thick, a cup at a time.

*Put the apples* and lime juice in the bowls and ladle the soup over the apples. Garnish with cilantro.

# Curried Lentil Soup

**T**HIS SOUP, eaten with a slice or two of Old-Fashioned Tecate Bread (page 217), is a warmly satisfying, complete meal. It is equally good if you replace the green lentils with red lentils.

PER SERVING:

*146 calories*

*2 g total fat (11% of calories)*

*0 g saturated fat*

*0 mg cholesterol*

*8 g protein (23% of calories)*

*24 g carbohydrates*

*(67% of calories)*

*2 g fiber*

*31 mg sodium*

**MAKES 8 SERVINGS**

2 teaspoons canola oil

½ cup chopped onions (2 ounces)

1 carrot, chopped (4 ounces)

2 ribs celery, chopped (5 ounces)

1 tablespoon curry powder

2 tomatoes, cored and chopped (9 ounces)

1 cup dried green lentils, rinsed

8 cups Vegetable Broth (page 280) or water, plus more if necessary

⅓ cup tomato puree

1 bay leaf

1 teaspoon kosher salt (optional)

1 cup diced peeled potatoes (5 ounces)

½ cup thinly sliced scallions (2 ounces) or chopped fresh flat-leaf parsley

*In a large pot,* heat the oil over medium heat. Add the onions, carrot, and celery and cook for about 5 minutes, stirring occasionally, until they begin to soften. Stir in the curry powder and cook for 1 to 2 minutes, stirring. Add the tomatoes, lentils, broth, tomato puree, bay leaf, and the salt, if desired. Bring to a boil over high heat, reduce the heat to medium-low, and simmer for about 40 minutes, or until the lentils are soft.

*Add the potatoes* and simmer for about 15 minutes, or until the potatoes are cooked through. Adjust the consistency of the soup if necessary by adding more broth. Taste and correct the seasonings if necessary.

*Ladle the soup* into heated bowls and sprinkle with the scallions.

# Watermelon Gazpacho

OST PEOPLE think of only tomatoes and celery when they think of gazpacho, but I like to add other fresh vegetables and fruit, such as watermelons. I make this chilled soup in the summer, when watermelons are plentiful and exceptionally sweet. The new seedless melons make it easy to prepare. Try it also with yellow watermelon.

1 cup thinly sliced peeled and seeded cucumbers
(2½ ounces)

¼ teaspoon kosher salt

6 cups cubed seeded watermelon (from about 2¼ pounds melon)

½ cup cranberry juice cocktail

1 red bell pepper, cored, seeded, and finely chopped
(4½ ounces)

1 red onion, finely chopped
(4 ounces)

1 rib celery, finely diced
(2 ounces)

¼ cup minced fresh flat-leaf parsley

2 to 3 tablespoons fresh lime juice

1 tablespoon sherry vinegar

8 fresh mint leaves

*In a small bowl,* toss the cucumbers with the salt. Set aside.

*In a blender* or food processor, combine the watermelon and cranberry juice cocktail. Pulse briefly until just blended. (Overprocessing will make the juice frothy and pale.) Pour through a sieve, set over a bowl, and press on the pulp to extract all of the juice. Discard the pulp.

*Stir the bell pepper,* onion, celery, parsley, lime juice, and vinegar into the watermelon juice. Cover and refrigerate for 1 hour to chill and give the flavors time to blend.

*Rinse the cucumbers* and pat dry.

*Ladle the soup* into chilled bowls and garnish with the cucumber slices and mint leaves.

# Gazpacho with Minted Grapefruit

**T**HIS UNUSUAL GAZPACHO is a refreshing start to any meal, made with juicy grapefruit freshly picked from our own citrus groves. Buy heavy, thin-skinned fruit for optimum juice. We serve this with low-sodium, low-cholesterol whole wheat crackers.

1½ cups fresh grapefruit juice (from 2 large grapefruit)

1 cucumber, peeled, seeded, and diced (5 ounces)

1 tomato, cored and diced (4½ ounces)

½ cup diced celery (4 ounces)

½ cup diced red bell pepper (2½ ounces)

¼ cup thinly sliced scallions (1 ounce)

2 tablespoons chopped fresh mint

2 tablespoons chopped fresh flat-leaf parsley

*In a bowl,* combine the grapefruit juice, cucumber, tomato, celery, red pepper, scallions, mint, and parsley and stir to mix. Cover and refrigerate for 2 hours to chill and give the flavors time to blend.

*Ladle the soup* into chilled bowls.

# Chilled Melon Soup with Mint

**N**O COOKING REQUIRED for this soup—only chilling time for the luscious blending of fresh fruit. I serve it as a first course or a refreshing lunch on hot summer days.

NOTE: *Honeydew or casaba melon can be substituted for the cantaloupe.*

1 cantaloupe (12 ounces), halved, seeded, peeled, and cut into large chunks

1 banana, sliced (3½ ounces)

½ cup fresh orange juice

1 green apple, such as Granny Smith, peeled, cored, and finely diced (4 ounces)

2 teaspoons fresh lime juice

2 teaspoons minced fresh mint

*Put the melon in a blender* or food processor, add the banana and orange juice, and process until smooth. Transfer to a glass or ceramic bowl, cover, and refrigerate for up to 1 hour.

*Meanwhile,* in a small bowl, toss the apple with the lime juice and mint. Cover and refrigerate for up to 1 hour.

*Ladle the soup* into chilled bowls and spoon the apples into the center of each.

# Salads

MANY FIRST-TIME GUESTS ARRIVE at our doorstep expecting to eat nothing but salad for a week. After all, they reason, they are in southern California at a "health spa"—of course they will be presented with a profusion of lettuces, raw vegetables, and sprouts. They are partly right: we love salads at the Door and I serve them frequently. I use organically grown greens and vegetables, herbs and edible flowers, succulent fruits, and flavorful seafood and chicken, all tossed with light and imaginative salad dressings. Our concern with balance in all things, however, extends to how we serve salads. Many are side salads, meant to be enjoyed alongside more substantial fare, while others are complete meals, perfect for lunch or, if you prefer, a light supper.

# California Gold Salad

**W**HEN I MAKE THIS SALAD at the Golden Door, I turn to our extensive gardens for inspiration, picking the greens and flowers that are in season. When you make it, rely on local farmers' markets—they are a cornucopia of incredible produce—or your own garden. Let nature's bounty be your guide when selecting the ingredients for the salad I call California Gold.

**PER SERVING:**

*179 calories*

*9 g total fat (46% of calories)*

*2 g saturated fat*

*3 mg cholesterol*

*4 g protein (9% of calories)*

*20 g carbohydrates*

*(45% of calories)*

*2 g fiber*

*67 mg sodium*

**MAKES 4 SERVINGS**

*NOTE: Society garlic is botanically known as tulbaghia violacea. It is commonly planted as a decorative border plant because its pungent aroma acts as a natural insect repellent. The mauve-colored flowers smell strongly but pleasantly of garlic and are wonderful in salads.*

### Salad

8 leaves radicchio (3 ounces)

4 cups mixed lettuces or mesclun mix (4 ounces)

1 cup edible flowers, such as nasturtiums, Johnny jump-ups, and/or society garlic flowers (see Note)

8 thin slices avocado (4 ounces)

2 grapefruits, peeled and sectioned, juice reserved

2 yellow or red tomatoes, cored and quartered (9 ounces)

### Dressing

¼ cup reserved grapefruit juice

1 tablespoon balsamic vinegar

1 tablespoon water

1 tablespoon olive oil

½ teaspoon freshly ground black pepper

2 tablespoons slivered fresh basil

1 cup radish sprouts (1 ounce)

2 tablespoons crumbled feta cheese

*To make the salad,* mound 2 radicchio leaves, 1 cup greens, and ¼ cup edible flowers (reserve some for garnish) on each of 4 chilled plates. Arrange the avocado, grapefruit, and tomatoes around the greens on the plates.

*To make the dressing,* in a small bowl, whisk the grapefruit juice with the balsamic vinegar, water, oil, and pepper. Whisk in the basil.

*Drizzle the dressing* over the salads. Top with the radish sprouts and a sprinkling of feta cheese and flowers.

## CALIFORNIA GREENS AND EDIBLE FLOWERS

California gardens offer a variety of tender lettuces such as oak leaf, Lollo Rossa, baby tatsoi, spinach, watercress, and mizuna. Combinations of these greens are now available in many grocery stores, packaged as mesclun. Combined with edible flowers, these greens become the base for any number of colorful and fresh salads. The flowers provide mild flavor but their primary role is to add glamour and a touch of whimsy. When selecting blooms from your garden to add to salads, be sure the flower is indeed edible. It's also important that the flower beds have not been sprayed with toxic insecticides. Some edible flowers that are commonly available include geraniums, nasturtiums, johnny jump-ups, rose petals, garlic flowers, and zucchini blossoms.

# Coleslaw

**I** PROMISE YOU won't miss the usual heavy creamy dressing so often tossed with cabbage to make coleslaw when you taste this one made crunchy with carrots and apples. Try it with the Turkey Patties on Garlic-Rosemary Buns on page 182 or with the Red Lentil and Seven-Grain Veggie Burgers with Grilled Onions on page 132.

Try it with the Turkey Patties on Garlic-Rosemary Buns on page 182 or with the Red Lentil and Seven-Grain Veggie Burgers with Grilled Onions on page 132.

PER SERVING:

*60 calories*

*0 g total fat (6% of calories)*

*0 g saturated fat*

*0 mg cholesterol*

*1 g protein (10% of calories)*

*10 g carbohydrates*

*(70% of calories)*

*1 g fiber*

*803 mg sodium*

**MAKES 4 SERVINGS**

½ head green or savoy cabbage, cored, quartered, and thinly sliced (12 ounces)

¼ head red cabbage, thinly sliced (3 ounces)

½ cup diced red onions (2 ounces)

1 carrot, grated (4 ounces)

1 tablespoon caraway seeds

2 teaspoons kosher salt

⅓ cup red wine vinegar or cider vinegar

1 green or red apple, unpeeled, cored, and grated (4 ounces)

2 tablespoons minced fresh flat-leaf parsley

*In a large bowl,* combine the cabbages, onions, carrot, caraway seeds, salt, and vinegar and toss to mix. Cover and set aside for about 1 hour to marinate.

*Drain the excess liquid* from the coleslaw. Add the apple and toss to mix. Serve sprinkled with the parsley.

# Celery Root and Apple Salad

**C**ELERY ROOT (or celeriac) hides its delicately flavored white flesh beneath knobby brown skin. Popular in Europe, it can also be found in this country, and I like to serve it with a tangy mustard dressing.

PER SERVING
(not including dressing):

*63 calories*

*1 g total fat (10% of calories)*

*0 g saturated fat*

*0 mg cholesterol*

*2 g protein (11% of calories)*

*12 g carbohydrates*

*(79% of calories)*

*1 g fiber*

*164 mg sodium*

**MAKES 4 SERVINGS**

2 to 3 celery roots, peeled and julienned (9 ounces)

1/3 cup Mustard Dressing (page 86)

1 tablespoon fresh lemon juice

1 tablespoon Dijon mustard

1/2 teaspoon freshly ground black pepper

1 green apple, unpeeled, cored and julienned

2 tablespoons chopped fresh flat-leaf parsley

4 cups torn Bibb lettuce (4 ounces)

6 radishes, thinly sliced (1 ounce)

6 sprigs fresh flat-leaf parsley

*In a bowl,* combine the celery root with the dressing, lemon juice, mustard, and pepper, tossing to coat. Cover and set aside for 1 hour.

*Add the apples* and parsley to the celery root and toss to combine.

*To serve,* spread the lettuce on 4 chilled salad plates. Spoon the salad in the center and garnish with the radishes and sprigs of parsley.

# Citus Salad

**A**T THE GOLDEN DOOR, we make this colorful winter salad with several citrus fruits, all of which grow in our organic mountainside groves. Here we suggest Meyer lemons, pink grapefruit, tangerines, and both blood and navel oranges. This mélange creates an unbeatable sweet-tart flavor that is offset perfectly by the sweet sherry dressing.

PER SERVING:

90 calories

0 g total fat (4% of calories)

0 g saturated fat

0 mg cholesterol

2 g protein (9% of calories)

20 g carbohydrates

(87% of calories)

1 g fiber

10 mg sodium

**MAKES 4 SERVINGS**

NOTE: *Meyer lemons, which grow in California, are scarce in most of the country, but can be found in specialty markets in the early spring and fall. You can substitute with lemons available everywhere.*

*Fructose is sold in health food stores. Substitute granulated sugar if necessary.*

Julienned zest of 1 orange

1 large navel orange (4 ounces)

1 blood orange (2 ounces)

1 large pink grapefruit (6 ounces)

2 Meyer lemons, peeled (5 ounces; see Note)

2 tangerines, peeled (3 ounces)

1 tablespoon sherry vinegar

1 tablespoon fructose, or to taste (see Note)

½ teaspoon freshly ground black pepper

1 tablespoon canola oil or walnut oil (optional)

2 tablespoons slivered fresh basil

4 cups mixed lettuces or mesclun mix (4 ounces)

*In a small saucepan* of boiling water, blanch the orange zest for 2 minutes. Drain and set aside.

*Working over a bowl,* peel, seed, and section each citrus fruit, cutting off the membrane, collecting the juices as you work. You should have about ½ cup citrus juice. Set the fruit aside.

*To make the dressing,* whisk the vinegar, fructose, pepper, and the oil, if using, into the citrus juice. Stir in the basil. If the fruit is very tart, add a few more drops of fructose to the dressing.

*To serve,* spread the greens on 4 chilled plates. Arrange the citrus sections on the greens, drizzle with the dressing, and garnish with the orange zest.

## A DISAPPEARING FRUIT SALAD

We use a great deal of fresh fruit at the Golden Door. We often place a fresh pear, apple, or banana in the rooms of guests who may awaken earlier than others (and grow hungry sooner) because they're from a different time zone.

Our favorite method of serving fruit, however, is to cut up many different kinds of fruit from our garden and create a large, fragrant fruit salad. Nothing disappears faster. The selection of the fruits at the peak of ripeness is a key, of course, but at home many of us find it difficult to find fruit that ripens properly. I urge you to search out a source for produce that selects fruit that is as close to on-the-tree ripeness as possible.

And, as we suggest elsewhere, follow the seasons. Stone fruits, for example, taste all the sweeter when you know that they'll soon be unavailable except by refrigerated air or sea cargo.

# Flageolet Beans with Marinated Tofu

**F**LAGEOLET BEANS ARE TINY, tender French kidney beans that can now be found in their dried form in this country. Prepare this salad at least an hour before serving to allow the marinade to flavor the beans. We serve it with marinated tofu, but it is also good with seared tuna or other grilled fish.

*Beans*

1 cup dried flageolets or small white beans, rinsed (6 ounces)

4½ cups Vegetable Broth (page 280) or water

1 bay leaf

*Tofu*

14 ounces firm tofu, cut into ¾-inch dice

1 teaspoon minced fresh ginger

1 teaspoon minced garlic

3 to 4 teaspoons low-sodium tamari or soy sauce

*Dressing*

1 tablespoon Dijon mustard

1 teaspoon minced garlic

2 tablespoons balsamic vinegar

1 tablespoon olive oil

2 teaspoons minced fresh oregano or 1 teaspoon dried

½ teaspoon freshly ground black pepper

2 tomatoes, cored and diced (9 ounces)

¼ cup chopped fresh flat-leaf parsley

½ to 1 teaspoon kosher salt (optional)

3 ounces mixed lettuces or mesclun mix

1 cup alfalfa sprouts (1 ounce)

1 lemon, cut into 6 wedges

*Soak the beans* in 4 cups of water for 1 hour. Drain and rinse well.

*In a large saucepan,* combine the beans with the broth and bay leaf. Bring to a boil over high heat, reduce the heat to low, and simmer, partially covered, for about 1¼ hours, or until the beans are very tender. Drain and transfer the beans to a bowl.

*Meanwhile,* in a bowl, combine the tofu, ginger, garlic, and tamari, tossing gently to mix. Cover and refrigerate for at least 1 hour.

*To make the dressing,* in a small bowl, whisk together the mustard, garlic, vinegar, oil, oregano, and pepper. Stir in the tomatoes and parsley. Add the salt, if desired. Add the dressing to the beans, stir gently to combine, and set aside for 1 hour.

*Spray a nonstick sauté pan* with vegetable oil spray and heat over medium-high heat. Add the tofu and its marinade and sauté for 2 to 4 minutes, until the tofu is lightly browned.

*Spread the greens* on 6 plates. Spoon the flageolet salad in the center, top with the tofu, and garnish with the sprouts and lemon wedges.

# Lebanese Green Lentil Salad

THE FRENCH GREEN LENTILS, called du Puy in France, are favored for salads, as they retain their shape and flavor during cooking and are well suited to spicy dishes such as this one.

PER SERVING:

201 calories

4 g total fat (19% of calories)

1 g saturated fat

0 mg cholesterol

11 g protein (22% of calories)

30 g carbohydrates

(59% of calories)

3 g fiber

640 mg sodium

MAKES 4 SERVINGS

**Lentils**

3/4 cup dried green lentils, rinsed (4 3/4 ounces)

1 bay leaf

1 teaspoon kosher salt

1 teaspoon red pepper flakes (optional)

**Salad**

1/2 cup diced onions (2 ounces)

2 ribs celery, peeled and diced (5 ounces)

1 carrot, diced (4 ounces)

2 teaspoons chopped fresh oregano

2 teaspoons ground cumin

1 teaspoon ground allspice

1/4 cup fresh lemon juice

1 tablespoon olive oil

1/2 cup chopped fresh flat-leaf parsley

1 tablespoon chopped fresh mint

1 head Bibb lettuce, leaves separated

1 tomato, cored and cut into 8 wedges (4 1/2 ounces)

2 tablespoons crumbled feta cheese (optional)

*To cook the lentils,* in a medium-sized saucepan, combine the lentils with 3 1/4 cups of water, the bay leaf, salt, and the pepper flakes, if desired. Bring to a boil over high heat, reduce the heat, and simmer for about 25 minutes, or until the lentils are tender but still hold their shape. Transfer 1/4 cup of the cooking liquid to a small bowl and set aside. Drain the lentils and transfer to a large bowl to cool.

*Spray a nonstick sauté pan* with vegetable oil spray and place over medium heat. Add the onions, celery, and carrot and cook for about 5 minutes, stirring occasionally, until the onions are translucent. Add the oregano, cumin, and allspice and cook, stirring, for 1 minute. Stir into the lentils.

*Add the lemon juice* and oil to the reserved lentil cooking liquid and whisk until combined. Pour the dressing over the lentils and toss gently to combine. Stir in the parsley and mint.

*Line 4 chilled plates* with the lettuce leaves. Spoon the lentils over the lettuce, arrange the tomatoes on top, and sprinkle with the cheese, if desired.

NOTE: *French green lentils are available in specialty food stores. Substitute regular green lentils if you cannot locate them and reduce the cooking time by 5 to 10 minutes.*

# Potato, Artichoke, and Apple Salad

**T**HIS UNUSUAL but robustly satisfying combination of flavors makes a fine accompaniment to broiled chicken breast or grilled fish.

**PER SERVING**
(not including dressing):

*169 calories*

*1 g total fat (4% of calories)*

*0 g saturated fat*

*0 mg cholesterol*

*5 g protein (11% of calories)*

*36 g carbohydrates*

*(84% of calories)*

*2 g fiber*

*152 mg sodium*

**MAKES 4 SERVINGS**

3 medium-sized red potatoes (14 ounces)

4 artichokes

2 tablespoons fresh lemon juice

1 tart apple, peeled, cored, and diced (4 ounces)

1 rib celery, diced

$^1/_3$ cup Mustard Dressing (page 86)

1 tablespoon Dijon mustard

2 tablespoons chopped fresh flat-leaf parsley

$^1/_2$ teaspoon freshly ground black pepper

4 large lettuce leaves

*Put the potatoes in a large saucepan,* add enough water to cover by several inches, and bring to a boil over high heat. Reduce the heat and simmer for 20 to 25 minutes, until the potatoes are fork-tender. Drain, cool, and dice the potatoes. Transfer to a large bowl.

*To prepare the artichokes,* trim the stems and break off all of the tough outer leaves. Cut off the inner core of pale green leaves. Put the artichokes in a large pot and add 1 tablespoon of the lemon juice and enough water to cover by several inches. Bring to a boil over high heat, reduce the heat, and simmer for about 20 minutes, until the artichokes are tender. Drain, cool, and scoop out the fuzzy chokes with a spoon. Cut the artichoke bottoms into 1-inch wedges and add them to the potatoes.

*Add the apple,* drizzle with the remaining 1 tablespoon lemon juice, and toss. Add the celery and toss again.

*In a small bowl,* whisk together the dressing, mustard, parsley, and pepper. Pour the dressing over the salad and toss gently to combine.

*To serve,* line 4 plates with the lettuce leaves. Spoon the potato salad in the center.

# Rotelle Pasta Salad

**S**ALADS ARE ALWAYS WELCOME at the Golden Door, where days are wonderfully sunny all year round. This pasta salad is lighter than most and is ideal on a buffet table.

PER SERVING:

*217 calories*

*4 g total fat (15% of calories)*

*1 g saturated fat*

*0 mg cholesterol*

*7 g protein (13% of calories)*

*39 g carbohydrates*

*(72% of calories)*

*2 g fiber*

*25 mg sodium*

**MAKES 6 SERVINGS**

1 cup slender green beans

8 ounces whole wheat or semolina rotelle

1 tablespoon pine nuts

4 tomatoes, cored and diced (18 ounces)

2 tablespoons thinly sliced soaked dry-packed sundried tomatoes (see Note)

2 tablespoons thinly sliced scallions (white part only)

2 teaspoons minced garlic

2 fresh artichoke hearts, diced (optional; see Note)

3 to 4 tablespoons balsamic vinegar

1 tablespoon olive oil

½ cup chopped fresh flat-leaf parsley

½ cup slivered fresh basil

1 teaspoon chopped fresh oregano

1 teaspoon kosher salt (optional)

½ teaspoon freshly ground black pepper

5 cups mixed lettuces or mesclun mix (5 ounces)

5 ounces yellow or red cherry tomatoes

*Bring a large pot* of lightly salted water to a boil. Add the beans and cook for 2 to 3 minutes, until bright green and crisp-tender. Remove with a slotted spoon, refresh under cold water, and set aside. Add the rotelle to the boiling water and cook at a rapid boil for 8 to 9 minutes, until al dente. Drain, rinse under cold running water, and set aside.

*In a small skillet,* toast the pine nuts over medium heat, shaking several times, for about 4 minutes, until pale golden and fragrant. Set aside.

*In a large bowl,* combine the diced tomatoes, sundried tomatoes, scallions, garlic, the artichoke hearts, if desired, vinegar, oil, parsley, basil, oregano, the salt, if using, and pepper. Add the cooked pasta and stir gently but thoroughly to combine.

*Line 6 chilled plates* with the greens. Spoon the salad over the greens and garnish each plate with the green beans, cherry tomatoes, and pine nuts.

NOTE: *To rehydrate dry-packed sundried tomatoes, soak them in warm water to cover for 15 to 20 minutes. Drain and slice. To prepare artichokes, see page 38.*

# Tabbouleh Salad

**B**ULGUR WHEAT IS GROUND to a fine, medium, or coarse texture. Tabbouleh is usually prepared with medium-grind bulgur, but if you are in a hurry and cannot take the time to soak the bulgur for at least two hours, use fine-ground bulgur and soak it for one hour. I recommend doubling the recipe so that you have plenty left over for tomorrow—it's that good!

NOTE: *There are a number of ways to prepare bulgur. If you prefer, pour 1 cup of boiling water over the bulgur and let it stand for about 30 minutes, until tender but still crunchy. Drain and cool.*

½ cup medium-grind bulgur

1 large tomato, cored and diced (6 ounces)

½ cup thinly sliced scallions (including green tops; 2 ounces)

6 radishes, diced

¾ cup chopped fresh flat-leaf parsley

2 tablespoons chopped fresh mint

1 tablespoon minced garlic

3 tablespoons fresh lemon juice

1 to 2 tablespoons olive oil

Pinch of cayenne pepper (optional)

6 large lettuce leaves

½ cucumber, thinly sliced (3 ounces)

*In a small bowl,* combine the bulgur with 1½ cups of water. Set aside to soak for at least 2 hours, or until the bulgur is tender but still slightly crunchy. Drain in a fine sieve and press out any excess water. Transfer to a large bowl.

*Add the tomato,* scallions, radishes, parsley, mint, and garlic to the bulgur and, using a large kitchen fork, fold together. Add the lemon juice, oil, and the cayenne, if using, and stir gently. Set aside at room temperature for about 1 hour to give the flavors time to blend.

*Line 6 chilled plates* with the lettuce leaves and spoon the tabbouleh over the lettuce. Garnish with the cucumber.

# Tomato Salad Oreganato

**B**OLDLY ACCENTED with garlic and oregano, this salad is a refreshing starter with unmistakable Italian flavor. I like to serve it before a pasta course. For best results, use vine-ripened tomatoes.

PER SERVING:

*84 calories*

*4 g total fat (45% of calories)*

*1 g saturated fat*

*0 mg cholesterol*

*2 g protein (10% of calories)*

*10 g carbohydrates*

*(46% of calories)*

*1 g fiber*

*82 mg sodium*

**MAKES 4 SERVINGS**

4 ripe tomatoes, cored (24 ounces)

1 tablespoon balsamic vinegar

1 tablespoon water

1 tablespoon olive oil

2 teaspoons Dijon mustard

1 teaspoon minced garlic

2 teaspoons dry or 2 tablespoons chopped fresh oregano

$1/4$ teaspoon freshly ground black pepper

2 tablespoons chopped fresh flat-leaf parsley

4 large lettuce leaves

*Bring a large pot* of water to a boil over high heat. Plunge the tomatoes into the water and blanch for about 30 seconds. Using a slotted spoon, lift the tomatoes from the water and immediately plunge them into a bowl of ice water. Drain, peel, and cut each tomato into 8 wedges. Set aside.

*In a bowl,* whisk together the vinegar, water, oil, mustard, garlic, oregano, and pepper. Add the tomatoes and stir gently to combine. Cover the bowl and refrigerate for at least 1 hour.

*Stir the chopped parsley* into the tomatoes. Line 4 chilled plates with the lettuce leaves and spoon the salad into the center of the plates.

# Fruit "Club Sandwich" with Cottage Cheese and Apple Filling

**T**HIS RECIPE HAS ALWAYS been popular with our guests, who often ask for it at lunchtime. It is also an ideal brunch dish.

*Filling*

2 cups 1% low-fat cottage cheese (16 ounces)

1 green apple, unpeeled, cored and grated (4 ounces)

½ teaspoon ground cinnamon

*Mango yogurt sauce*

1 mango, peeled and pitted (8 ounces)

1 cup nonfat plain yogurt

1 teaspoon honey

1 teaspoon fresh lime juice

*Sandwiches*

Four ⅓-inch-thick cantaloupe rings (10 ounces; see Note)

Four ⅓-inch-thick pineapple rings (10 ounces)

Four ¼-inch-thick slices peeled grapefruit (6 ounces)

Four ¼-inch-thick slices peeled orange (5 ounces)

Four ¼-inch-thick slices peeled kiwi (2 ounces)

4 strawberries, hulled (1 ounce)

4 large lettuce leaves

¼ cup Raspberry Coulis (page 247)

12 mini rice crackers

*To make the filling,* in a small bowl, whisk together the filling ingredients.

*To make the sauce,* combine the mango, yogurt, honey, and lime juice in a food processor or blender and process until smooth and creamy.

*To assemble the sandwiches,* line a tray or baking sheet with plastic wrap. Arrange the cantaloupe rings on the tray and spoon ¼ cup of the cottage cheese mixture into the center of each. Top with the pineapple rings and spoon 2 tablespoons of the cottage cheese filling into the center of each. Top with the grapefruit slices and spoon 2 tablespoons of cottage cheese filling over each one. Top each stack with an orange, kiwi and a strawberry. Insert a toothpick through each strawberry to secure the sandwiches.

*Line 4 plates* with the lettuce leaves. Using a spatula, slide a sandwich onto each plate. Drizzle 1 tablespoon of the coulis over the top of each. Surround with the rice crackers and serve the yogurt sauce on the side.

NOTE: *To prepare cantaloupe rings, slice the melon crosswise, remove the seeds, and peel. Slice the melon into rings.*

# Lobster-Filled Papaya

**G**UESTS AT THE SPA love this salad, whether I make it with lobster or, as I sometimes do, with shrimp. I serve it with the Tabbouleh Salad on page 75 or the Wild Rice Pilaf with Pineapple and Ginger (page 202).

PER SERVING:

*162 calories*

*3 g total fat (18% of calories)*

*0 g saturated fat*

*51 mg cholesterol*

*17 g protein (42% of calories)*

*16 g carbohydrates*

*(40% of calories)*

*2 g fiber*

*308 mg sodium*

**MAKES 4 SERVINGS**

NOTE: *You can substitute 10 ounces chopped cooked shrimp for the lobster, or combine shrimp and lobster for a rich seafood filling.*

2 ribs celery, chopped (5 ounces)

8 snow peas (1 ounce)

2 papayas, halved lengthwise and seeded (16 ounces)

10 ounces cooked lobster meat, diced

2 teaspoons fresh lemon juice

1½ to 2 teaspoons curry powder

2 tablespoons thinly sliced chives

2 tablespoons lightly toasted sunflower seeds

2 cups mixed lettuces or mesclun mix (2 ounces)

4 orange wedges

*In a saucepan of boiling water,* blanch the celery for 1 minute. Using a slotted spoon, lift the celery from the water, drain, refresh under cold running water, and set aside. Blanch the snow peas for 1 minute, drain, refresh under cold running water, and set aside.

*Using a melon baller,* scoop out balls from the papaya halves, leaving enough flesh in the skin that the shells retain their shape.

*In a large bowl,* combine the papaya balls with the celery, lobster, lemon juice, curry powder, chives, and sunflower seeds. Mix gently but thoroughly. Spoon the lobster mixture into the papaya shells.

*Line 4 chilled plates* with the lettuce. Place the filled papaya shells on the greens and spoon a scoop of tabbouleh on the side of each. Garnish with the orange wedges and snow peas.

# Crunchy Chicken Salad with Apples and Bulgur

**T**HIS CHICKEN SALAD is not only delicious, but has the added advantage of being rich in fiber, in the form of bulgur.

PER SERVING
(including dressing):

*227 calories*

*6 g total fat (22% of calories)*

*1 g saturated fat*

*67 mg cholesterol*

*29 g protein (51% of calories)*

*15 g carbohydrates*

*(27% of calories)*

*1 g fiber*

*130 mg sodium*

**MAKES 4 SERVINGS**

*Bulgur topping*

¼ cup fine- or medium-grind bulgur

1 tablespoon chopped fresh mint

*Salad*

14 ounces skinless, boneless chicken breast halves

1 teaspoon olive oil

¼ teaspoon dried basil or tarragon

¼ teaspoon freshly ground black pepper

1 green apple, peeled, cored, and diced (4 ounces)

1 tablespoon fresh lime juice

1 cup diced celery (6 ounces)

¼ cup chopped fresh flat-leaf parsley

2 teaspoons chopped fresh tarragon

½ cup Silken Tofu Mayonnaise (page 289)

4 cups mixed lettuces or mesclun mix (4 ounces)

2 tablespoons slivered edible flowers, such as nasturtiums or Johnny jump-ups

*To prepare the bulgur,* bring ½ cup of water to a boil over high heat. Put the bulgur in a bowl and pour the boiling water over it. Let stand for about 30 minutes, or until the bulgur is swollen and tender but still slightly crunchy. Drain in a fine sieve and press out any excess water. Just before serving, stir in the mint.

*Prepare a charcoal or gas grill* or preheat a stove-top grill. Preheat the oven to 350°F.

*Rub the chicken* with the oil, basil, and pepper. Grill the chicken for 2 to 3 minutes to make diamond or square grill marks on both sides. Transfer to a baking pan and bake, uncovered, for 8 to 10 minutes, or until the juices run clear when the meat is pierced with a fork or sharp knife. Cool, cut into ½-inch cubes, and transfer to a large bowl.

*Add the apple* to the bowl and drizzle with the lime juice. Add the celery, parsley, and tarragon and toss to coat. Add the mayonnaise and toss gently but thoroughly.

*Line 4 chilled plates* with the lettuce. Spoon the chicken salad over the lettuce and sprinkle with the bulgur-mint mixture. Garnish with the slivered flowers.

# Tuna Salad with Cottage Cheese

**T**HIS SALAD, on the menu since the Golden Door opened in the late 1950s, is still very much in demand. I like to serve it with the potato salad from Grilled Ahi Tuna Niçoise on page 81.

PER SERVING
(not including dressing):

193 calories

3 g total fat (15% of calories)

1 g saturated fat

40 mg cholesterol

31 g protein (63% of calories)

10 g carbohydrates

(21% of calories)

1 g fiber

292 mg sodium

**MAKES 4 SERVINGS**

One 13-ounce can unsalted white tuna in water, drained

½ cup 1% low-fat cottage cheese

¼ cup diced celery (2 ounces)

2 tablespoons chopped flat-leaf fresh parsley

1 tablespoon Dijon mustard

2 teaspoons fresh lemon juice

1 head Bibb or oak leaf lettuce, torn into bite-sized pieces

2 tomatoes, cored and quartered (9 ounces)

½ seedless (English) cucumber, cut into 8 thin slices (3 ounces)

1 cup broccoli florets, blanched

1 carrot, shredded (4 ounces)

1 cup alfalfa sprouts (1 ounce)

4 lemon wedges

Nonfat Pinto Bean–Oregano Dressing (page 89)

*With a fork,* flake the tuna into a bowl. Add the cottage cheese, celery, parsley, mustard, and lemon juice and mix well.

*Arrange the lettuce,* tomatoes, cucumber, broccoli, carrot, sprouts, and lemon wedges on 4 plates. Scoop the tuna mixture off-center onto the plates and drizzle with the dressing.

# Grilled Ahi Tuna Niçoise

**I** SERVE AHI TUNA with a light potato salad, fresh tomatoes, and green beans to make a California version of classic Tuna Niçoise. I also like ahi cooked medium-rare and served simply with buttery lettuce, summer-ripe tomatoes, and a little creamy horseradish on the side.

PER SERVING
(not including dressing):

342 calories

9 g total fat (25% of calories)

2 g saturated fat

42 mg cholesterol

30 g protein (35% of calories)

34 g carbohydrates
(40% of calories)

2 g fiber

134 mg sodium

**MAKES 4 SERVINGS**

*Potato salad*

1 pound red or new potatoes, halved or quartered

1 tablespoon olive oil

3 tablespoons water

2 tablespoons cider vinegar

2 teaspoons Dijon mustard

1 teaspoon freshly ground black pepper

½ cup sliced scallions (including green tops)

1 teaspoon coarsely chopped drained capers

*Tuna*

Four 4-ounce ahi tuna steaks, about ½ inch thick

1 teaspoon olive oil (optional)

1 teaspoon coarsely ground black pepper

4 large lettuce leaves

4 ounces green beans, blanched

2 tomatoes, cored and quartered (9 ounces)

1 cup alfalfa sprouts (1 ounce)

4 lemon wedges

Nonfat Pinto Bean–Oregano Dressing (page 89) or Roasted Tomato–Basil Dressing (page 92)

*Prepare a charcoal or gas grill* or preheat a stove-top grill.

*Bring a large saucepan* of salted water to a boil. Add the potatoes and cook for about 15 minutes, or until fork-tender. Drain, cool, and slice.

*In a bowl,* whisk together the olive oil, water, vinegar, mustard, and pepper. Add the potatoes, scallions, and capers and mix well.

*Spray the grill* with vegetable oil spray. Brush the tuna on both sides with the olive oil, if using, and sprinkle with the pepper. Grill for about 3 minutes on each side, turning to make square or diamond grill marks on both sides.

*Line 4 chilled plates* with the lettuce leaves and spoon the potato salad onto the lettuce. Set the grilled tuna opposite the potato salad and garnish the plates with the green beans, tomatoes, alfalfa sprouts, and lemon wedges. Serve the dressing on the side.

*NOTE: You can use a heavy cast-iron pan to cook the tuna.*

# Lobster and Shrimp Salad with Lime-Ginger Dressing

**T**HIS DELICATE SALAD IS INSPIRED by Vietnamese cuisine, which relies on light fresh flavors. I suggest lobster here, but it is equally good with shrimp or monkfish that has been cooked in a little broth and lemon juice. Whether lobster, shrimp, or monkfish, the results are outstanding.

**PER SERVING**
(not including dressing):

*322 calories*

*8 g total fat (22% of calories)*

*2 g saturated fat*

*144 mg cholesterol*

*31 g protein (39% of calories)*

*31 g carbohydrates*

*(38% of calories)*

*2 g fiber*

*668 mg sodium*

**MAKES 4 SERVINGS**

NOTE: *Mung bean Asian noodles are sold in Asian markets. Substitute other Asian noodles if necessary, or use vermicelli.*

*To make papaya fans, halve and seed the papaya. Cut each piece lengthwise in half and peel. Set each quarter on a cutting board and make several evenly spaced vertical cuts, stopping 2 inches from the stem end. To serve, spread the fruit into fans and lift onto the plates.*

3 ounces mung bean Asian noodles (see Note)

2 tablespoons rice vinegar

1/2 cup thinly sliced scallions (including green tops; 2 ounces)

1/2 red bell pepper, julienned (2 ounces)

1 leek (white part only), julienned (3 ounces)

8 slender stalks asparagus, trimmed (3 ounces)

4 to 8 large Romaine or butter lettuce leaves

1 cup sliced Bibb or leaf lettuce (2 ounces)

12 ounces cooked lobster meat

4 large cooked shrimp (6 ounces before peeling and cooking)

1 papaya, cut into 4 fans (8 ounces; see Note)

Lime-Ginger Dressing (page 88)

1 tablespoon black sesame seeds

1 lime, cut into 4 wedges

4 sprigs fresh cilantro

*Bring a saucepan of water* to a boil over high heat and drop the noodles into the water. Immediately remove the pan from the heat and let the noodles stand in the hot water for 15 minutes, or until softened.

*Drain the noodles* and rinse under cool running water. Shake off the excess water and transfer the noodles to a small bowl. Add the rice vinegar and scallions, toss, and set aside.

*In a steaming basket* set over boiling water, steam the pepper, leek, and asparagus for 1 to 2 minutes, until fork-tender. Drain, rinse under cool running water, and set aside.

*Line 4 plates* with the lettuce leaves and cover the base of each leaf with the sliced lettuce. Top with the noodles and arrange the steamed vegetables around the noodles. Arrange a quarter of the lobster meat on top of each serving of noodles and lay a shrimp next to the lobster. Arrange a papaya fan on the side of each plate. Drizzle with the dressing and sprinkle with the sesame seeds. Garnish each plate with a lime wedge and cilantro sprig.

# Salad Dressings

MY YEARS AS A CHEF have taught me any number of valuable lessons, not the least of which is that many people drown otherwise perfect salads in heavy, oily dressings. At the Golden Door, we pride ourselves on our varied and full-flavored dressings that rely more on vinegars, just-squeezed citrus juices, fresh herbs, and potent infusions than on oils for flavor and body. I use these liberally throughout the book and urge you to try them on your own salads, or drizzled over simple grilled chicken breasts, grilled vegetables, and fish steaks for bold flavor with plenty of zip.

# Balsamic Vinaigrette

2 tablespoons balsamic vinegar

1½ tablespoons water

1½ tablespoons Dijon mustard

¼ teaspoon crumbled dried basil

¼ teaspoon freshly ground black pepper

1 tablespoon olive oil or canola oil

*In a small bowl,* whisk together the vinegar, water, mustard, basil, and pepper. Gradually add the oil in a thin stream, whisking vigorously.

*Cover and refrigerate* until ready to use. (This dressing will keep for up to 2 weeks.)

# Mustard Dressing

¼ cup water

1½ tablespoons cider vinegar

1 shallot, sliced

1 tablespoon canola oil

2½ teaspoons Dijon mustard

1½ teaspoons honey (optional)

¼ teaspoon freshly ground black pepper

¼ teaspoon dried tarragon or thyme

1 tablespoon chopped fresh flat-leaf parsley

*In a blender* or food processor, combine the water, vinegar, shallot, oil, mustard, the honey, if using, and pepper. Process until smooth. Add the tarragon and parsley and pulse until combined.

*Cover and refrigerate* until ready to serve. (This dressing will keep for up to 1 week.)

# Lemon Dressing

PER TABLESPOON:

*25 calories*

*2 g total fat (82% of calories)*

*0 g saturated fat*

*0 mg cholesterol*

*0 g protein (1% of calories)*

*1 g carbohydrates*

*(17% of calories)*

*0 g fiber*

*1 mg sodium*

**MAKES ABOUT 1/3 CUP**

NOTE: *Xanthan gum is made from fermented corn sugar and is used as a thickener, emulsifier, and stabilizer in foods such as dairy products and salad dressings. It is sold in health food stores, although you may have to special-order it.*

1/4 cup water

2 tablespoons fresh lemon juice

1 tablespoon canola oil

1/2 teaspoon fructose

1/2 teaspoon dried basil or tarragon

1/4 teaspoon freshly ground black pepper

1/8 teaspoon xanthan gum (see Note; optional)

1 tablespoon minced fresh flat-leaf parsley

*In a small bowl,* combine the water, lemon juice, oil, fructose, basil, and pepper. If using, sprinkle the xanthan gum over the mixture and whisk vigorously until blended. Stir in the parsley.

*Cover and refrigerate* until ready to use. (This dressing will keep for up to 1 week.)

# Lime-Ginger Dressing

PER TABLESPOON:

*8 calories*

*0 g total fat (1% of calories)*

*0 g saturated fat*

*0 mg cholesterol*

*0 g protein (2% of calories)*

*1 g carbohydrates*

*(56% of calories)*

*0 g fiber*

*1 mg sodium*

**MAKES ABOUT 1/3 CUP**

2 tablespoons fresh lime juice

2 tablespoons mirin
(sweet rice wine)

1 tablespoon rice vinegar

1/2 teaspoon fructose

Dash of hot chili sauce
(see page 22)

1/4 teaspoon Chinese toasted
sesame oil (optional)

1/4 teaspoon xanthan gum
(see Note page 87; optional)

1/2 teaspoon chopped
Japanese pickled ginger
(*shoga*)

*In a small bowl,* combine the lime juice, mirin, rice vinegar, fructose, chili sauce, and the sesame oil, if desired. If using, sprinkle the xanthan gum over the mixture and whisk vigorously until smooth. Stir in the pickled ginger.

*Cover and refrigerate* until ready to use. (This dressing will keep for up to 1 week.)

# Nonfat Pinto Bean–Oregano Dressing

**PER TABLESPOON:**

*4 calories*

*0 g total fat (11% of calories)*

*0 g saturated fat*

*0 mg cholesterol*

*0 g protein (19% of calories)*

*1 g carbohydrates*

*(70% of calories)*

*0 g fiber*

*61 mg sodium*

**MAKES ABOUT 1 CUP**

¼ cup dried pinto beans, rinsed and soaked for 1 hour

1 small bay leaf

¼ teaspoon salt

1½ teaspoons Dijon mustard

1 tablespoon plus 1 scant teaspoon cider vinegar

1½ teaspoons minced shallots

1 tablespoon chopped fresh oregano or 1 teaspoon dried

2 tablespoons coarsely chopped fresh flat-leaf parsley

¼ teaspoon freshly ground black pepper

*In a small saucepan,* combine the pinto beans with 3 cups of water, the bay leaf, and salt. Bring to a boil over high heat, reduce the heat to low, and simmer, covered, for about 2 hours, or until the beans are tender and the water just barely covers the cooked beans. (Add more water if necessary while cooking the beans.) Drain, reserving the cooking liquid. Set aside to cool.

*In a blender* or food processor, combine 6 tablespoons of the cooked beans, 6 tablespoons of the reserved cooking liquid, the mustard, vinegar, and shallots. Reserve the remaining beans for another use. Process until smooth.

*Add the oregano,* parsley, and pepper and pulse to combine. If the dressing is too thick, thin with a little additional bean broth or water before serving.

*Cover and refrigerate* until ready to serve. (This dressing will keep for up to 1 week.)

# Peanut-Ginger-Honey Dressing or Sauce

*Fabulous! 9/07 made at Miltm's 60th party.*

NOTE: *You can substitute the same quantity of Thai or Vietnamese chili paste.*

1 tablespoon minced fresh ginger

1/2 teaspoon minced garlic

1 tablespoon mirin (sweet rice wine)

1 to 1 1/2 tablespoons low-sodium tamari or soy sauce

1 tablespoon rice vinegar

1 1/2 teaspoons red wine vinegar

1 tablespoon honey

1/4 teaspoon dried basil

1/2 teaspoon cracked Szechwan peppercorns (see Note)

1 tablespoon chunky peanut butter

1 tablespoon water

*In a blender* or food processor, combine the ginger, garlic, mirin, tamari, rice vinegar, red wine vinegar, honey, basil, peppercorns, peanut butter, and water. Process until smooth.

*Cover and refrigerate* until ready to use. (This dressing will keep for up to 1 week.)

# Raspberry Vinaigrette

PER TABLESPOON:

*14 calories*

*1 g total fat (37% of calories)*

*0 g saturated fat*

*0 mg cholesterol*

*0 g protein (1% of calories)*

*2 g carbohydrates*

*(62% of calories)*

*0 g fiber*

*0 mg sodium*

MAKES ABOUT 1/2 CUP

⅓ cup fresh raspberries or frozen unsweetened raspberries

1½ teaspoons unsweetened apple juice or water

2 tablespoons Raspberry-Vinegar Infusion (page 94) or raspberry vinegar

1½ tablespoons water

1 teaspoon fructose

1 teaspoon canola oil

⅛ teaspoon freshly ground black pepper

*In a blender* or food processor, pulse the raspberries with the apple juice 2 to 3 times until the berries are just broken up. Strain through a fine sieve set over a small bowl, pressing on the seeds to extract as much puree as possible. Discard the seeds. (You should have about ¼ cup puree.)

*Whisk the raspberry vinegar,* water, fructose, oil, and pepper into the raspberry puree.

*Cover and refrigerate* until ready to serve. (This dressing will keep for up to 1 week.)

# Red Pepper Dressing

PER TABLESPOON:

*19 calories*

*2 g total fat (81% of calories)*

*0 g saturated fat*

*0 mg cholesterol*

*0 g protein (2% of calories)*

*1 g carbohydrates*

*(16% of calories)*

*0 g fiber*

*8 mg sodium*

MAKES ABOUT ¹/₂ CUP

¹/₂ roasted red bell pepper (see page 99), chopped (2 ounces)

1 tablespoon chopped shallots

1 tablespoon olive oil

1 tablespoon sherry vinegar or red wine vinegar

¹/₂ teaspoon Dijon mustard

¹/₈ teaspoon hot chili sauce (see page 22), or to taste

¹/₄ cup water

*In a blender* or food processor, combine the bell pepper, shallots, oil, vinegar, mustard, chili sauce, and water. Process until quite smooth. Season to taste with additional chili sauce, if desired.

*Cover and refrigerate* until ready to use. (This dressing will keep for up to 5 days.)

# Roasted Tomato–Basil Dressing

PER TABLESPOON:

*4 calories*

*0 g total fat (10% of calories)*

*0 g saturated fat*

*0 mg cholesterol*

*0 g protein (13% of calories)*

*1 g carbohydrates*

*(77% of calories)*

*0 g fiber*

*1 mg sodium*

MAKES ABOUT ²/₃ CUP

1 tomato, cored (4¹/₂ ounces)

1 teaspoon chopped shallots

¹/₄ teaspoon minced garlic

1 tablespoon water

2 teaspoons balsamic vinegar

¹/₈ teaspoon freshly ground black pepper

1 tablespoon slivered fresh basil

*Preheat a gas grill,* broiler, or stove-top grill. Grill the tomato, turning often, until the skin begins to blister and char. Set aside to cool.

*Quarter the tomato* and combine in a blender or food processor with the shallots, garlic, water, vinegar, and pepper. Pulse just until the tomato is coarsely pureed. Add the basil and pulse to combine.

*Cover and refrigerate* until ready to use. (This dressing will keep for up to 5 days.)

# Caesar Dressing

PER 2 TABLESPOONS:

*14 calories*

*0 g total fat (18% of calories)*

*0 g saturated fat*

*1 mg cholesterol*

*1 g protein (38% of calories)*

*2 g carbohydrates*

*(45% of calories)*

*0 g fiber*

*65 mg sodium*

MAKES ABOUT 1 CUP

2 to 3 anchovy fillets, rinsed and patted dry (¼ ounce)

½ cup low-fat buttermilk or nonfat plain yogurt

2 tablespoons 1% low-fat cottage cheese

1 small minced shallot

1 clove minced garlic

4 teaspoons fresh lime juice

½ teaspoon white wine Worcestershire sauce

¼ teaspoon freshly ground black pepper

1 to 3 drops hot pepper sauce

¼ cup coarsely chopped fresh flat-leaf parsley

*In a blender* or food processor, combine the anchovies, buttermilk, cottage cheese, shallot, garlic, lemon juice, Worcestershire sauce, pepper, and hot pepper sauce and process until smooth and creamy. Add the parsley and pulse just to combine. (Do not overprocess, or the dressing will turn a uniform green.)

*Cover and refrigerate* until ready to use. (This dressing will keep for up to 1 week.)

# Buttermilk-Dill Dressing

PER TABLESPOON:

*8 calories*

*0 g total fat (12% of calories)*

*0 g saturated fat*

*0 mg cholesterol*

*1 g protein (33% of calories)*

*1 g carbohydrates*

*(55% of calories)*

*0 g fiber*

*14 mg sodium*

MAKES ABOUT ½ CUP

¼ cup low-fat buttermilk

2 tablespoons nonfat plain yogurt

1 teaspoon minced shallots

¼ teaspoon minced garlic

¼ teaspoon fresh lemon juice

1½ teaspoons minced fresh dill

2 drops hot pepper sauce, or to taste

*In a small bowl,* whisk together the buttermilk, yogurt, shallots, garlic, lemon juice, dill, and pepper sauce.

*Cover and refrigerate* until ready to use. (This dressing will keep for up to 1 week.)

# Creamy Ranch Dressing

PER TABLESPOON:

*10 calories*

*0 g total fat (21% of calories)*

*0 g saturated fat*

*1 mg cholesterol*

*1 g protein (49% of calories)*

*1 g carbohydrates*

*(31% of calories)*

*0 g fiber*

*41 mg sodium*

**MAKES ABOUT 1/2 CUP**

¼ cup 1% low-fat cottage cheese

3 tablespoons low-fat buttermilk

1½ teaspoons fresh lemon juice

1½ teaspoons water

1½ teaspoons freshly grated Parmigiano-Reggiano

1 small shallot, sliced

1 clove garlic, crushed

Pinch of freshly ground black pepper

1 teaspoon chopped fresh basil or ½ teaspoon dried

*In a blender* or food processor, combine the cottage cheese, buttermilk, lemon juice, water, cheese, shallot, garlic, and pepper and process until smooth and creamy. Add the basil and oregano and pulse just to combine.

*Cover and refrigerate* until ready to use. (This dressing will keep for up to 1 week.)

# Raspberry-Vinegar Infusion

PER TABLESPOON:

*20 calories*

*0 g total fat (3% of calories)*

*0 g saturated fat*

*0 mg cholesterol*

*0 g protein (2% of calories)*

*5 g carbohydrates*

*(95% of calories)*

*0 g fiber*

*0 mg sodium*

**MAKES ABOUT 1 CUP**

1 cup sherry vinegar

1¼ cups fresh raspberries (6¼ ounces) or 1 cup frozen unsweetened raspberries

3 tablespoons fructose

*In a small saucepan,* bring the sherry vinegar to a simmer over medium heat. Stir in the raspberries and remove from the heat. Transfer to a bowl, stir in the fructose, and set aside to cool.

*Strain the mixture* through a fine sieve set over a bowl, pressing on the raspberries with a large spatula or wooden spoon to extract as much liquid as possible. Transfer to a sterilized glass bottle. Cover and refrigerate until ready to use. (This infusion will keep for up to 2 weeks.)

# Strawberry-Basil-Balsamic Infusion

PER TABLESPOON:

*6 calories*

*0 g total fat (4% of calories)*

*0 g saturated fat*

*0 mg cholesterol*

*0 g protein (4% of calories)*

*1 g carbohydrates*
*(92% of calories)*

*0 g fiber*

*0 mg sodium*

MAKES ABOUT 4 CUPS

1½ cups quartered hulled strawberries (7½ ounces)

1 cup packed fresh basil leaves

3 cups balsamic vinegar

1 cup water

*Force the strawberries* into a sterilized 1-quart bottle or spoon them into a sterilized 1-quart Mason jar. Push the basil leaves into the bottle or jar.

*In a saucepan,* heat the vinegar over medium heat until simmering. Remove from the heat and add the water.

*Using a funnel,* pour the hot vinegar mixture into the bottle or jar. Allow to cool, then cover and let stand at room temperature for 8 hours, or overnight. Transfer to a glass jar. Refrigerate until ready to use. (This infusion will keep for up to 2 weeks.)

# Vegetarian Main Courses

MANY OF OUR GUESTS CHOOSE a vegetarian menu every day. I am so glad they do, because over the years I have enjoyed the challenge of developing these recipes. I usually begin with a visit to our extensive organic gardens, selecting what is in season and at its peak of ripeness, and proceed to add herbs, spices, and other ingredients until I am satisfied with the overall dish. What pleases me most is when new guests realize that vegetarian meals are more than tofu and brown rice. We serve a wide and constantly changing range of vegetarian main dishes. In the autumn and winter, I cook with squash and root vegetables such as onions, potatoes, and beets. In the spring and summer, mushrooms, corn, tomatoes, beans, and greens appear on the menu with happy regularity. With each changing season, I continue to discover new combinations of flavors and textures to make these some of the most interesting and memorable dishes on our menu.

# Focaccia Sandwich with Grilled Vegetables Provençal

**W**HEN I LIVED IN THE SOUTH OF FRANCE near the Italian border, I would take the train to the region around San Remo. At a little trattoria near the coast, I had focaccia with grilled vegetables. The tantalizing memory of the smell and taste of the mingled olive oil, garlic, and basil, enjoyed with a glass of red wine, is still with me—and life is pleasant and tranquil. To save time, you could saunter over to an Italian bakery and buy a few pieces of focaccia for your sandwiches instead of baking your own.

PER SERVING
(not including Focaccia):

*208 calories*

*12 g total fat (52% of calories)*

*3 g saturated fat*

*8 mg cholesterol*

*6 g protein (12% of calories)*

*19 g carbohydrates*
*(36% of calories)*

*2 g fiber*

*58 mg sodium*

**MAKES 4 SERVINGS**

2 tablespoons olive oil

1½ tablespoons fresh lemon juice

1 eggplant, sliced lengthwise into six ¼-inch slices (8 ounces)

4 small zucchini (14 ounces)

2 portobello mushrooms, stemmed and halved (4 ounces)

8 small scallions, trimmed (4 ounces)

2 tomatoes, cored and sliced into ½-inch slices

1 teaspoon dried oregano

1 teaspoon dried basil

½ teaspoon freshly ground black pepper

2 teaspoons balsamic vinegar

2 roasted red bell peppers (see page 99; 9 ounces)

8 large fresh basil leaves

1½ ounces mozzarella cheese, sliced into 4 thin slices

½ Focaccia (page 214)

Roasted Garlic (page 290)

*Garnish*

Oak leaf lettuce leaves, fresh parsley and basil leaves, rosemary blossoms, and/or sunflower sprouts

*Preheat the oven* to 325°F. Prepare a charcoal or gas grill.

*In a small bowl,* mix together the oil and lemon juice.

*In a large baking pan,* arrange the eggplant, zucchini, mushrooms, scallions, and tomatoes in a single layer. Brush the eggplant with the olive oil–lemon juice mixture. Sprinkle the oregano, basil, and pepper over the other vegetables.

*Spray the grill* with vegetable oil spray and grill the vegetables for 4 to 8 minutes, turning, until they are crisp-tender. (The zucchini and eggplant will require more time than the mushrooms and tomatoes.) Sprinkle the underside of the mushroom caps with balsamic vinegar.

*Make 4 stacks* of the grilled vegetables in the baking pan, starting with the eggplant and then layering the zucchini, mushrooms, scallions, and tomato slices on top. Top the stacks with the roasted peppers, basil leaves, and mozzarella cheese. Keep warm in the oven.

*Cut the focaccia* into 4 equal pieces and split each horizontally. Grill, turning once, for 2 to 3 minutes, just long enough to make grill marks on both sides. Spread the roasted garlic in the focaccia. Enclose each vegetable-cheese stack in 2 pieces of focaccia, garnishing the sandwiches with lettuce, parsley, basil, or any other selection of the garnishes.

## ROASTING BELL PEPPERS AND CHILIES

To roast bell peppers and chili peppers, set the peppers over an open flame or under the broiler and grill or broil, turning every few minutes, until charred on all sides. Transfer to a plastic bag, close it tightly, and let the peppers steam for about 5 minutes. Peel by rubbing off the charred skin. (It is easier to peel the peppers under gently running cool water, but the water will dilute their flavor and wash away some nutrients.) Lay the peppers on a cutting board and slice them in half. Scrape out the seeds and cut away the membranes. Cover and refrigerate until ready to use. The peppers will keep in the refrigerator for up to two days.

# Calzone

ALTHOUGH A TRADITIONAL CALZONE is shaped like a half-moon, I toss tradition to the wind with my version by forming it into a folded rectangle. And I make it with a relatively thin dough rather than thick chewy traditional dough. Inside, I layer various vegetables and herbs and add just a sprinkling of bold-tasting Asiago cheese. No one has ever complained about my nonconformist technique!

## Dough

1 tablespoon active dry yeast (one $\frac{1}{4}$-ounce package)

$\frac{1}{2}$ teaspoon granulated sugar or honey

$\frac{3}{4}$ cup lukewarm water

1 teaspoon kosher salt

1 teaspoon olive oil

$\frac{3}{4}$ cup unbleached all-purpose flour, plus more for dusting

$\frac{1}{2}$ cup whole wheat flour

## Filling

2 onions, thinly sliced (14 ounces)

$\frac{1}{4}$ cup dry-packed sundried tomatoes

2 cups sliced white mushrooms (6 ounces)

1 teaspoon minced garlic

$\frac{1}{4}$ teaspoon dried oregano

$\frac{1}{4}$ teaspoon freshly ground black pepper

6 cups loosely packed thinly sliced spinach leaves or Swiss chard (6 ounces)

1 cup low-fat ricotta cheese

$\frac{1}{2}$ cup thinly sliced scallions (2 ounces)

$\frac{1}{8}$ teaspoon freshly grated nutmeg

$\frac{1}{4}$ cup cornmeal for sprinkling on pan

$\frac{1}{2}$ cup Marinara Sauce (page 284)

$\frac{1}{4}$ cup finely sliced fresh basil

2 tablespoons freshly grated Asiago cheese

1 large egg white, lightly beaten

*To make the dough,* in a bowl of an electric mixer fitted with a dough hook, dissolve the yeast and sugar in the water.

*With the mixer running,* add the salt, oil, and flours. Mix until the dough forms a ball, pulls away from the sides of the bowl, and is smooth and elastic. Transfer to an oiled bowl, cover, and let rise in a warm area for about 20 minutes until puffy.

*To prepare the filling,* in a saucepan sprayed with vegetable oil spray, sauté the onions for 5 to 6 minutes, until softened and lightly browned. Transfer to a bowl and set aside to cool.

*In another small bowl,* soak the sundried tomatoes in warm water to cover for about 20 minutes, until plumped. Drain and slice.

*In the pan used earlier,* sauté the mushrooms and garlic for about 5 minutes, until the mushrooms release their liquid and begin to brown. Transfer to another bowl and set aside to cool.

*Sauté the spinach* in the same saucepan for 2 to 3 minutes, until wilted. Cool, squeeze out the excess moisture, and coarsely chop.

*In a small bowl,* combine the ricotta cheese, scallions, and nutmeg. Set aside.

*Preheat the oven* to 375°F. Spray a baking sheet with vegetable oil spray and sprinkle the sheet with the cornmeal.

*Turn the dough out* onto a lightly floured work surface and knead for 2 to 3 minutes. Using a rolling pin, roll the dough into a 10-by-16-inch rectangle. The dough will be quite thin. Transfer to the prepared baking sheet.

*Spread the onions* over the top half of the dough, top with the mushroom-garlic mixture, leaving a 1-inch border, and sprinkle with the oregano and black pepper. Spoon the sauce over the vegetables and then spoon dollops of the ricotta mixture over the sauce. Scatter the sundried tomatoes and basil over the top. Sprinkle with the Asiago cheese.

*Brush the edges* of the dough with the egg white and then fold the bottom half of the dough over the filling. Crimp the edges with a fork to seal. Brush the top of the calzone with egg white.

*Bake* for 30 to 40 minutes, until the crust is crispy and golden brown. Cool slightly and slice to serve.

# Rice Noodle and Tempeh Salad with Lime-Ginger Dressing

**D**URING ITS BRIEF STINT IN THE OVEN, the tempeh soaks up the marinade and turns temptingly moist and flavorful, thus making this one of the tastiest as well as one of the prettiest salads we serve at the Door. While we usually reserve salads for lunchtime, this makes a light supper too. If so inclined, you can substitute a grilled chicken breast or fillet of white-fleshed fish for the tempeh.

PER SERVING
(not including dressing):

*285 calories*

*5 g total fat (16% of calories)*

*1 g saturated fat*

*40 mg cholesterol*

*16 g protein (22% of calories)*

*44 g carbohydrates*

*(61% of calories)*

*2 g fiber*

*413 mg sodium*

**MAKES 4 SERVINGS**

3 tablespoons low-sodium tamari or soy sauce

2 tablespoons frozen apple juice concentrate, thawed

2 tablespoons balsamic vinegar

1 clove garlic

6 ounces tempeh (see Note)

6 ounces rice noodles

¼ cup Vegetable Broth (page 280) or water

4 cups crisp lettuce, such as Romaine

Double recipe Lime-Ginger Dressing (page 88)

½ cup julienned blanched red bell pepper (2 ounces)

½ cup small green beans, blanched (2 ounces)

¼ cup sliced water chestnuts

12 thin slices cucumber (3 ounces)

2 scallions, thinly sliced on the diagonal (1 ounce)

*To make the marinade,* combine the tamari, apple juice concentrate, vinegar, and garlic in a shallow bowl. Place the tempeh in the marinade, turn to coat, and set aside.

*Bring a large pot* of water to a boil. Put the noodles in a large bowl and pour the water over them. Let stand for 10 minutes, or until the noodles are al dente. Drain and cool under cold running water. Drain again.

*Preheat the oven* to 350°F.

*Remove the tempeh* from the marinade, reserving the marinade. In a small nonstick ovenproof sauté pan, brown the tempeh on both sides.

*Mix the broth* with the marinade and pour over the tempeh. Bake for about 5 minutes, until the tempeh is heated through and has absorbed

NOTE: *Tempeh is packaged in 6-ounce rectangles. Substitute 12 ounces boneless, skinless chicken breasts, seafood, or tofu for the tempeh.*

most of the liquid. Cool, then cut the tempeh into 1-inch cubes and return to the pan with the remaining marinade in it.

*Line the plates* or large shallow bowls with the greens. Toss the cooked noodles with half of the dressing. Arrange the noodles, tempeh, bell pepper, beans, water chestnuts, and cucumber on the greens. Drizzle with the remaining dressing and sprinkle with the scallions.

## THE CHANGING DINING ROOM

Only thirty-nine guests experience the Door each week, allowing us to serve dinner in one sitting, like a fine, small restaurant. We especially enjoy the camaraderie that develops over seven days and have found that eating at large, long tables refectory-style is conducive to conversation. (We also have some smaller tables for four or six.)

Each night we arrange our tables in a different pattern, a subtlety that some guests don't notice at all, but that we believe makes a difference. A "mixer" atmosphere develops, and guests often find themselves sitting with intriguing dinner companions.

Each dinner, ideally, should be a special occasion. Simply shifting your perspective can be awakening. Try it at home. If you haven't moved your dining table in years or changed the position of the chair you sit in, perhaps it's time: a different view out the window . . . the way the sunlight falls across the table . . . is not unlike a new herb—invigorating, delightful!

# Moussaka with Tzatziki

IN THE SPRING OF 1996 my wife, Irma, joined me on the cruise ship *Vistafjord,* where I was guest chef. The ship docked in Athens, Greece, and Irma and I happily explored the local restaurants. When I returned to my kitchen at the Golden Door, I eagerly set about developing both a traditional and a meatless moussaka that met spa standards of low fat and low calories. This vegetarian version, made with mushrooms, is especially popular with our guests. Take care to cook it partially covered so that the bread crumbs and ricotta do not dry out.

**PER SERVING:**

*380 calories*

*11 g total fat (25% of calories)*

*5 g saturated fat*

*26 mg cholesterol*

*21 g protein (22% of calories)*

*50 g carbohydrates*

*(53% of calories)*

*4 g fiber*

*850 mg sodium*

**MAKES 4 SERVINGS**

*Duxelles*

1 pound mixed mushrooms, such as white, cremini, and shiitake, cleaned, trimmed, and quartered

2 shallots, coarsely chopped (1 ounce)

1 teaspoon minced garlic

1 teaspoon dried oregano

¼ teaspoon salt, or to taste

¼ teaspoon freshly ground black pepper, or to taste

6 tablespoons bulgur or cracked wheat

4 cups packed spinach leaves (8 ounces)

¼ cup tomato puree

2 tablespoons freshly grated Asiago or Parmesan cheese

2 teaspoons minced lemon zest

*Eggplant and tomato*

1 eggplant, peeled and sliced lengthwise into ¼-inch slices (1½ pounds)

1 cup low-fat ricotta cheese

⅛ teaspoon freshly grated nutmeg

3 tablespoons dry bread crumbs

Pinch of dried basil

¼ teaspoon minced garlic

Pinch of dried oregano

2 tomatoes, cored and thinly sliced

*Tzatziki*

1 cucumber, peeled, seeded, and shredded, diced, or thinly sliced (10 ounces)

⅛ teaspoon salt, or to taste

1 cup low-fat plain yogurt

1 teaspoon minced garlic

1 teaspoon chopped fresh mint, dill, or oregano

1 cup Marinara Sauce (page 284), heated

*To prepare the duxelles,* combine the mushrooms, shallots, garlic, oregano, salt, and pepper in a food processor and process until the mushrooms are coarsely chopped. Transfer to a saucepan, cover, and cook over medium heat for 1 to 3 minutes, until the mushrooms release their juices. Stir in the bulgur, reduce the heat, and cook, covered, stirring occasionally, for 10 minutes, or until the mixture is quite dry. Set aside to cool.

*In a large nonstick sauté pan,* cook the spinach over medium-high heat until it wilts. (If necessary, add 2 tablespoons of water to the spinach.) Drain in a colander and cool.

*When the spinach is cool* enough to handle, squeeze out the excess liquid. Coarsely chop the spinach and stir into the duxelles. Add the tomato puree, cheese, and lemon zest, mix well, and set aside.

*To cook the eggplant,* prepare a charcoal or gas grill or preheat a stove-top grill. Preheat the oven to 350°F.

*Spray the eggplant* with vegetable oil spray and grill for 2 to 3 minutes on each side, until marked with grill marks and beginning to soften. Set aside.

*In a small bowl,* whisk the ricotta cheese and nutmeg until light and fluffy.

*In another small bowl,* combine the bread crumbs, basil, garlic, and oregano.

*Layer half the eggplant* in an 8-by-12-inch baking pan. Spread the duxelles over the eggplant and then layer with the tomatoes. Top with the remaining eggplant. Evenly spread the ricotta over the eggplant and sprinkle with the herbed bread crumbs. Bake for about 35 minutes, or until the duxelles layer bubbles gently. Set aside to cool for 10 to 15 minutes before cutting into squares.

*Meanwhile,* to make the tzatziki, in a bowl, combine the cucumber, salt, yogurt, garlic, and mint. Cover and refrigerate until ready to serve.

*Ladle* about ¼ cup of the warm sauce onto each plate. Set the squares of moussaka on top and spoon the tzatziki next to the moussaka.

*NOTE: As an alternative, spray a nonstick sauté pan with vegetable oil spray and cook the eggplant over medium-high heat for 2 to 3 minutes on each side, until softened.*

# Bulgur with Red Cabbage, Minted Peas, and Yogurt

**T**HIS DELICIOUS, SATISFYING MEAL will please vegetarians and nonvegetarians alike. The sweet-and-sour cabbage combined with the textures and flavors of bulgur and minted peas is scrumptious.

PER SERVING
(not including
Sweet-and-Sour Red Cabbage):

266 calories

3 g total fat (11% of calories)

1 g saturated fat

1 mg cholesterol

11 g protein (17% of calories)

48 g carbohydrates
(72% of calories)

3 g fiber

37 mg sodium

**MAKES 4 SERVINGS**

*Bulgur*

1 teaspoon olive oil

1 tablespoon minced shallots

1 cup medium-grind bulgur
(6¼ ounces)

1 teaspoon ground allspice

2 cups Vegetable Broth
(page 280) or water

½ cup minced fresh flat-leaf
parsley

*Peas*

2 cups fresh or frozen peas
(10 ounces)

1 to 2 teaspoons olive oil

Pinch of kosher salt
(optional)

¼ cup minced fresh mint

½ recipe Sweet-and-Sour Red
Cabbage (page 192)

½ cup nonfat plain yogurt

*To cook the bulgur,* in a saucepan, heat the olive oil over medium heat. Sauté the shallots until translucent. Stir in the bulgur, allspice, and 1½ cups of the broth, reduce the heat, cover, and simmer for 10 to 15 minutes, or until the broth is absorbed. Add the remaining ½ cup broth, cover, and set aside. Just before serving, fluff with a fork and fold in the parsley.

*To prepare the peas,* bring a saucepan of water to a boil over high heat and blanch the peas in the boiling water just until vivid green. Discard the water. Drain the peas and return to the saucepan. Stir in the olive oil, the salt, if using, and mint.

*Spoon warm cabbage* onto 4 warmed plates. Spoon the bulgur next to the cabbage and surround with the peas. Spoon a dollop of yogurt onto each serving of bulgur.

# Butternut Squash Baked with Maple Syrup

ONE DAY, a few of our guests suggested that I serve this squash dish as a main course. The idea quickly caught on and it became a standing favorite. It is easy to make, and butternut squash is rich in cancer-fighting beta carotene.

*Squash*

1 butternut squash, halved lengthwise and seeded (1½ to 2 pounds)

4 teaspoons maple syrup

2 teaspoons ground cinnamon

1 teaspoon olive oil

½ cup diced onions (2 ounces)

¾ cup bulgur (4⅔ ounces)

½ teaspoon ground allspice

1¼ cups Vegetable Broth (page 280) or water

2 tablespoons chopped fresh flat-leaf parsley

*Swiss chard*

1 teaspoon olive oil

1 teaspoon minced garlic

4 large Swiss chard leaves, stemmed and cut into 2-inch pieces (4 ounces)

1 to 2 tablespoons Vegetable Broth (page 280) or water (optional)

¼ teaspoon freshly ground black pepper

*Preheat the oven to 350°F.*

*To prepare the squash,* in a shallow baking pan, arrange the squash cut side up. Add enough water to fill the pan to a depth of ½ inch. Drizzle the squash with the maple syrup and sprinkle with the cinnamon. Cover and bake for about 45 minutes, or until fork-tender.

*Meanwhile,* in a saucepan, heat the olive oil over medium heat. Sauté the onions until translucent. Add the bulgur, allspice, and broth. Cover and simmer over low heat for about 10 minutes, until the liquid is absorbed. Remove from the heat, fluff with a fork, fold in the parsley, and cover to keep warm.

*To cook the Swiss chard,* in a sauté pan, heat the olive oil over medium heat. Add the garlic and sauté briefly (do not brown). Add the Swiss chard and stir-fry for 3 to 4 minutes, until it wilts; if necessary, add 1 to 2 tablespoons of broth to the pan to prevent scorching. Sprinkle the chard with the pepper.

*Serve the squash* on warmed plates, with the bulgur and Swiss chard on the side.

NOTE: *Substitute cracked wheat for the bulgur if desired. Use a little more broth and cook the wheat for 15 to 20 minutes.*

# Curried Ratatouille with Tofu and Quinoa

Yummy los

**I** FIRST TASTED CURRIED RATATOUILLE in Paris, of all places, and found it fascinating that such a traditional Provençal dish adapted so easily to the exotic. I like making it with nutritious quinoa, which is as easy to prepare as one-two-three.

*Tofu*

14 ounces firm tofu, cut crosswise into 16 thin slices

1 tablespoon low-sodium tamari or soy sauce

1/4 teaspoon freshly ground black pepper

*Ratatouille*

2 teaspoons olive oil

1/2 cup diced onions (2 ounces)

1 green or red bell pepper, cored, seeded, and diced (4 ounces)

1 red serrano chili, seeded and diced

2 teaspoons minced garlic

1 tablespoon dried basil

1 to 2 tablespoons curry powder

1/2 cinnamon stick

1 whole star anise

1 bay leaf

1 small eggplant, peeled and diced (12 ounces)

1 zucchini, diced (10 ounces)

1 large Yellow Finnish or red potato, cut into 1-inch cubes (8 ounces)

4 plum tomatoes, cored and diced (12 ounces)

1/4 cup tomato puree

1/4 cup Vegetable Broth (page 280) or water

1/2 cup slivered fresh basil

1 1/2 cups hot cooked quinoa (page 203)

2 tablespoons sliced fresh chives

2 teaspoons black sesame seeds

*To prepare the tofu,* lay the slices in a single layer in a shallow dish. Sprinkle with the tamari and pepper, cover, and refrigerate.

*To make the ratatouille,* in a large heavy saucepan, heat the olive oil over medium heat. Add the onions, bell pepper, chili, garlic, and dried basil and sauté for 4 to 5 minutes, stirring occasionally, until the onions are translucent. Add the curry powder and mix well, then add the cinnamon stick, star anise, and bay leaf. Stir in the eggplant, zucchini, potato, tomatoes, tomato puree, and broth, cover, reduce the heat, and simmer for about 15 minutes, or until the vegetables are fork-tender.

*Remove from the heat* and let stand, covered, for 10 minutes. Just before serving, remove and discard the cinnamon stick, star anise, and bay leaf. Reheat if necessary, and sprinkle with the fresh basil.

*Meanwhile,* in a nonstick sauté pan sprayed with vegetable oil spray, sauté the tofu over medium heat for 2 to 3 minutes on each side, until golden brown. Drain the tofu on paper towels.

*Make a ring of quinoa* on each plate and sprinkle with the chives. Spoon the ratatouille into the center of the rings and arrange 2 slices of tofu on each side of the ratatouille. Sprinkle with the sesame seeds.

# Grilled Portobello Mushrooms with Couscous

**I**T SHOULD COME AS NO SURPRISE that we frequently cook with mushrooms at the Golden Door. They lend flavor and body without fat or lots of calories. Fresh mushrooms are delivered to us every week from a nearby farm and I adjust my menu to incorporate those that are included in the order. Large portobellos are particularly popular because of their meaty taste and texture. Because we use very little oil, the mushrooms are only half done on the grill and then transferred to the oven to continue cooking in balsamic vinegar and vegetable broth to soften them. I prefer whole wheat couscous with this dish, but basmati rice, pasta, or another grain would work equally well.

**PER SERVING**
(not including Two-Pepper Coulis):

*164 calories*

*7 g total fat (39% of calories)*

*1 g saturated fat*

*0 mg cholesterol*

*5 g protein (12% of calories)*

*20 g carbohydrates*

*(49% of calories)*

*1 g fiber*

*7 mg sodium*

**MAKES 4 SERVINGS**

2 tablespoons olive oil

2 teaspoons fresh lemon juice

4 large portobello mushrooms, cleaned and stemmed (4 ounces)

½ teaspoon freshly ground black pepper

4 teaspoons balsamic vinegar

¾ cup Vegetable Broth (page 280) or water, plus more if necessary

½ cup whole wheat couscous (3 ounces)

1 tablespoon minced fresh flat-leaf parsley

1 tablespoon chopped fresh basil or scallions

Sixteen 2-inch asparagus tips, blanched (6 ounces)

Two-Pepper Coulis (page 285)

*Prepare a charcoal or gas grill* or stove-top grill. Preheat the oven to 300°F.

*Spray the grill* with vegetable oil spray. In a small bowl, whisk together the olive oil and lemon juice and brush over the tops of the mushroom caps. Grill, smooth side down, for 3 to 4 minutes, turning to make square or diamond grill marks, until the mushrooms are limp and begin to release their juices. Sprinkle the pepper over the inside of the mushroom caps, and transfer them, smooth side down, to a shallow baking pan. (Keep the grill hot.)

*Drizzle the balsamic vinegar* over the inside of each mushroom cap. Add ¼ cup of the broth to the pan, cover with aluminum foil, and place in the oven for up to 10 minutes to keep warm.

NOTE: *When grilling the asparagus tips, take care they do not fall through the grill. If possible, grill them in a small-mesh grilling basket.*

**VEGETARIAN MAIN COURSES**

*In a saucepan,* bring the remaining $\frac{1}{2}$ cup broth to a boil. Put the couscous in a bowl and pour the hot broth over it. Cover and let stand for 5 minutes. Fluff with a fork and fold in the parsley and basil. Add more broth if couscous seems dry.

*Meanwhile,* spray the grill once more with vegetable oil spray and briefly grill the asparagus tips, just until lightly browned (see Note).

*Place the grilled mushroom caps,* smooth side down, on warmed plates. Mound the couscous on the mushrooms. Ladle the pepper coulis on either side of the mushrooms and arrange the asparagus on top of the coulis.

## THE GOOD EARTH

At the Golden Door, we grow most of our fruits and vegetables in our mountainside gardens and orchards. All are grown organically, without chemical pesticides or herbicides. Not only are organic foods better for you, their flavors are more intense.

Buy organic produce whenever possible. It's available in health food stores, many green grocers and farmers markets, and in an ever-increasing number of supermarkets. If you can, grow your own. Organic produce may not look as picture perfect as its chemically enhanced counterparts because it grows as nature intended it to and may be smaller or slightly misshapen. But its flavor and healthfulness will compensate for any blemishes.

*9/03 Only pretty good!! Robert & Susan*

# Marinated Tofu with Basil and Red Onion Glaze

**D**URING THE YEARS I HAVE BEEN COOKING at the Golden Door, I have had numerous occasions to cook for Deborah, the founder of the spa, at her house in San Diego. I have learned my employer's likes when it comes to good food, and together we have spent many pleasurable hours discovering our shared passion. This dish is one of her favorites.

### Tofu

14 ounces firm tofu, pressed to remove excess water and cut crosswise into 8 slices

1 teaspoon minced fresh ginger

1 teaspoon minced garlic

2 tablespoons low-sodium tamari or soy sauce

1 tablespoon fresh lime juice

1 teaspoon light brown sugar

$\frac{1}{2}$ teaspoon Thai or Vietnamese chili paste

$\frac{1}{4}$ teaspoon toasted sesame oil

### Glaze

1 teaspoon canola oil

1 large red onion, halved lengthwise and thinly sliced (8 ounces)

1 whole star anise or $\frac{1}{2}$ teaspoon anise seeds ✓

2 tablespoons light brown sugar

2 teaspoons arrowroot or cornstarch ✓

1 tablespoon low-sodium tamari or soy sauce

1 tablespoon balsamic vinegar

$\frac{3}{4}$ cup Vegetable Broth (page 280) or water, plus more if necessary

$\frac{1}{4}$ cup fresh basil leaves

Deborah's Basmati Rice (page 201)

*To prepare the tofu,* lay the slices in a single layer in a shallow dish.

*In a small bowl,* combine the ginger, garlic, tamari, lime juice, brown sugar, chili paste, and oil. Mix well and pour over the tofu. Cover and refrigerate.

*Preheat the oven* to 300°F.

*To prepare the glaze,* in a nonstick sauté pan, heat the oil over medium heat and sauté the onions for 5 to 6 minutes, until they soften and begin to brown. Add the anise and brown sugar and cook for 2 to 3 minutes longer, until the onions brown and caramelize.

*Mix the arrowroot* with the tamari and vinegar. Stir the arrowroot mixture and broth into the onions and cook until slightly thickened. Add the basil, stir gently, and remove from the heat. Spoon into an 8-by-8-inch baking pan and spread evenly over the bottom of the pan.

*In a nonstick sauté pan* sprayed with vegetable oil spray, cook the marinated tofu over medium heat for 1 to 2 minutes on each side, until lightly browned. Arrange in a single layer over the onions. Bake, loosely covered with aluminum foil, for about 20 minutes.

*Spoon the rice* onto warmed plates. Arrange 2 slices of tofu on each plate and spoon the onions and glaze over them.

# Mexican Flautas with Potatoes, Onions, Zucchini, Tomatoes, and Mushrooms

**I**N BEAUTIFUL SANTA BARBARA, there is an unassuming cantina called *La Super-Rica Taqueria* made famous by Julia Child's praise for its authentic Mexican cuisine. It's a simple spot where customers line up to taste great food, each dish prepared to order. This recipe captures the essence of the dishes served there, with its sautéed vegetables and pungent ancho chili sauce.

PER SERVING:

*368 calories*

*4 g total fat (9% of calories)*

*1 g saturated fat*

*2 mg cholesterol*

*12 g protein (13% of calories)*

*72 g carbohydrates*

*(78% of calories)*

*5 g fiber*

*493 mg sodium*

**MAKES 4 SERVINGS**

*Chili sauce*

1 dried ancho chili

½ teaspoon canola oil

½ cup diced onions (2 ounces)

1 carrot, diced (4 ounces)

3 cloves garlic

1 tablespoon ground cumin

1 teaspoon dried oregano

3 tomatoes, cored and halved (14 ounces)

1 red serrano chili, stemmed (optional)

⅓ cup tomato puree

⅓ cup Vegetable Broth (page 280) or water

Kosher salt to taste

*Flautas*

Yellow Finnish, purple, or red potatoes (12 ounces) (see Note)

1 red onion, thinly sliced (3 ounces)

1 red or yellow bell pepper or Anaheim chili, cored, seeded, and sliced into ¼-inch slices (4½ ounces)

2 medium-sized zucchini or yellow squash, quartered and sliced into ¼-inch slices (4 to 6 ounces)

1 cup trimmed oyster mushrooms or stemmed and thickly sliced small white mushrooms (2 ounces)

2 tablespoons dried oregano

1 to 2 teaspoons chili powder

1 teaspoon ground cumin

¼ teaspoon kosher salt

3 plum tomatoes, cored and quartered (8 ounces)

¾ cup shredded Swiss chard or spinach (1 ounce)

Four 10-inch whole wheat tortillas (7 ounces)

4 teaspoons crumbled feta cheese (¼ ounce)

4 sprigs fresh cilantro

*To make the chili sauce,* soak the ancho chili in water to cover for about 1 hour, until softened. Drain, stem, and seed.

*Prepare a charcoal or gas grill* or preheat the broiler.

NOTE: *A large potato weighs about 8 to 10 ounces.*

*In a saucepan,* heat the oil over medium-low heat. Add the onions, carrot, garlic, cumin, and oregano and sauté for 5 to 6 minutes, until the vegetables begin to soften.

*Meanwhile,* grill the tomatoes and the serrano chili, if using, turning often, until soft and lightly charred.

*Add the tomatoes* and serrano chili to the sautéed vegetables and stir with a wooden spoon, gently crushing the tomatoes and chili with the back of the spoon. Add the ancho chilies, tomato puree, broth, and salt; stir to mix. Cover and simmer for about 45 minutes, until the flavors are well blended, stirring frequently. Cool.

*Transfer the chili sauce* to a blender or food processor and process until smooth. Set aside.

*To prepare the flautas,* put the potatoes in a large saucepan and add cold water just to cover. Bring to a boil over high heat. Reduce the heat and simmer for about 15 minutes, until the potatoes are tender but still firm. Drain and cool. When cool enough to handle, slice the potatoes: if they are small, slice into ¼-inch rounds; if large, quarter and cut into ¼-inch slices. Set aside.

*Preheat the oven* to 300°F.

*Spray a large cast-iron frying pan* or nonstick sauté pan with vegetable oil spray. Set over medium-high heat and when hot, sauté the red onion for 1 to 2 minutes, just until slightly softened. Add the pepper and sauté for 2 to 3 minutes. Add the potatoes, zucchini, and mushrooms. Sprinkle with the oregano, chili powder, cumin, and salt and, using a spatula, toss and cook for about 10 minutes, until the vegetables are crisp-tender. Add the tomatoes and cook for 1 minute. Add the Swiss chard and sauté for 1 minute longer, or until the chard begins to wilt. Remove from the heat.

*To assemble the flautas,* briefly warm the tortillas on both sides on a hot stove-top griddle or over an open flame. Spray a large baking pan with vegetable oil spray. Place a tortilla on a work surface. Mound about ¾ cup of the vegetables on it. Ladle 2 tablespoons of the ancho chili sauce over the vegetables. Sprinkle with 1 teaspoon of the feta cheese. Roll up the tortilla and place seam side down in the baking pan. Brush some sauce on top of the tortilla. Repeat with the remaining tortillas and put in the oven to keep warm. Serve garnished with cilantro sprigs.

# Caramelized Red Onion Pizza

**H**OW COULD I HOLD UP MY CULINARY HEAD in southern California without serving pizza? Here is pizza with a difference: moist and full-flavored, but without a smothering layer of cheese—just a tantalizing hint of feta and a glorious crown of sweet, caramelized red onions. Our guests love this.

PER SERVING
(including pizza dough):

*390 calories*

*8 g total fat (18% of calories)*

*3 g saturated fat*

*11 mg cholesterol*

*12 g protein (12% of calories)*

*68 g carbohydrates*

*(70% of calories)*

*2 g fiber*

*1482 mg sodium*

**MAKES 6 SERVINGS**

NOTE: *Alternatively, the pizza dough can be divided into 6 pieces and rolled out to make 6 individual pizzas.*

1 teaspoon olive oil

3 large red onions, thinly sliced (28 ounces)

1 tablespoon pure maple syrup or light brown sugar

1 tablespoon balsamic vinegar

2 teaspoons dried basil

2 cups Marinara Sauce (page 284)

Pizza Dough (page 216), rolled into an 18- to 19-inch round

4 cups shredded Swiss chard or spinach (4 ounces)

½ cup slivered fresh basil

½ cup feta cheese, crumbled (2½ ounces)

½ teaspoon dried oregano

¼ teaspoon freshly ground black pepper, or to taste

*In a large nonstick sauté pan,* heat the olive oil over medium-high heat. Add the onions and sauté, stirring frequently, for 9 to 10 minutes, or until caramelized to a deep golden brown and soft. Stir in the maple syrup, vinegar, and basil and set aside.

*Preheat the oven* to 375°F.

*Spread the marinara sauce* over the pizza dough, leaving a ½-inch border. Arrange the Swiss chard on top and top with the onions. Sprinkle with the basil, feta cheese, oregano, and pepper.

*Bake* for 30 to 35 minutes, until the crust is crisp. Cut into wedges to serve.

# Penne Primavera

**T**RY USING A WHOLE-GRAIN PASTA for this recipe. Whole grains, in general, reduce food cravings because they provide long-lasting energy, a plus for anyone wanting to lose weight. I cook these pastas for a shorter time than regular pasta and serve them immediately after adding the sauce.

PER SERVING:

*323 calories*

*6 g total fat (15% of calories)*

*1 g saturated fat*

*42 mg cholesterol*

*13 g protein (16% of calories)*

*56 g carbohydrates*

*(69% of calories)*

*3 g fiber*

*594 mg sodium*

**MAKES 4 SERVINGS**

2 teaspoons kosher salt (optional)

8 ounces whole wheat, kamut, or quinoa-corn penne

2 carrots, julienned (8 ounces)

2 ribs celery, peeled and julienned (5 ounces)

½ red bell pepper, julienned (3 ounces)

8 green beans or snow peas (4 ounces)

½ cup julienned scallions

1¼ cups Marinara Sauce (page 284)

2 tablespoons slivered fresh basil

2 tablespoons freshly grated Parmigiano-Reggiano cheese (optional; see Note.)

¼ cup minced fresh flat-leaf parsley

*In a large saucepan* of boiling water, with the salt added, if desired, cook the pasta according to the package directions until al dente. Drain.

*Meanwhile,* in a steaming basket set over boiling water, combine the carrots, celery, and bell pepper and steam for 3 to 5 minutes, until crisp-tender. Drain and set aside. Steam the beans and scallions for about 3 minutes, until crisp-tender.

*In a saucepan,* heat the marinara sauce. Stir in the basil.

*Ladle half the sauce* into 4 shallow bowls. Spoon the pasta on top of the sauce and surround with the vegetables. Ladle the remaining sauce over the pasta. Sprinkle with the cheese, if using, and parsley.

NOTE: *You may omit the cheese and substitute Spa Pesto (page 286).*

# Polenta with Sundried Tomatoes, Garlic, Corn, and Caramelized Red Onions

**T**HE CONTRAST OF caramelized red onions and tomato concassé with firm, juicy vine-ripened tomatoes is seductively satisfying. The juices from the vegetables seep into the polenta, mingling deliciously.

**PER SERVING**
(not including Caramelized Red Onions):

*249 calories*

*6 g total fat (21% of calories)*

*1 g saturated fat*

*0 mg cholesterol*

*7 g protein (11% of calories)*

*43 g carbohydrates*

*(68% of calories)*

*3 g fiber*

*669 mg sodium*

**MAKES 4 SERVINGS**

*Polenta*

2½ cups water

1 teaspoon kosher salt

2 teaspoons olive oil

2 teaspoons minced garlic

2 teaspoons minced fresh rosemary or sage

¼ cup fresh corn kernels (1¼ ounces)

2 tablespoons chopped dry-packed sundried tomatoes, soaked in warm water to cover for 15 to 20 minutes

¾ cup yellow cornmeal

*Tomato concassé*

2 teaspoons olive oil

2 teaspoons minced garlic

4 tomatoes, cored and diced (18 ounces)

1 teaspoon kosher salt (optional)

¼ teaspoon freshly ground black pepper

¼ cup slivered fresh basil

¾ cup fresh or frozen peas (3½ ounces)

½ cup fresh corn kernels (2½ ounces)

½ cup diced celery (4 ounces)

½ cup diced carrots (4 ounces)

¼ cup sliced scallions (1 ounce)

2 teaspoons crumbled feta cheese (optional)

Caramelized Red Onions (page 194)

¼ cup chopped fresh flat-leaf parsley

*To cook the polenta,* in a saucepan, bring the water and salt to a boil over high heat.

*Meanwhile,* in a nonstick sauté pan, heat the olive oil over medium heat. Add the garlic and rosemary and sauté for 2 to 3 minutes, until the garlic softens. Add to the boiling water along with the corn and sundried tomatoes. Briskly whisk in the cornmeal and continue whisking for 5 to 7 minutes, until the mixture is thick and bubbly.

*Spray a 5-by-9-inch loaf pan* with vegetable oil spray. Pour the polenta into the pan, smooth the surface, and spray it lightly with vegetable oil spray. Cover with plastic wrap and set aside to cool.

*Prepare a charcoal or gas grill* or preheat a stove-top grill.

*To make the concassé,* in a nonstick saucepan, heat the olive oil over high heat. Stir in the garlic and then quickly add the tomatoes. Sauté just until the tomatoes are heated through. Add the salt, if desired, and black pepper. Mix in the basil.

*Meanwhile,* in a steaming basket set over boiling water, steam the peas, corn, celery, and carrots for 3 to 5 minutes until fork-tender. Drain and mix in the scallions.

*Invert the polenta* onto a work surface and cut into 8 squares.

*Spray the grill* with vegetable oil spray. Grill the polenta squares for 2 to 3 minutes on each side, turning to make diamond or square grill marks. To make sure the polenta is heated through, place in the oven for 4 to 5 minutes, until hot. Remove from the oven and sprinkle with the feta cheese, if desired.

*Ladle the concassé* into the center of warmed plates. Place the polenta on the concassé and top with the onions. Surround with the steamed vegetables and sprinkle with the chopped parsley.

NOTE: *If you prefer, cook the squares of polenta in an ovenproof nonstick skillet sprayed with vegetable oil spray for 2 to 3 minutes on each side. Then cover and bake in a preheated 350°F oven for 4 to 5 minutes, until hot.*

# Wonton Ravioli

**O**UR GUESTS ARE OFTEN SURPRISED to discover that I occasionally use store-bought products such as wonton wrappers or flour or corn tortillas. Products such as these are very good and significantly reduce the labor and time required to make any number of dishes. (If you prefer, you can of course make the dough for the wonton wrappers and cut the ravioli shapes yourself.) I fill these delightful ravioli with a mouth-watering combination of spinach, mozzarella cheese, tomatoes, basil, and, for earthy richness, a generous measure of mushrooms.

PER SERVING:

*253 calories*

*8 g total fat (29% of calories)*

*2 g saturated fat*

*35 mg cholesterol*

*10 g protein (15% of calories)*

*35 g carbohydrates*

*(56% of calories)*

*2 g fiber*

*999 mg sodium*

**MAKES 8 SERVINGS**

12 cups loosely packed spinach leaves (10 ounces)

12 ounces shiitake, cremini, or white mushrooms, cleaned, trimmed, and coarsely chopped

1 shallot, minced (1 ounce)

2 teaspoons olive oil

1/2 teaspoon freshly ground black pepper

1/8 teaspoon freshly grated nutmeg

2 ounces mozzarella cheese, grated (1/2 cup)

1/4 cup finely ground cornmeal, or semolina flour

About 1 pound 3 1/2-inch square wonton wrappers (68 wrappers)

2 egg whites, lightly beaten

2 medium-sized zucchini, sliced into 1/4-inch slices (14 to 16 ounces)

4 cups Marinara Sauce (page 284), heated

1/4 cup minced fresh basil

*Heat a large nonstick skillet* over medium-high heat. Sauté the spinach for 2 to 3 minutes, until wilted. Set aside to cool and then press out the excess liquid. Finely chop and set aside.

*In a food processor,* process the mushrooms and shallot until coarsely chopped. Set aside.

*In a saucepan,* heat the olive oil over medium heat. Add the mushroom-shallot mixture, season with the pepper and nutmeg, cover, and cook for about 10 minutes, until the mushrooms release their liquid. Simmer, uncovered, until the liquid has almost evaporated. Add the spinach and cheese, mix well, and set aside to cool.

*NOTE:* You can double the recipe easily to fill 128 wonton wrappers. Pack the extras in layers between sheets of lightly oiled parchment paper, place in freezer bags, and freeze for up to 2 months. Drop the frozen ravioli into boiling water and cook for 7 to 10 minutes, until al dente.

*Sprinkle the cornmeal* on a baking sheet. Set aside.

*On a large work surface,* arrange an even number of wonton wrappers in rows. Brush some beaten egg white over the wrappers. Place 1 heaping tablespoon of the ravioli filling in the center of half the wrappers. Cover with the remaining wrappers, egg-brushed-side down. Gently press the wrappers together, releasing any air pockets and pressing with your fingers to seal. Transfer to the baking sheet. Cover with plastic wrap and refrigerate. Repeat with the remaining wonton wrappers and filling until you have 32 ravioli.

*Bring a large pot* of boiling water to a boil. Immerse the ravioli in the water and boil for 5 to 7 minutes, or until the wonton wrappers are al dente. Drain. You will have to do this in batches.

*Meanwhile,* in a nonstick sauté pan sprayed with vegetable oil spray, sauté the zucchini over medium heat for 5 to 6 minutes, until browned and crisp-tender.

*Ladle sauce* into 8 shallow bowls. Arrange 4 ravioli in each. Ladle sauce over the ravioli, arrange the zucchini around them, and sprinkle with the basil.

# Twice-Baked Potatoes

**H**ERE IS THE EVER-POPULAR TWICE-BAKED POTATO—a perennial favorite at the Golden Door. It's a nicely filling comfort food, but it is low in both fat and calories. In place of the carrots and broccoli, you can substitute fresh corn, celery, asparagus, or whatever seasonal vegetable strikes your fancy. The potatoes can be prepared in advance.

PER SERVING
(not including
Caramelized Red Onions):

*340 calories*

*3 g total fat (8% of calories)*

*1 g saturated fat*

*4 mg cholesterol*

*15 g protein (17% of calories)*

*64 g carbohydrates*

*(75% of calories)*

*3 g fiber*

*287 mg sodium*

**MAKES 4 SERVINGS**

4 russet potatoes, scrubbed and dried (2 pounds)

1 tablespoon canola oil

1¹/₂ cups chopped broccoli (4¹/₂ ounces)

¹/₂ cup diced carrots (4 ounces)

¹/₂ cup sliced scallions (2 ounces)

1 cup 1% low-fat cottage cheese

2 tablespoons nonfat plain yogurt (optional)

1 tablespoon Dijon mustard

¹/₄ teaspoon freshly ground black pepper, or to taste

2 tablespoons grated low-fat mozzarella cheese

8 baby carrots (4 ounces)

4 ounces green beans

Sixteen 2-inch asparagus tips (6 ounces)

Caramelized Red Onions (page 194)

*Preheat the oven* to 350°F.

*Rub the potato skins* with the canola oil. Lay potatoes in a shallow baking pan and bake for about 1 hour and 15 minutes, or until tender. Remove the potatoes from the oven and raise the oven temperature to 375°F.

*Meanwhile,* bring a saucepan of water to a boil over high heat. Blanch the broccoli for 1 to 2 minutes, until bright green and just tender. Remove with a slotted spoon, drain, and coarsely chop. Blanch the diced carrots in the boiling water, drain, and set aside.

*While the potatoes are still hot* but cool enough to handle, cut off the tops. Scoop out the potato flesh, leaving about ¹/₂-inch-thick shell.

*In a bowl,* combine the scooped-out potato flesh, the blanched vegetables, the scallions, cottage cheese, the yogurt, if desired, mustard, and pepper. Spoon into the potato shells, mounding the mixture so that the potatoes are well rounded. Sprinkle with the cheese. Return to the oven for about 15 minutes, or until heated through and golden brown on top.

*Meanwhile,* in a steaming basket set over boiling water, steam the baby carrots, green beans, and asparagus tips until crisp-tender.

*Place the potatoes* on warmed plates and arrange the steamed vegetables next to them. Serve with the onions.

NOTE: *To serve the potatoes as a side dish, cut the potatoes in half and fill both halves.*

# Three-Bean Chili with Rice and Corn

**T**HE COMBINATION OF BEANS AND RICE is classic and this chili is no exception, but the proportions of rice to beans and the addition of corn make it lighter than others. I top it with aromatic onions and red peppers, for one of our most popular dishes.

**PER SERVING:**

*291 calories*

*4 g total fat (14% of calories)*

*1 g saturated fat*

*0 mg cholesterol*

*9 g protein (13% of calories)*

*54 g carbohydrates*

*(74% of calories)*

*4 g fiber*

*262 mg sodium*

**MAKES 6 SERVINGS**

½ cup dried pinto beans, rinsed

½ cup dried white beans, such as cannellini, rinsed

¼ cup dried red beans, such as kidney or Anasazi, rinsed

1 bay leaf

½ teaspoon red pepper flakes

1 tablespoon olive oil

1 large onion, diced (6 ounces)

2 teaspoons minced garlic

1 carrot, diced (4 ounces)

1 green bell pepper, cored, seeded, and diced (4 ounces)

1 red serrano chili, seeded and minced

2 tablespoons chili powder

1 tablespoon ground cumin

2 teaspoons dried oregano

3 tomatoes, cored and diced (14 ounces)

½ cup tomato sauce

2 cups fresh corn kernels (from 3 ears; 10 ounces)

½ red bell pepper, diced (2 ounces)

1½ cups hot cooked medium-grain brown rice

1 cup diced red onions (4 ounces)

6 sprigs fresh cilantro

*In a large bowl,* soak the beans in water to cover for at least 6 hours, or overnight. Change the water several times during soaking if possible. Drain.

*In a large saucepan,* combine the beans, 7 cups of water, the bay leaf, and pepper flakes. Bring to a boil and simmer, covered, for about 1 hour and 20 minutes, or until tender. You may have to add more water while the beans are cooking, but by the time they are done, the water should barely cover the beans. Remove and discard the bay leaf.

*In a large pan,* heat the olive oil over medium heat. Add the onion, garlic, carrot, green bell pepper, and serrano chili and sauté for 8 to 10 minutes, until softened. Stir in the chili powder, cumin, and oregano. Add the tomatoes and tomato sauce and simmer for about 10 minutes.

*Add the beans* and their liquid and simmer for 10 to 15 minutes; add more water if the chili becomes too dry.

*Meanwhile,* in a steaming basket set over boiling water, steam the corn for 1 to 2 minutes. Remove and set aside. Put the red bell pepper in the basket and steam for 1 to 2 minutes. Set aside.

*Spoon* about ½ cup of rice onto each warmed plate. Spoon the chili next to the rice. Sprinkle with the corn and red bell peppers. Mound the red onions on top of the chili and garnish with the cilantro sprigs.

# Rancho La Puerta Whole Wheat Tortilla Lasagne

**T**HIS MEXICAN-STYLE LASAGNE made with whole wheat tortillas was developed at our sister spa, Rancho La Puerta, which is located only an hour from San Diego in Baja California, Mexico. The spiciness of the tomatillo sauce blends well with the sweet corn and the tortillas.

PER SERVING:

*337 calories*

*10 g total fat (26% of calories)*

*6 g saturated fat*

*32 mg cholesterol*

*19 g protein (23% of calories)*

*43 g carbohydrates*

*(51% of calories)*

*3 g fiber*

*397 mg sodium*

**MAKES 4 SERVINGS**

1 cup thinly sliced white mushrooms (2 ounces)

1 teaspoon dried oregano

1 large zucchini, thinly sliced (10 ounces)

1½ cups low-fat ricotta cheese

1 cup fresh corn kernels (5 ounces)

½ cup thinly sliced scallions (2 ounces)

¼ teaspoon freshly ground black pepper

Three 10-inch whole wheat tortillas (5¼ ounces)

2 cups Tomatillo Chili Sauce (page 288) or commercial green taco sauce

1 cup shredded Swiss chard (1 ounce)

⅓ cup low-fat, low-sodium mozzarella cheese, grated (1 ounce)

4 sprigs fresh cilantro

*In a nonstick sauté pan* sprayed with vegetable oil spray, sauté the mushrooms over medium-high heat for 4 to 5 minutes, until softened. Sprinkle with ½ teaspoon of the oregano and set aside.

*In another nonstick sauté pan* sprayed with vegetable oil spray, sauté the zucchini over medium-high heat for 5 to 6 minutes, until softened. Sprinkle with the remaining ½ teaspoon oregano and set aside.

*In a bowl,* combine the ricotta, corn, scallions, and pepper and mix well. Set aside.

*Preheat the oven* to 350°F. Spray an 8-by-8-inch baking pan or 10-inch pie pan with vegetable oil spray.

*Briefly warm the tortillas* on both sides on a griddle or over an open flame. Lay on a work surface and, using a pastry brush, liberally coat both sides of the tortillas with sauce.

*Lay a tortilla* in the prepared pan. (The tortilla will outsize the pan, but let it climb the sides of the pan.) Spread half the ricotta mixture on the tortilla, and top with the mushrooms and half the Swiss chard.

*Top with another tortilla* and spread with the remaining ricotta mixture. Layer with the zucchini and the remaining Swiss chard. Lay the last tortilla on top. Spread with a quarter of the remaining sauce and sprinkle with mozzarella cheese.

*Loosely cover* with aluminum foil and bake for 20 to 30 minutes, until the sauce bubbles. Let stand for 10 minutes before cutting into squares and serving on warmed plates. Garnish with the cilantro sprigs and serve with remaining sauce.

# Spinach-Zucchini-Asparagus Lasagne

**I**N THIS RICH AND SATISFYING DISH, wide whole wheat pasta lasagna noodles are rolled around ricotta cheese and grilled vegetables rather than being layered as in a more traditional lasagne.

PER SERVING:

*357 calories*

*11 g total fat (28% of calories)*

*4 g saturated fat*

*15 mg cholesterol*

*16 g protein (18% of calories)*

*48 g carbohydrates*

*(54% of calories)*

*2 g fiber*

*919 mg sodium*

**MAKES 4 SERVINGS**

4 whole wheat or durum wheat dried lasagna noodles (5$^1$/$_3$ ounces)

6 cups loosely packed spinach leaves (5 ounces)

6 ounces low-fat ricotta cheese ($^3$/$_4$ cup)

$^1$/$_8$ teaspoon freshly grated nutmeg

1 small zucchini, quartered (4 ounces)

8 stalks asparagus, trimmed

2 cups Marinara Sauce (page 284)

1 teaspoon olive oil

6 ounces white mushrooms, cleaned, trimmed, and thinly sliced

1 teaspoon fresh lemon juice

2 to 3 tablespoons Vegetable Broth (page 280) or water

$^1$/$_2$ ounce Asiago cheese, grated (4 teaspoons)

2 tablespoons chopped fresh flat-leaf parsley

*Bring a large saucepan* of lightly salted water to a boil and cook the lasagna noodles for 8 to 10 minutes, or until al dente. Drain, rinse with cold water, drain, and set aside.

*Prepare a charcoal* or gas grill.

*In a large nonstick sauté pan,* sauté the spinach over medium heat for 2 to 3 minutes, until wilted. Drain and chop into small pieces.

*In a bowl,* combine the ricotta, spinach, and nutmeg and mix well. Set aside.

*Spray the grill* with vegetable oil spray and grill the zucchini and asparagus for 3 to 4 minutes until al dente.

*In a saucepan,* heat the sauce over medium-low heat until warm.

*In a nonstick sauté pan,* heat the olive oil over medium heat. Add the mushrooms and sauté for 3 to 4 minutes, until they begin to release their juices. Drizzle with the lemon juice and broth and stir into the sauce.

*Preheat the oven* to 350°F.

*Spread enough sauce* in a shallow medium-sized baking pan to cover the bottom of the pan.

*Lay a noodle on a work surface* and spoon a quarter of the ricotta mixture close to one end of it. Arrange a piece of zucchini and 2 stalks of asparagus across the ricotta.

*Roll up the noodle,* beginning at the end with filling, so that the filling is encased by one layer of pasta. Trim any excess pasta and set the rolled noodle, seam side down, on top of the sauce in the baking pan. Repeat with the remaining 3 noodles and filling.

*Spoon* about ½ cup of the remaining sauce over each noodle and sprinkle with the cheese. Cover with aluminum foil and bake for 25 to 30 minutes, until the sauce is bubbling. Let stand for 10 minutes before serving.

*Set the rolled lasagna noodles* on warmed plates. Ladle the remaining sauce over them and sprinkle with the parsley.

# Sultan's Curry

**T**HIS CURRY IS A PROVOCATIVE MARRIAGE of a little spice, a little heat, and a little sweet allowed to blend and simmer slowly. It is the dish that converts many of our guests to part-time vegetarians!

PER SERVING:

*299 calories*

*2 g total fat (7% of calories)*

*0 g saturated fat*

*0 mg cholesterol*

*13 g protein (18% of calories)*

*56 g carbohydrates*

*(75% of calories)*

*5 g fiber*

*151 mg sodium*

**MAKES 6 SERVINGS**

³/₄ cup dried green lentils, rinsed

4¹/₂ to 5 cups Vegetable Broth (page 280) or water

2 pinches cayenne pepper

1 teaspoon canola oil

1 onion, coarsely chopped (4 ounces)

2 cloves garlic, thinly sliced

1 jalapeño pepper, seeded and minced (1 ounce)

1¹/₂ tablespoons curry powder, or to taste

2 whole cloves

1 whole star anise

¹/₂ cinnamon stick

1 cardamom seed, cracked (optional)

1 bay leaf

1 pound plum tomatoes, cored and quartered

12 ounces red or purple potatoes, cut into 1-inch chunks

1 small eggplant, peeled and cut into 1-inch chunks (12 ounces)

1 large zucchini, cut into 1-inch chunks (10 ounces)

2 carrots, sliced (8 ounces)

3 ribs celery, cut into 1-inch pieces (6 ounces)

1 green bell pepper or Anaheim chili, cored, seeded, and cut into 1-inch pieces (4 ounces)

One 8³/₄-ounce can chickpeas, drained (³/₄ cup)

¹/₄ cup tomato puree

¹/₂ cup currants

¹/₄ cup chopped fresh cilantro

1 lemon or lime, cut into 6 wedges

*In a saucepan,* combine the lentils, 2¹/₂ cups of the broth, and a pinch of cayenne and bring to a boil over medium-high heat. Reduce the heat and simmer for 45 minutes to 1 hour, until the lentils are tender. Cover to keep warm and set aside.

*Meanwhile,* in a wide saucepan, heat the oil over medium heat. Add the onion, garlic, and jalapeño and sauté for about 5 minutes, until the onion is translucent. Sprinkle with the curry powder. Add the cloves, star anise, cinnamon stick, the cardamom, if using, bay leaf, and remaining pinch of cayenne and cook for about 1 minute, stirring and taking care not to burn the spices.

*Add the tomatoes,* potatoes, eggplant, zucchini, carrots, celery, bell pepper, chickpeas, tomato puree, and 2 cups broth. Cover and simmer for 30 to 35 minutes, until the potatoes and eggplant are fork-tender. Add more broth if necessary. Add the currants and simmer, covered, for about 5 minutes longer to soften the currants. Remove from the heat and set aside for 20 minutes. Remove and discard the cloves, star anise, cinnamon stick, the cardamom, if you used it, and bay leaf.

*Spoon the lentils* into warmed shallow bowls and ladle the vegetable curry over them. Garnish with the cilantro and lemon wedges.

# Red Lentil and Seven-Grain Veggie Burgers with Grilled Onions

**G**OOD NEWS: these burgers don't require a bun to satisfy the "burger urge." Try them with pungent salsa or a little guacamole, or serve them with a baked potato or yam for an increased intake of complex carbohydrates.

*Burgers*

¾ cup Kashi Breakfast Pilaf (see Note)

⅓ cup dried red lentils, rinsed

1 teaspoon fennel seeds

Pinch of red pepper flakes

2½ cups Vegetable Broth (page 280) or water

2 teaspoons miso

3 slices whole wheat bread

1 tablespoon dried basil

2 teaspoons dried oregano

½ teaspoon dried thyme

1 tablespoon olive oil or canola oil

1 onion, minced (4 ounces)

2 ribs celery, minced (5 ounces)

1 carrot, minced (4 ounces)

¼ cup chopped fresh flat-leaf parsley

2 teaspoons liquid amino acids (see Note)

1½ tablespoons Dijon mustard

2 tomatoes, cored and cut into 12 thin slices (9 ounces)

*Onions*

2 onions, halved and thinly sliced (8 ounces)

Pinch of salt (optional)

*To make the burgers,* in a saucepan, combine the Kashi, lentils, fennel seeds, red pepper flakes, and broth. Cover, bring to a simmer over medium heat, and cook for about 55 minutes, or until the Kashi and lentils are very soft and mushy. Stir in the miso and set aside.

*Preheat the oven* to 250°F.

*Lay the bread* on an oven rack and bake for 10 to 15 minutes, until thoroughly dry. Transfer to a food processor and process until very fine. Add the basil, oregano, and thyme and pulse to mix. Set aside.

*In a sauté pan,* heat the oil over medium heat and sauté the onion for about 5 minutes, until softened. Add the celery, carrot, and parsley and sauté for 1 or 2 minutes, just until they begin to soften. Add the Kashi-lentil mixture and cook, stirring, until mixed. Remove from the heat and add the bread crumbs and liquid amino acids.

NOTE: *Kashi Breakfast Pilaf, a prepared grain mixture, is sold in many health food stores and some supermarkets. Do not confuse it with Kashi Puffed Grain Cereal. You can substitute wheat berries or medium-grain brown rice for the pilaf.*

*If you find it easier, mince the carrots and celery in a food processor.*

*Liquid amino acids are sold under the brand name Bragg Amino Acid and are available in health food stores. They provide a meaty flavor.*

*Spray* 2 pieces of parchment paper with vegetable oil spray and lay 1 piece, oiled side up, on a baking sheet or tray. Scoop twelve 1/4-cupfuls of the lentil mixture onto the paper and lay the other piece of paper, oiled side down, on top. Flatten the burgers by pressing on the parchment paper. Freeze for at least 2 hours, until solid.

*Preheat the oven* to 350°F.

*Spray* a stove-top griddle or large cast-iron pan with vegetable oil spray and heat over medium-high heat. Sauté the burgers for 2 to 3 minutes on each side, until browned but still cold in the center. Transfer the burgers to a shallow baking pan. Spread a thin layer of mustard over each burger and top with a tomato slice. Bake for 5 to 10 minutes, just until heated through.

*Meanwhile,* to cook the onions, spray the griddle or cast-iron pan with a little more vegetable oil spray and heat over medium-high heat. Cook the onions, tossing with a large spatula, for 5 to 7 minutes, until they brown and soften. Take care not to burn the onions. Season with the salt, if using.

*Serve the burgers* with the grilled onions.

# Red Lentil Dhal and Basmati Rice with Scallions

**D**HAL, HERE MADE WITH RED LENTILS and heady spices, and brown basmati rice are an ideal combination: both are flavorful and nutritionally satisfying. We suggest serving them with steamed Swiss chard or bok choy, brightened with steamed green beans, carrots, and a sprinkling of toasted sesame seeds.

PER SERVING:

*321 calories*

*3 g total fat (10% of calories)*

*0 g saturated fat*

*0 mg cholesterol*

*15 g protein (19% of calories)*

*57 g carbohydrates*

*(71% of calories)*

*4 g fiber*

*108 mg sodium*

**MAKES 4 SERVINGS**

2 teaspoons canola oil

½ cup diced onions (2 ounces)

2 cloves garlic, minced

1 jalapeño pepper, seeded and minced (1 ounce)

1 large tomato, cored and diced (6 ounces)

1 cup dried red lentils, rinsed (6½ ounces)

1 tablespoon curry powder

2 teaspoons ground cumin

¼ teaspoon freshly ground black pepper, or to taste

2¼ cups Vegetable Broth (page 280) or water, plus more if necessary

4 large Swiss chard leaves, steamed (6 ounces)

½ cup finely sliced scallions

1½ cups hot cooked brown basmati rice

*In a saucepan,* heat the oil over medium heat. Add the onions, garlic, and jalapeño and sauté for 2 to 3 minutes, until the onions begin to soften. Stir in the tomato, lentils, curry powder, cumin, black pepper, and broth.

*Simmer* for about 25 minutes, or until the lentils are soft. Mix with a wooden spatula until very smooth, adding more broth or water if necessary.

*Spread a Swiss chard leaf* on each warmed plate. Stir the scallions into the rice. Spoon the dhal onto the chard leaves and spoon the rice next to it.

## ORANGES ON A BOULDER

A day at the Door begins just before sunrise for many guests: time for the mountain hike! Awake at 5:30 A.M., they slip into sturdy hiking shoes, ease their room doors open, and step onto the wood deck *engawa*, which surrounds a garden courtyard. Waterfalls thread musically through boulders and cobbled stream beds, masking footfalls.

Hikers make their way quietly, but with some haste, to the Wisteria Lounge. Unlike many events and meetings in life that seem to start ten to twenty minutes late, the hikes leave promptly at 5:45. A sunrise—a new day—doesn't wait.

Several members of the fitness staff arrive equally promptly (they seem so *awake!*), and it's off to the trail head for a brief warm-up stretch. Soon the group walks briskly up the valley, past the vegetable garden, and turns to follow one of the many trails that lead up the hillside above the Door.

Dawn glows behind the ridge line. The group hasn't eaten yet, but there are no cravings. Sips of water are more than enough.

Views open up across the fragrant chaparral. At times the trail plunges through an avocado grove. The walk is challenging but not impossible: hikers of all abilities and fitness levels have found their pace between the leader and the trailing guide. Some chatter amiably despite breathing hard. Others fall into a quiet rhythm.

At the top, all gather on the massive, gently rounded granite boulders that crown the Door's mountainside. Sliced oranges appear magically from a guide's knapsack. Never have they tasted so good.

Breakfast will come later, after descending back to the Door, but at this moment—with the sun warming their faces, leg muscles a-tingle—the guests feel as though few meals can match this simple orange from our own groves, this slice of a new day.

# Seafood

SEAFOOD IS ONE OF THE MOST VALUABLE FOODS in a low-fat, healthful diet. It's a spectacular source of protein and nutrients and is very low in fat and cholesterol. I particularly like to cook with fish and shellfish because their subtle flavors marry so well with various sauces, marinades, and vegetables. We are lucky to be located not far from the California coast so that I have access to fresh Pacific fish and shellfish. Without doubt, freshness is key when selecting fish. If you have a choice, always choose the freshest fish available and, if possible, cook it on the day you buy it.

# Grilled Swordfish with Papaya-Kiwi Salsa

**W**HEN I GRILL SWORDFISH, I prefer to cook it so that it stays a little moist in the center.

Salsa

1 cup peeled, seeded, and diced papaya (8 ounces)

1 kiwi, peeled and diced (2 ounces)

2 tablespoons minced shallots (½ ounce)

¼ cup fresh orange juice

1 tablespoon fresh lime juice

2 tablespoons chopped fresh cilantro

2 to 3 drops hot chili sauce (see page 22)

Four 4-ounce swordfish steaks or other firm white fish, cut ½ inch thick

Quinoa with Parsley (page 203)

*To make the salsa,* in a bowl, combine the papaya, kiwi, shallots, juices, cilantro, and chili sauce. Mix, cover, and refrigerate for about 1 hour.

*Prepare a charcoal or gas grill* or preheat the broiler.

*Spray the grill* with vegetable oil spray and grill the swordfish for about 3 minutes on each side, turning to make diamond or square grill marks, until cooked through.

*Serve the fish* with the salsa and quinoa on the side.

# Grilled Salmon with
# Spinach and Yogurt-Dill Sauce

**W**ITHOUT QUESTION, SALMON IS a great favorite at the Golden Door. Even those guests who profess to dislike seafood appreciate the firm texture and subtle flavor of this glorious fish. Salmon takes so well to grilling, I find I rarely prepare it any other way——although it lends itself nicely to other cooking methods. To round out this indulgent yet surprisingly light meal, I serve the fillets on a bed of barely wilted spinach and spoon smooth satisfying Potato-Parsnip Puree next to them. The fish is topped with a refreshing yogurt sauce, made lively with a dash of horseradish.

PER SERVING:

*174 calories*

*8 g total fat (44% of calories)*

*1 g saturated fat*

*47 mg cholesterol*

*18 g protein (42% of calories)*

*6 g carbohydrates*

*(14% of calories)*

*1 g fiber*

*115 mg sodium*

**MAKES 4 SERVINGS**

½ cup nonfat plain yogurt

1 teaspoon prepared horseradish

1 teaspoon minced fresh dill

Four 2½-ounce salmon fillets

2 teaspoons olive oil

2 teaspoons minced garlic

10 cups loosely packed spinach leaves (8 ounces)

Pinch of freshly grated nutmeg

Pinch of freshly ground black pepper

4 sprigs fresh dill

4 lemon wedges

Potato-Parsnip Puree (page 194)

*Prepare a charcoal or gas grill* or preheat a stove-top grill.

*In a small bowl,* whisk together the yogurt, horseradish, and dill. Set aside.

*Spray the grill* with vegetable oil spray and grill the salmon for about 2 minutes on each side, turning to make square or diamond grill marks, until the fish is cooked through.

*Meanwhile,* in a large sauté pan, heat the olive oil over medium-low heat. Add the garlic and sauté for about 1 minute. Add the spinach and sauté for 2 to 3 minutes, until the spinach turns bright green and wilts; add 1 to 2 tablespoons of water to prevent sticking if necessary. Sprinkle with the nutmeg and pepper.

*Spoon the spinach* onto warmed plates and arrange the salmon to cover the spinach partially. Ladle the yogurt sauce over the salmon and garnish with the dill and lemon wedges. Serve the puree next to the salmon.

# Grilled Mahi-Mahi with Pineapple Curry Sauce

**T**HE SAUCE IS MADE WITH a heady mixture of vegetables and fruits for a decisively sweet-and-sour effect that tastes just right with the light and tender mahi-mahi.

### Sauce

1 teaspoon toasted sesame oil

½ cup coarsely chopped onions (2 ounces)

1 tablespoon minced garlic

½ green bell pepper, coarsely chopped (2 ounces)

1 carrot, coarsely chopped (2 ounces)

1 small tomato, cored and cut into 1-inch chunks (2 ounces)

1 rib celery, coarsely chopped (2 ounces)

2 to 3 teaspoons curry powder

½ cup diced fresh or canned pineapple (3½ ounces)

½ papaya, coarsely chopped (3 ounces; optional)

½ apple, cored and coarsely chopped (2 ounces)

½ banana, sliced (1¾ ounces)

1 tablespoon tomato paste

1 whole star anise

1¼ cups Vegetable Broth (page 280) or water, plus more if necessary

½ cup unsweetened pineapple juice

1 teaspoon low-sodium tamari or soy sauce

¼ teaspoon hot chili sauce (see page 22; optional)

### Mahi-Mahi

Four 4-ounce mahi-mahi steaks

10 cups fresh spinach leaves (8 ounces)

1 teaspoon minced garlic

8 baby carrots (4 ounces)

1½ cups hot cooked brown rice

*In a saucepan,* heat the oil over medium heat. Add the onions, 1 tablespoon of the garlic, the bell pepper, carrot, tomato, celery, and curry powder and sauté for 5 to 6 minutes, until the onions are translucent.

*Stir in the pineapple,* the papaya, if using, apple, banana, tomato paste, and star anise. Add the broth, pineapple juice, and tamari and simmer, partially covered, over low heat for 25 to 30 minutes. Remove and discard the star anise.

*Transfer to a blender* or food processor and process to a coarse consistency. If necessary, add more broth. Season with the chili sauce, if desired, cover, and set aside to keep warm.

*Prepare a charcoal or gas grill* or preheat a stove-top grill. Preheat the oven to 375°F.

*Grill the steaks* on both sides just long enough to make square or diamond grill marks on each side. Spray a baking pan just large enough to hold the steaks in a single layer with vegetable oil spray. Lay the steaks in the pan and bake for 5 to 10 minutes, or until cooked through. Cover and set aside to keep warm.

*Meanwhile,* in a nonstick sauté pan, sauté the spinach with the remaining 1 teaspoon garlic for 2 to 3 minutes, until soft.

*In a saucepan* of boiling water, blanch the baby carrots for 1 minute, or until fork-tender.

*Spoon the rice* onto warmed plates. Arrange the mahi-mahi to cover half of the rice. Place the spinach and carrots next to the fish. Spoon the sauce over the fish.

# Roasted Mahi-Mahi with Tomatillo Sauce

**M**AHI-MAHI IS A MILD-FLAVORED fish that marries well with any number of sauces and chutneys. The sauce is made from tomatillos, a close relative of the gooseberry, with a papery husk that must be removed.

*Sauce*

1 teaspoon canola oil

½ cup diced onions (2 ounces)

1 Anaheim chili, seeded and diced

1 jalapeño pepper, seeded and diced

12 tomatillos, husked, rinsed (12 ounces)

½ teaspoon salt (optional)

¼ cup Vegetable Broth (page 280) or water

6 sprigs fresh cilantro, chopped

*Mahi-mahi*

Four 4-ounce mahi-mahi steaks or other firm white fish, such as red snapper or sea bass

1 to 2 teaspoons canola oil

1 teaspoon fresh lemon juice

4 baby carrots, halved lengthwise (4 ounces)

2 cups broccoli florets (10 ounces)

Spanish Rice (page 199)

*To make the sauce,* in a saucepan, heat the oil over medium-high heat. Add the onions and the Anaheim and jalapeño peppers and sauté for 4 to 5 minutes, until softened. Add the tomatillos, the salt, if desired, and broth, cover, and simmer for about 25 minutes, or until the vegetables are soft. Cool.

*Transfer the sauce* to a blender or food processor and blend just until barely mixed; do not crush the tomatillo seeds. Add the chopped cilantro.

*To prepare the fish,* heat a nonstick sauté pan over medium heat and coat it with vegetable oil spray. Rub the fish with the oil and sprinkle with the lemon juice. Sauté the fish on both sides just until lightly browned. Cover and cook over medium-low heat for about 10 minutes, or until cooked through.

*Meanwhile,* in a steaming basket set over boiling water, steam the carrots for 4 to 5 minutes, until crisp-tender. Remove and set aside. Steam the broccoli for 2 to 3 minutes, until crisp-tender.

*Ladle* about 3 tablespoons of sauce onto each warmed plate. Arrange the fish on top and spoon the rice next to the fish. Place the carrots and broccoli between the fish and rice.

**Vegetarian Wontons with Plum Sauce**  PAGE 24

**Hummus** PAGE 33 **Eggplant Caviar with Pita Chips** PAGE 32
**Cucumber Filled with Smoked Salmon and Ricotta** PAGE 21
**Spinach and Red Pepper Paté** PAGE 36, **and Iced Red Zinger Tea**

**Creamy Corn Soup** PAGE 42

**Fruit "Club Sandwich" with Cottage Cheese and Apple Filling**  PAGE 77

**Lobster-Filled Papaya** PAGE 78

**Focaccia Sandwich with Grilled Vegetables Provençal** PAGE 98

**Yoshe Nobe** PAGE 152

**Old-Fashioned Tecate Bread**
**Garlic-Rosemary Baguette**

**Exotic Fruit Salad with Mint and Gingersnap Crumble**  PAGE 229

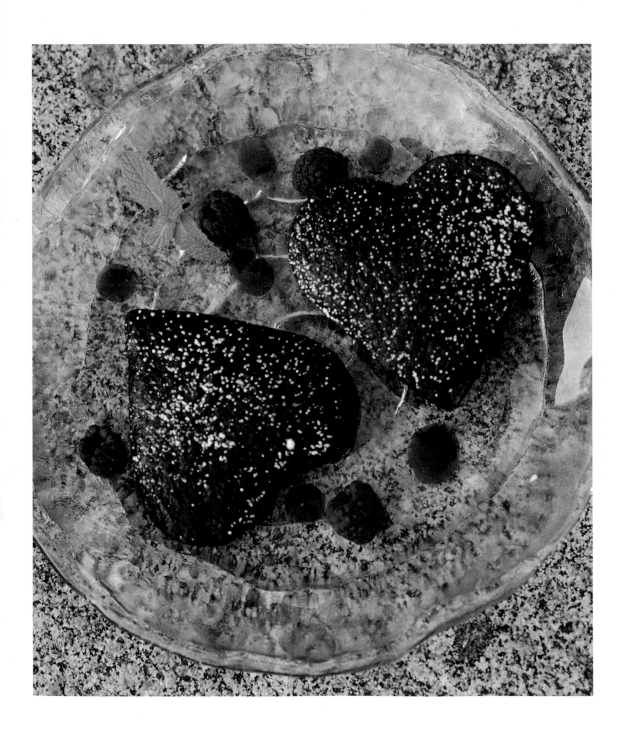

**Chocolate Madeleines**  PAGE 263

# Baked Halibut on Savoy Cabbage

**S**AVOY CABBAGE, bright green, crisp, and sweet, is ideal with fish. It is a loose and full head, with crinkled leaves and a mild flavor. This dish is excellent served with small steamed potatoes with chervil or parsley.

½ cup nonfat plain yogurt

2 teaspoons prepared horseradish, or to taste

½ teaspoon olive oil

½ cup thinly sliced red onions (2 ounces)

Four 4-ounce halibut steaks or other firm white fish

½ cup dry white wine or fish stock

¼ teaspoon freshly ground black pepper

4 sprigs fresh lemon thyme or ½ teaspoon dried

8 small inner leaves savoy or Napa cabbage (4 ounces)

1 lemon, quartered

*Preheat the oven* to 350°F.

*In a small bowl,* mix the yogurt with the horseradish. Set aside.

*In a nonstick sauté pan,* heat the olive oil over medium heat. Sauté the onions for 4 to 5 minutes, until translucent. Lay the fish over the onions, add the wine, and season with the pepper and lemon thyme. Cover tightly and bake for about 10 minutes, or until the fish is opaque and cooked through.

*Meanwhile,* in a steaming basket set over boiling water, steam the cabbage leaves for 8 to 10 minutes, until they soften but are still a vivid green.

*Arrange* 2 cabbage leaves on each plate. Center the fish and onions over them and ladle some of the cooking liquid over the fish. Spoon a dollop of the horseradish sauce onto each steak and garnish with a lemon wedge.

# Sea Bass with Three-Pepper Basquaise Sauce and Kamut Pasta

**W**HEN I DEVISE RECIPES for our guests, I naturally consider the taste, texture, and aroma of the dish, as well as its appearance. It's important to consider how all the senses are affected by a dish. The sauce for the bass is especially colorful and lively and as such is ideal for serving with pasta.

PER SERVING:

*326 calories*

*5 g total fat (12% of calories)*

*1 g saturated fat*

*86 mg cholesterol*

*28 g protein (35% of calories)*

*43 g carbohydrates*

*(53% of calories)*

*1 g fiber*

*397 mg sodium*

**MAKES 4 SERVINGS**

*Sauce*

¹/₂ teaspoon olive oil

²/₃ cup sliced onions
(3 ounces)

1 clove garlic, minced

¹/₂ red bell pepper, thinly
sliced (3 ounces)

¹/₂ green bell pepper, thinly
sliced (3 ounces)

¹/₂ yellow bell pepper, thinly
sliced (3 ounces)

2 tomatoes, cored and diced
(10 ounces)

¹/₄ cup tomato puree

¹/₂ teaspoon dried thyme

¹/₄ cup Vegetable Broth
(page 280) or water

¹/₂ teaspoon salt

¹/₄ teaspoon freshly ground
black pepper, or to taste

¹/₄ cup chopped fresh flat-leaf
parsley

*Pasta*

8 ounces kamut pasta
(see Note)

1 tablespoon olive oil
(optional)

¹/₄ cup Vegetable Broth
(page 280) or water

¹/₄ cup chopped fresh flat-leaf
parsley

¹/₄ cup chopped fresh basil

Freshly ground black pepper

Four 4-ounce sea bass fillets

*Prepare a charcoal or gas grill* or preheat the broiler. Preheat the oven to 350°F.

*To make the sauce,* in a saucepan, heat the olive oil over medium-high heat. Add the onions, garlic, and bell peppers and sauté for 4 to 6 minutes, until softened. (If the onions and peppers stick to the pan, add a little water or vegetable broth.)

*Add the tomatoes,* tomato puree, thyme, broth, salt, and pepper. Reduce the heat and simmer gently for about 10 minutes, until the flavors are well blended. Stir in the parsley and cover to keep warm.

*To cook the pasta,* bring a large pot of water to a boil and add the kamut pasta. Reduce the heat slightly and cook for 4 to 5 minutes, until al dente. Drain and shake the pasta to remove excess moisture. Return to the pot and sprinkle with the olive oil and vegetable broth. Toss with the parsley and basil and season to taste with pepper.

*Spray the grill* with vegetable oil spray and grill the bass for 1 to 2 minutes on each side, just long enough to make square or diamond grill marks. Transfer the fish to a shallow baking pan and bake for about 5 minutes, or until cooked through.

*Ladle the sauce* onto warmed plates and top with the bass. Arrange the pasta next to the bass.

## A BOUQUET FOR THE EYE

We often garnish salads and other dishes at the Golden Door with fresh edible flowers such as borage, nasturtiums, society garlic, squash blossoms, onion flower, and many more. Other favorite garnishes are sprigs of fresh herbs, especially rosemary, chopped tomatoes, slivered red and yellow peppers, chopped red and green onions, and colorful citrus zest to add interest, aroma, and flavor to each plate. Fresh cilantro is a great garnish, and those who develop a taste for this Latin American favorite will soon crave its pungent, distinctive flavor.

Keep a dish's ingredients in mind when garnishing. Use fresh thyme, slices of lime, or chopped peppers if these flavors are part of a dish. For sweets, we use fresh berries and mint sprigs.

Parsley? A last resort, if that.

# Cabrilla in Green Sauce

IN MY HOMELAND OF BELGIUM, we pride ourselves on our preparation for "eels in green." However, for this recipe I substitute a firm white fish, such as cabrilla (the Mexican sea bass), monkfish, or bluenose for the eel.

PER SERVING:

*126 calories*

*2 g total fat (14% of calories)*

*0 g saturated fat*

*41 mg cholesterol*

*18 g protein (57% of calories)*

*7 g carbohydrates*

*(22% of calories)*

*1 g fiber*

*76 mg sodium*

**MAKES 4 SERVINGS**

1 teaspoon olive oil

Four ½-inch-thick firm white fish fillets, such as cabrilla, monkfish, or bluenose, cut into ½- to ¾-inch pieces (14 to 16 ounces)

¼ to ½ teaspoon freshly ground black pepper

1 teaspoon fresh lemon juice

2 shallots, coarsely chopped (1 ounce)

¼ cup dry white wine

1 cup Vegetable Broth (page 280), Fish Stock (page 283), or water

1 cup chopped spinach leaves (½ ounce)

¼ cup chopped sorrel leaves

¼ cup chopped fresh flat-leaf parsley

¼ cup chopped fresh basil

1 scallion (including green tops), thinly sliced (½ ounce)

1 teaspoon minced fresh tarragon

⅛ teaspoon freshly grated nutmeg

2 teaspoons cornstarch or arrowroot, dissolved in 3 tablespoons water

1 cup baby carrots, or sliced carrots (5 ounces)

Winter Vegetable Mashed Potatoes (page 195)

*In a large nonstick sauté pan,* heat the olive oil over medium heat. Put the fish in the pan and season with the pepper. Sauté for 2 to 3 minutes until opaque throughout. Sprinkle with the lemon juice, remove from the pan, and set aside.

*In the same pan,* sauté the shallots for 1 minute. Add the white wine and simmer for 1 minute, stirring to scrape up any brown bits stuck to the pan. Add the broth and simmer to reduce slightly. Return the fish to the pan. Add the spinach, sorrel, parsley, basil, scallion, tarragon, nutmeg, and the cornstarch mixture and simmer for 1 to 2 minutes, just until the sauce is thickened.

*Meanwhile,* in a steaming basket set over boiling water, steam the carrots for 2 to 3 minutes, until crisp-tender.

*Spread the mashed potatoes* over a quarter of each plate. Spoon the fish over the potatoes and ladle the sauce over all. Garnish with the carrots.

# Monkfish with Saffron, Tarragon, and Tomato over Spelt Pasta

**A**LTHOUGH FEW AMERICANS had even heard of monkfish a decade ago, it is becoming quite popular because of its firm texture and similarity to lobster meat. I agree that it is incredibly delicious and love to cook with it.

PER SERVING:

*278 calories*

*3 g total fat (10% of calories)*

*0 g saturated fat*

*82 mg cholesterol*

*24 g protein (34% of calories)*

*36 g carbohydrates*

*(52% of calories)*

*0 g fiber*

*79 mg sodium*

**MAKES 4 SERVINGS**

1 teaspoon olive oil

14 to 16 ounces ½-inch-thick firm white fish fillets, such as monkfish, bluenose or snapper, cut into small pieces

Pinch of saffron

1 shallot, minced (½ ounce)

1 tomato, cored, seeded, and diced (4½ ounces)

1 teaspoon chopped fresh tarragon or ½ teaspoon dried

¼ to ½ teaspoon freshly ground black pepper, or to taste

8 ounces spelt pasta (see Note)

¼ cup dry white wine

1½ cups Vegetable Broth (page 280), Fish Stock (page 283), or water

1 tablespoon fresh lemon juice

1 tablespoon cornstarch, dissolved in 3 tablespoons water

¼ cup minced fresh flat-leaf parsley

*In a nonstick sauté pan,* heat the oil over medium heat. Put the fish in the pan and crumble the saffron over them. Sauté for 2 to 3 minutes on each side. Remove the fish from the pan and set aside. Add the shallot to the pan and sauté for 1 to 2 minutes. Add the tomato, tarragon, and pepper and cook until the tomato begins to soften.

*Meanwhile,* bring a large pot of water to a boil and cook the pasta for 8 to 10 minutes, or until al dente. Drain.

*Deglaze the sauté pan* with the wine and simmer for 1 minute. Add the broth and lemon juice and simmer for 2 to 3 minutes, to reduce slightly. Return the fish to the pan and stir in the cornstarch mixture. Cook for 1 to 2 minutes, to thicken the sauce.

*Spoon the pasta* into shallow bowls and spoon the fish and sauce over the pasta. Garnish with the parsley.

NOTE: *Spelt pasta, made from the highly nutritious grain, is sold in natural food stores and some specialty markets. You can substitute whole wheat pasta.*

# Salmon and Shrimp Paupiettes with Indian Dhal and Ginger Sauce

**W**E PREPARED THIS RECIPE at the La Quinta Resort near Palm Springs, California, for four hundred guests at the International Spa Association's annual gathering. The Indian-style vegetable dhal is excellent, and there is enough to ensure leftovers—how wonderful!

*Salmon and shrimp*

Four 2-ounce salmon fillets

4 large shrimp, peeled, deveined, and butterflied (6 ounces before peeling)

2 tablespoons chopped cilantro

1 tablespoon minced garlic

2 tablespoons low-sodium tamari or soy sauce

2 tablespoons mirin (sweet rice wine)

1 teaspoon toasted sesame oil

*Dhal*

2 teaspoons canola oil

1/2 cup minced onions (2 ounces)

2 teaspoons minced garlic

1 jalapeño pepper, seeded and minced (1 ounce)

1 large tomato, cored and diced (6 ounces)

1 cup dried red lentils, rinsed (6 1/2 ounces)

1 tablespoon curry powder

2 teaspoons ground cumin

1/4 teaspoon freshly ground black pepper, or to taste

2 1/4 cups Vegetable Broth (page 280) or water, plus more if necessary

Four 8-inch round rice sheets (see Note)

1/2 cup Vegetable Broth (page 280), Fish Stock (page 283), or water, heated

1 red bell pepper, julienned (4 1/2 ounces)

6 ounces carrots, julienned (3/4 cup)

3/4 cup sliced asparagus (1 ounce)

*Sauce*

2 teaspoons minced fresh ginger

1 teaspoon minced garlic

1 tablespoon fresh lime juice

1 tablespoon miso

1 tablespoon fructose or honey

2 to 3 drops hot chili sauce (see page 22)

1/4 cup reserved cooking liquid from salmon and shrimp

2 tablespoons chopped fresh chives

*To prepare the salmon* and shrimp, combine them with the cilantro, garlic, tamari, mirin, and sesame oil in a glass or ceramic bowl. Cover and refrigerate for no longer than 2 hours.

*To make the dhal,* in a saucepan, heat the oil over medium heat. Add the onions, garlic, and jalapeño and sauté for 2 to 3 minutes, until softened. Stir in the tomato, lentils, curry powder, cumin, pepper, and broth and simmer for about 25 minutes, or until the lentils are soft. Mix with a wooden spatula, mashing until smooth, adding more broth or water if necessary. Set aside, covered to keep warm.

*Preheat the oven* at 350°F.

*Soak the rice sheets* in cold water for 2 to 3 minutes, until softened and flexible. Dampen a work surface with water and lay the soaked rice papers on it. Arrange a salmon fillet and a shrimp in the center of each paper, sprinkle with some of the marinade, and fold the rice paper over the salmon and shrimp like a package.

*Place the packets,* seam side down, in a nonstick baking pan just large enough to hold them. Ladle the broth over the packets and bake, covered with aluminum foil or parchment paper, for 12 to 15 minutes, until the salmon is cooked through.

*Meanwhile,* in a steaming basket set over boiling water, steam the red pepper and carrots until crisp-tender for 4 to 5 minutes. Steam the asparagus for 2 to 3 minutes.

*To make the sauce,* in a blender or food processor, combine the ginger, garlic, lime juice, miso, fructose, chili sauce, and reserved cooking liquid and blend until smooth. Set aside and keep warm.

*Spoon* about ½ cup of the dahl onto each warmed plate. Place each edible, unopened paupiette next to the dahl. Ladle 1 tablespoon of sauce on top. Surround with the steamed asparagus, pepper, and carrots and sprinkle with the chopped chives.

NOTE: *Rice sheets, also called rice paper, are available in Asian markets and specialty stores.*

*You can wrap the fish in the rice paper, arrange the paupiettes in the baking dish, cover with plastic or foil, and refrigerate for several hours before baking. Sprinkle a few drops of water or broth over the paupiettes before covering the dish.*

# Grilled Shrimp with Lemon Thyme and Olive Oil

**T**HE AROMA OF FRESH LEMON THYME fills the kitchen with a bright citrusy fragrance that I love and which goes beautifully with seafood. However, you can substitute ordinary thyme to create delicious results.

1 tablespoon minced fresh lemon thyme or thyme

3 tablespoons fresh lemon or lime juice

1 tablespoon olive oil

1 teaspoon freshly ground black pepper

16 medium-to-large shrimp, peeled and deveined (12 ounces after peeling)

Green Rice (page 200)

Lemon wedges

*In a bowl,* combine the lemon thyme, lemon juice, olive oil, and pepper. Add the shrimp and toss. Cover and refrigerate for 1 to 2 hours.

*Prepare a charcoal or gas grill* or preheat the broiler.

*Spray the grill* with vegetable oil spray. Lay the shrimp on the grill (see Note) and cook for 3 to 4 minutes, turning several times, until opaque.

*Serve* with the rice and garnish with lemon wedges.

# Bouillabaisse with Shrimp, Sea Bass, Clams, and Lobster

OLIVE OIL, SAFFRON, tarragon, and the variety of seafood give this one-pot fish stew a definite Mediterranean flavor. All the ingredients can be prepared a few hours ahead and refrigerated until you are ready to cook. A flavorful fish stock and homemade marinara sauce are essential for this bouillabaisse.

2 teaspoons olive oil

2 teaspoons minced garlic

2 ribs celery, julienned (5 ounces)

1 leek (white part only), julienned (3 ounces)

1 carrot, julienned (4 ounces)

1 bulb fennel, sliced (5 ounces)

8 medium shrimp, peeled and deveined (5 ounces after peeling)

4 to 5 ounces sea bass fillets, cut into 1-inch pieces

16 Manila clams, scrubbed (see Note)

3½ ounces cooked lobster meat, cut into 1-inch pieces

½ cup dry white wine (optional)

Pinch of saffron, or to taste

¾ cup Marinara Sauce (page 284)

5 cups Fish Stock (page 283), heated

½ teaspoon Pernod

¼ cup minced fresh flat-leaf parsley

1 teaspoon minced fresh tarragon or ½ teaspoon dried

*In a large stockpot,* heat the olive oil over medium heat. Add the garlic, celery, leek, carrot, and fennel and sauté for 5 to 6 minutes, until the vegetables begin to soften.

*Add the shrimp,* sea bass, clams, and lobster. Sprinkle with the white wine and saffron and stir in the marinara sauce and fish stock. Simmer gently for about 10 minutes, until the clams open and the fish is opaque throughout.

*Sprinkle the Pernod,* parsley, and tarragon over the bouillabaisse and serve.

NOTE: *Manila clams are small, sweet, tender clams. If you cannot find them in the fish market, substitute littlenecks.*

# Yoshe Nobe

**T**O ME, this recipe epitomizes many tenets of my style of cooking at the Golden Door. It's a one-pot seafood dish that relies on Asian ingredients such as tofu, soy sauce, and shiitake mushrooms, yet the method and underlying idea are essentially European, reflecting my heritage. If you have all the ingredients ready, this can be made in minutes.

2 teaspoons canola oil

1 onion, halved and thinly sliced lengthwise (4 ounces)

1 clove garlic, minced

1 teaspoon minced fresh ginger

12 ounces firm white fish fillets, such as sea bream, sea bass, or mahi-mahi, cut into 1-inch pieces

12 Manila clams, scrubbed

8 medium shrimp, peeled and deveined (5 ounces before peeling), or 5 ounces cooked lobster meat, cut into 1-inch pieces

6 cups Vegetable Broth (page 280), Fish Stock (page 283), or water

½ cup rice wine (sake; optional)

½ teaspoon salt

8 small inner leaves Napa cabbage, blanched (4 ounces)

1 carrot, peeled and cut on the diagonal into ¼-inch slices (4 ounces)

4 ounces spinach (see Note)

4 large shiitake mushrooms, cleaned, trimmed, and quartered (6 ounces)

4 ounces firm tofu, cut into ½-inch cubes

A few drops of tamari or low-sodium soy sauce

2 scallions (including green tops), thinly sliced (1 ounce)

1 lime, quartered

*In a wide heavy saucepan* or skillet, heat the oil over medium heat. Sauté the onion, garlic, and ginger for 2 to 3 minutes, until the onion is translucent. Arrange the fish, clams, and shrimp separately over the onion and add the broth, the sake, if desired, tamari, and salt. Bring to a simmer and skim off the fat.

*Lay the cabbage leaves* on a work surface and roll into tight cylinders.

*Arrange the cabbage rolls,* carrot, spinach, and mushrooms separately over the seafood and simmer for 5 minutes longer, or until the vegetables are crisp-tender. Remove from the heat.

*Add the tofu* and let it sit in the hot broth until heated through. Sprinkle with the scallions and serve in shallow bowls, garnished with the lime quarters.

*NOTE: If the market carries fresh baby spinach with the roots still attached, buy it this way for a prettier presentation.*

# Paella with Shrimp, Lobster, Monkfish, and Clams

**P**AELLA IS A GREAT PARTY MEAL. I use basmati rice for the base, which I cook separately and then add to the cooked seafood. Traditionally, poultry or even rabbit is used, but I use only seafood here. If you want to combine meat of some sort with the seafood, I suggest turkey sausage.

PER SERVING:

*325 calories*

*4 g total fat (11% of calories)*

*1 g saturated fat*

*129 mg cholesterol*

*28 g protein (34% of calories)*

*42 g carbohydrates*

*(52% of calories)*

*2 g fiber*

*285 mg sodium*

MAKES 4 SERVINGS

2 teaspoons olive oil or canola oil

½ cup diced onions (2 ounces)

2 teaspoons minced garlic

2 ribs celery, diced (5 ounces)

1 teaspoon fennel seeds

8 medium-sized shrimp, peeled and deveined (6 ounces after peeling)

4 to 5 ounces firm white fish fillets, such as monkfish, cut into 1-inch pieces

8 Manila or littleneck clams, scrubbed

½ teaspoon saffron

½ teaspoon freshly ground black pepper

¼ cup dry white wine

4 ounces cooked lobster meat, cut into 1-inch pieces

1 cup heated peas (5 ounces)

2 teaspoons finely chopped lemon zest

2 cups hot cooked basmati rice

½ cup minced fresh flat-leaf parsley

*In a wide stockpot,* heat the oil over medium heat. Add the onions, garlic, celery, and fennel seeds and sauté for 2 to 3 minutes. Add the shrimp, monkfish, and clams and sprinkle with the saffron, pepper, and white wine. Simmer, covered, for 5 to 7 minutes, until the seafood is cooked through and the clams have opened. Add the lobster and stir gently until heated through.

*Using a kitchen fork,* mix the peas and lemon zest into the cooked rice. Spread the rice evenly over the seafood and shake the pot to combine the ingredients. Sprinkle with the parsley and serve.

# Scallops with Sweet Corn–Curry Sauce and Citrus Couscous with Apricots

**I** RELY ON cooked corn and a little coconut milk to make this subtle curry sauce creamy and full-bodied. Be sure the scallops are impeccably fresh and tender. Make sure to remove the small muscle still attached to fresh scallops—it originally attached the bivalve to the shell.

*Sauce*

2 teaspoons canola oil

1 tablespoon shallots (½ ounce)

1 to 2 teaspoons curry powder

1½ cups fresh corn kernels (from 2 ears; 7½ ounces)

1½ cups Vegetable Broth (page 280) or water, plus more if necessary

2 teaspoons arrowroot or cornstarch, dissolved in 2 tablespoons water

Pinch of cayenne pepper

2 tablespoons low-fat coconut milk

*Couscous*

½ cup chopped, dried apricots (2½ ounces)

1¼ cups Vegetable Broth (page 280) or water

1 cup whole wheat couscous (6 ounces)

1 teaspoon ground cumin

1 tablespoon finely chopped orange zest

½ cup minced fresh flat-leaf parsley

12 sea scallops (14 ounces)

6 ounces green beans

3 tablespoons thinly sliced red bell pepper

1 tablespoon sliced fresh chives

*Prepare a charcoal or gas grill* or preheat the broiler.

*To make the curry sauce,* in a saucepan, heat the oil over medium heat. Add the shallots and curry and stir until the consistency of a paste. Add the corn and broth and simmer for about 20 minutes, stirring occasionally, until the flavors are well blended.

*Strain the sauce* through a fine sieve. Return it to the pan, add the arrowroot mixture, and stir over heat until thickened. Add the cayenne and coconut milk, with a bit more broth if the sauce is too thick. Set aside and keep warm.

*Meanwhile,* to prepare the couscous, in a small bowl, combine the apricots with enough warm water to cover. Set aside for 15 to 20 minutes to plump. Drain.

*In a saucepan,* bring the broth to a boil. In a bowl, mix together the couscous and cumin. Pour 1 cup of the hot broth into the couscous. Cover and let stand for 5 minutes. Fluff with a fork while adding the apricots, orange zest, and parsley. Add the remaining vegetable broth if necessary to loosen the couscous. Keep warm.

*To cook the scallops,* spray the grill with vegetable oil spray and grill the scallops for about 2 minutes on each side (see Note). Take care not to overcook, or the scallops will be stringy and tough. Set aside and keep warm.

*Meanwhile,* in a steaming basket set over boiling water, steam the beans and red peppers until crisp-tender.

NOTE: *If the grilling grid is too wide, grill the scallops in a grilling basket or on a stove-top griddle.*

*Ladle* 3 tablespoons of curry sauce onto each warmed plate. Arrange the scallops on the sauce. Arrange the green beans around the scallops. Sprinkle the red bell pepper over the sauce and the chives over the scallops. Spoon the couscous next to the scallops.

# Chicken and Turkey

WHILE NO RED MEAT IS SERVED at the Golden Door, we offer a variety of chicken, turkey, and other poultry dishes. Chicken is the bird of choice, although I find I am serving more turkey than in years gone by. I also prepare game birds, duck, and Cornish game hens on occasion, which add to the interest and variety of the overall menu. Primarily I serve skinless chicken and rarely stray from white meat, which has less fat than dark meat. As every home cook knows, chicken and other poultry are excellent foils for sauces and glazes, vegetables, and fruits. I usually accompany the birds with grain dishes, although I also serve them with legumes and vegetable side dishes. Buy free-range, organically raised poultry. These birds have far more flavor and less fat than others.

# Stir-Fried Tamarind Chicken and Shiitake Mushrooms

**D**ELICIOUS, WITH JUST A LITTLE "TANG," this stir-fry is a great favorite at the Golden Door. We serve it with quinoa, or with rice.

### Chicken

2 teaspoons minced garlic

2 teaspoons minced fresh ginger

1 tablespoon low-sodium tamari or soy sauce

2 large boneless, skinless chicken breast halves, fat trimmed and cut into ³/₄-inch pieces (8 ounces)

### Tamarind mixture

¹/₄ cup rice vinegar

2 tablespoons mirin (sweet rice wine)

1 tablespoon light brown sugar

1 tablespoon low-sodium tamari or soy sauce

1¹/₂ tablespoons tamarind pulp (see Note)

### Vegetables

2 teaspoons canola oil

6 ounces shiitake mushrooms (about 6 mushrooms), cleaned, trimmed, and sliced into ¹/₄-inch slices

¹/₂ to ³/₄ cup Vegetable Broth (page 280) or Chicken Stock (page 282)

¹/₂ cup thinly sliced drained canned water chestnuts (2³/₄ ounces)

2 teaspoons arrowroot, dissolved in 2 tablespoons water

3 scallions, cut on the diagonal into ¹/₂-inch pieces

1 cup hot cooked brown rice

2 carrots, shredded (8 ounces)

³/₄ cup snow peas, blanched

¹/₄ cup fresh corn kernels, blanched

Toasted black sesame seeds (optional)

*To prepare the chicken,* in a glass or ceramic bowl, combine the garlic, ginger, and tamari. Add the chicken and toss. Cover and refrigerate for at least 1 hour and up to 8 hours.

*To make the tamarind mixture,* in a small nonreactive saucepan, combine the vinegar, mirin, brown sugar, tamari, and tamarind. Bring to a simmer over medium-low heat and cook for 5 to 6 minutes, stirring, until reduced by half. Strain through a fine sieve, pressing against the solids to extract as much liquid as possible. Set aside.

*To stir-fry the chicken* and vegetables, in a wok or large sauté pan, heat the oil over medium-high heat. Add the chicken and its marinade and cook for 2 to 3 minutes, turning, until lightly browned. Add the mushrooms and cook for about 1 minute. Add about $1/3$ cup broth and cook, stirring to scrape up any browned bits sticking to the pan. Add the tamarind mixture and the water chestnuts and stir-fry for 1 minute. Add the arrowroot mixture and stir until the sauce thickens. Add just enough additional broth to thin the sauce a little. Stir in the scallions.

*Spoon the rice* onto 4 plates and top each serving with chicken and vegetables. Garnish with the carrots, snow peas, corn, and the sesame seeds, if using, and serve immediately.

*NOTE: Tamarind pulp, an import from Southeast Asia, is available in Latin, Asian, and Middle Eastern markets. It is sold in cakes and will keep in the refrigerator for a week or longer.*

## HOLD THE OIL; LOWER THE HEAT; WATCH THE CLOCK

One of the most effective ways to reduce fat and calories when cooking is to use high-quality nonstick pans sprayed lightly with vegetable oil spray. This significantly reduces the amount of oil you will use during cooking. If you prefer to use oil from a bottle, use only a drop or two—do not pour it into the pan with abandon. The oil does not evaporate during cooking; it is absorbed by the food. Be sure to lower the heat under the pan; foods cooked over high heat will burn if not sufficiently lubricated with oil. If cooked more slowly, a little oil augmented by broth or water will provide adequate moisture—and far fewer grams of fat.

Cooking foods with less fat than you are used to also means calculating the cooking times carefully. Food cooked with less oil can overcook and dry out quickly and so must be watched carefully. I provide ranges for cooking times in the recipes that do not allow much latitude. Your stove, your idea of medium or medium-low heat, and your pans may vary from mine and so you will have to be the final judge of when the food is done. I try to give you a visual or textural test for doneness to help you determine when a dish is cooked to perfection, but keep a careful watch.

# Orange-Ginger Chicken with Citrus-Apricot Couscous

**T**HE COMBINATION OF INGREDIENTS might seem exotic to some, but our guests, who generally are adventurous eaters, have given this chicken dish an enthusiastic nod of approval. It's served with couscous, which is a welcome alternative to rice and contrasts with the bolder flavors of the chicken.

*Chicken*

½ cup fresh orange juice

2 tablespoons low-sodium tamari or soy sauce

2 teaspoons minced fresh ginger

4 boneless, skinless chicken breast halves, fat trimmed (1 pound)

*Couscous*

½ cup diced dried apricots

¼ cup fresh orange juice

1¼ cups Vegetable Broth (page 280) or water

1 cup whole wheat couscous

2 teaspoons ground cumin

Pinch of cayenne pepper

1 tablespoon finely chopped orange zest

12 snow peas (1¼ ounces)

½ red bell pepper, julienned (2 ounces)

1 teaspoon canola oil

¼ cup Chicken Stock (page 282) or Vegetable Broth (page 280)

4 sprigs fresh mint

*To prepare the chicken,* in a glass or ceramic bowl, combine the orange juice, tamari, and ginger and mix well. Add the chicken breasts, cover, and refrigerate for at least 1 hour, turning the chicken several times.

*To prepare the couscous,* in a small bowl, combine the apricots and orange juice and set aside for about 20 minutes.

*In a saucepan,* bring the vegetable broth to a boil. In a bowl, combine the couscous, cumin, and cayenne. Add 1 cup of the boiling broth, cover, and let stand for 5 minutes. Fluff the couscous with a fork and add more broth to loosen the couscous if necessary. Stir in the apricots with any juice and the zest.

*In a steaming basket* set over boiling water, steam the snow peas and bell pepper for 2 to 3 minutes, until fork-tender.

*In a nonstick sauté pan,* heat the canola oil over medium heat. Lift the chicken breasts from the marinade, reserving the marinade, and sauté the chicken for 2 to 3 minutes on each side, until golden brown. Drizzle the reserved marinade over the breasts. Cover, reduce the heat, and simmer for 5 to 8 minutes, or until the juices run clear when the meat is pierced with a fork or sharp knife.

*Transfer the breasts* to a warmed platter. Add the chicken broth to the pan drippings and cook over medium heat for 2 to 3 minutes, until slightly reduced.

*Spoon the couscous* onto plates and place the chicken in the center of the couscous. Coat the chicken with the sauce and garnish with the snow peas, red bell pepper, and mint sprigs.

# Chicken Yakitori and Asian Stir-Fry

IN THE SUMMER OF 1975, the Golden Door moved to its present lovely location, with Japanese-inspired architecture and museum-quality Japanese art. I changed my menu a little, too, adding dishes with obvious Asian flair. Here is one of the first of those early creations—it remains a favorite today.

PER SERVING
(Chicken):

*376 calories*

*5 g total fat (13% of calories)*

*1 g saturated fat*

*67 mg cholesterol*

*32 g protein (34% of calories)*

*49 g carbohydrates*

*(52% of calories)*

*3 g fiber*

*518 mg sodium*

**MAKES 4 SERVINGS**

### Chicken

2 teaspoons low-sodium tamari or soy sauce

2 teaspoons sake (rice wine)

1 teaspoon mirin (sweet rice wine)

1/2 teaspoon gingerroot, minced

1/2 teaspoon minced garlic

4 boneless, skinless chicken breast halves, fat trimmed and cut into 3/4-inch pieces (14 ounces)

1 large zucchini, cut into eight 3/4-inch rounds (10 ounces; see Note)

2 tablespoons Vegetable Broth (page 280) or Chicken Stock (page 282)

### Stir-fry

1 teaspoon canola oil

2 teaspoons minced garlic

1/2 teaspoon minced fresh ginger

1 cup diagonally sliced celery (3 1/2 ounces)

1 cup diagonally sliced carrots (3 1/2 ounces)

3/4 cup sliced red bell peppers (2 ounces)

1 cup sliced shiitake mushrooms (2 ounces)

2/3 cup snow peas (1 3/4 ounces)

1/2 cup diagonally sliced scallions (including green tops; 1 ounce)

1 cup mung bean sprouts (2 ounces)

4 teaspoons low-sodium tamari or soy sauce

1/4 cup Vegetable Broth (page 280) or water

2 teaspoons arrowroot or cornstarch, dissolved in 2 tablespoons water

1 1/2 cups hot cooked medium-grain brown rice

2 teaspoons black sesame seeds

*To prepare the chicken,* in a glass or ceramic bowl, combine the tamari, sake, mirin, ginger, and garlic. Add the chicken pieces and toss. Cover and refrigerate for at least 1 hour.

*Soak four 8-inch bamboo skewers* in water for at least 15 minutes.

*Prepare a charcoal or gas grill* or preheat the broiler. Preheat the oven to 350°F.

*Thread 4 to 5 chicken pieces* onto each of the bamboo skewers. Anchor each end with a round of zucchini. Spray the grill with vegetable oil spray. Grill the chicken for 2 to 3 minutes on each side until lightly browned.

*Transfer the chicken* and zucchini, still on the skewers, to a shallow baking pan. Sprinkle the broth over the chicken and zucchini. Bake for about 5 minutes, or until the juices run clear when the chicken is pierced with a fork or sharp knife.

*Meanwhile,* to make the stir-fry, heat the oil in a wok or large skillet over high heat. Add the garlic, ginger, celery, carrots, and bell peppers and stir-fry for 2 to 3 minutes  Add the mushrooms, snow peas, scallions, and bean sprouts and cook for another 2 to 3 minutes. Stir in the tamari and the broth. Slowly pour the arrowroot mixture over the vegetables. Bring to a simmer and cook for a few minutes, until the broth is thickened.

*Spoon the stir-fry* onto 4 plates. Mix the rice with the sesame seeds and spoon on top of the vegetables. Brush some of the broth from the stir-fry over the chicken, still on the skewers. Lay one skewer on top of each serving of rice.

## SHRIMP YAKITORI AND ASIAN STIR-FRY

Substitute 16 medium-to-large shrimp, peeled and deveined (12 ounces before peeling), for the chicken. Omit the zucchini. Omit the sake and mirin from the marinade and add 1 teaspoon soy sauce and 2 to 3 drops hot pepper sauce. Grill the shrimp for 3 to 4 minutes total, turning several times.

*NOTE: You can substitute half an eggplant (about 10 ounces) for the zucchini. Cut the eggplant into eight ³⁄₄-inch cubes.*

PER SERVING
(Shrimp):

*317 calories*

*3 g total fat (10% of calories)*

*1 g saturated fat*

*166 mg cholesterol*

*25 g protein (31% of calories)*

*47 carbohydrate*

*(59% of calories)*

*3 g fiber*

*687 mg sodium*

MAKES 4 SERVINGS

# Lemon-Chicken Couscous

**W**HILE TRAVELING THROUGH MARRAKESH and the Moroccan desert, I ate couscous practically every day and always enjoyed it. The *souks* (markets) are filled with mounds of spices, bright in color and very aromatic, and therein lies the secret of Morocco's flavorful cuisine. I have fond memories of this friendly and fascinating land.

PER SERVING:

*484 calories*

*6 g total fat (11% of calories)*

*1 g saturated fat*

*48 mg cholesterol*

*32 g protein (26% of calories)*

*71 g carbohydrates*

*(59% of calories)*

*4 g fiber*

*234 mg sodium*

**MAKES 4 SERVINGS**

1 teaspoon olive oil

1 onion, diced (4 ounces)

1 tablespoon minced garlic

2 carrots, sliced into ½-inch rounds (8 ounces)

2 small turnips, sliced into ½-inch rounds (5 ounces)

3 to 4 boneless, skinless chicken breast halves, fat trimmed (10 ounces)

3 large plum tomatoes, cored and quartered (10 ounces)

2 teaspoons ground cumin

2 teaspoons dried oregano

Pinch of cayenne pepper

Pinch of ground cloves or 1 whole clove

1 bay leaf

½ cinnamon stick

½ cup dry white wine

3 cups Chicken Stock (page 282) or Vegetable Broth (page 280)

4 small pieces ½-inch-thick butternut squash (4 ounces)

2 medium zucchini, cut into 1-inch rounds

¾ cup cooked or drained canned garbanzos

2 tablespoons dried currants

Pinch of saffron

1 teaspoon fresh lemon juice

*Couscous*

1¼ cups Vegetable Broth (page 280) or water

1 cup whole wheat couscous

¼ cup chopped fresh cilantro

4 lemon wedges

*To prepare the chicken,* in a large saucepan or small stockpot, heat the olive oil over medium-high heat. Add the onion and garlic and sauté for 2 to 3 minutes until the onion softens. Stir in the carrots and turnips.

*Lay the chicken* in the pan. Add the tomatoes, cumin, oregano, cayenne, cloves, bay leaf, cinnamon stick, wine, and broth and simmer, partially covered, for about 20 minutes. Add the butternut squash and zucchini and simmer for another 15 minutes. Stir in the chickpeas, currants, and saffron, remove from the heat, and let stand, covered, for 15 to 20 minutes, until the flavors blend. When ready to serve, cut the chicken into bite-sized pieces and return to the pan. Add the lemon juice to the pan.

*Meanwhile,* to make the couscous, in a large saucepan, bring the broth to a boil over high heat.

*Put the couscous in a bowl* and pour 1 cup of the hot broth over it. Cover and let stand for 5 minutes. Fluff with a fork and add more broth to loosen the couscous if necessary.

*Serve the chicken* and vegetables over the couscous in shallow pasta bowls, garnished with the cilantro and lemon wedges.

# Grilled Chicken Breasts with Salsa Verde

**B**ECAUSE WE ARE SO CLOSE TO MEXICO, many of the dishes I prepare are influenced by its delightful cuisine. This simple chicken dish is one of the most requested at the Door. It's not overly spicy, but does have a small nip of heat.

*Salsa*

1 teaspoon canola oil

½ cup diced onions
(2 ounces)

1 teaspoon minced garlic

1 jalapeño pepper, seeded
and chopped (1 ounce)

1½ cups chopped roasted
Anaheim chilies (see page 99)

2 teaspoons minced fresh or
1 teaspoon dried oregano

½ teaspoon ground cumin

1 teaspoon kosher salt
(optional)

1¼ to 2 cups Vegetable Broth
(page 280) or water

1 to 2 tablespoons chopped
fresh cilantro

4 boneless, skinless chicken
breast halves, fat trimmed
(1 pound)

1 teaspoon canola oil

1 to 2 teaspoons fresh lemon
juice

1 teaspoon chili powder, plus
more for sprinkling

Spanish Rice with Corn
(page 199)

4 large Romaine lettuce
leaves, shredded

1 small jicama, peeled and
cut into thick sticks
(12 ounces)

1 tablespoon fresh lime or
orange juice

3 tablespoons finely chopped
red onion

¼ cup nonfat plain yogurt

4 radishes, thinly sliced
(1 ounce), for garnish

*Prepare a charcoal or gas grill* or preheat a stove-top grill.

*To make the salsa,* heat the oil in a saucepan over medium heat. Add the onions, garlic, and jalapeño and sauté for 4 to 5 minutes, until softened.

*Add* ¾ cup of the Anaheim chilies, the oregano, cumin, and the salt, if desired. Add the broth and simmer for about 20 minutes, until the vegetables are very tender. Let cool slightly.

*Transfer the salsa* to a blender and blend until smooth. (You may have to do this in batches.) Finely dice the remaining Anaheim chilies and add them to the salsa with the cilantro. Set aside.

*Spray the grill* with vegetable oil spray. Rub the chicken with the oil and lemon juice and grill, turning once, just long enough to make diamond or square grill marks on both sides. Transfer to a deep skillet just large enough to hold the breasts. Sprinkle with the 1 teaspoon chili powder, cover, and cook over medium heat for 8 to 10 minutes, until cooked through.

*Spoon* about 1/2 cup of the rice onto each plate. Slice the breasts on the diagonal and fan next to the rice. Arrange the lettuce and jicama next to the chicken. Drizzle with the lime juice and top with the onion. Sprinkle with chili powder. Ladle the salsa over the chicken and top with the yogurt. Garnish with the radishes.

## SALT: TO SHAKE OR NOT TO SHAKE

As you read the recipes on these pages you will notice that, with very few exceptions, salt is optional. At the Golden Door, we only bring a salt shaker to the table if a guest requests one. Instead, I flavor the food with fresh herbs, aromatic spices, fruit juices, and citrus zest. The absence of salt makes the food taste fresh and clean and, after only a day or two, few guests miss it.

In general, Americans consume more salt (sodium chloride) than they need, and eliminating the salt shaker from the dinner table is an effective way to reduce our intake. (Studies show that as much as a quarter of the salt consumed by the average American is added once the food is served.) While there is little evidence of a link between sodium and hypertension for much of the population, there are benefits to limiting salt (protecting against edema, for example) and, because more than adequate amounts are available in the foods included in a balanced diet, I recommend leaving the salt shaker in the recesses of a dark cupboard.

When I use salt, I usually call for kosher salt, which is coarser than table salt and which I think tastes better. You could substitute sea salt for kosher salt.

# Black Bean–Chicken Enchiladas with California Chili Sauce

**W**HEN PLANNING THIS MEAL, keep in mind that I recommend soaking the dried beans for at least eight hours, or overnight. Soaking the California chilies for about an hour is also important both for flavor and to soften them, so plan your time accordingly. If you must substitute chili powder for the dried chilies, I strongly urge you to look for New Mexico–style chili powder, which is more robust than generic chili powder.

**PER SERVING**
(including chili sauce):

*331 calories*

*5 g total fat (14% of calories)*

*1 g saturated fat*

*35 mg cholesterol*

*22 g protein (26% of calories)*

*50 g carbohydrates*

*(60% of calories)*

*4 g fiber*

*831 mg sodium*

**MAKES 6 SERVINGS**

*Beans*

³/₄ cup dried black beans, rinsed, or one 16-ounce can low-sodium black beans, drained and rinsed

Pinch of red pepper flakes

¹/₂ cup diced onions (2 ounces)

2 teaspoons dried oregano

*Chili sauce*

2 dried California chilies or 2 tablespoons chili powder, preferably New Mexico–style

1 teaspoon canola oil

¹/₂ cup diced onions (2 ounces)

2 teaspoons minced garlic

1 carrot, sliced (4 ounces)

1 tablespoon ground cumin

2 teaspoons dried oregano

4 to 5 tomatoes, cored and halved (18 to 20 ounces)

1 red serrano chili (optional)

¹/₃ cup tomato puree

¹/₃ cup Vegetable Broth (page 280) or water

¹/₂ teaspoon kosher salt (optional)

*Cabbage*

1 small head cabbage, shredded (1 pound)

1 teaspoon kosher salt

¹/₄ cup fresh lime juice

*Chicken*

2 boneless, skinless chicken breast halves, fat trimmed (10 ounces)

1 teaspoon fresh lemon juice

2 tablespoons Vegetable Broth (page 280) or water

1 teaspoon dried oregano

*Enchiladas*

Six 10-inch whole wheat tortillas (10¹/₂ ounces)

1¹/₂ cups shredded Swiss chard or spinach (1¹/₂ ounces)

3 tablespoons crumbled feta cheese (1 ounce)

¹/₄ cup nonfat plain yogurt

6 radishes, thinly sliced (1¹/₂ ounces)

6 sprigs fresh cilantro

*To prepare the beans,* if using dried beans, soak in cold water to cover for at least 8 hours, or overnight. Change the water several times during soaking. Drain and rinse.

*Transfer the beans* to a saucepan and add 3 cups of water and the pepper flakes. Bring to a boil over high heat, reduce the heat, and simmer for 1½ hours, or until the beans are tender. Drain and set aside.

*Spray a small sauté pan* with vegetable oil spray and sauté the onions over medium heat for 4 to 5 minutes, until translucent. Stir into the black beans (cooked or canned), season with the oregano, and set aside. (If using canned beans, season with pepper flakes now.)

*To make the chili sauce,* put the dried chilies in a shallow bowl, cover with cold water, and set aside to soak for 1 hour. Drain.

*Prepare a charcoal or gas grill* or preheat the broiler.

*In a medium-sized saucepan,* heat the oil over medium-low heat. Add the onions, garlic, carrot, cumin, and oregano and cook for 4 to 5 minutes, until the onions are translucent.

*Spray the grill* with vegetable oil spray. Grill the tomatoes and serrano chili, if using, for 8 to 10 minutes, until softened and lightly charred, turning several times.

*Add the tomatoes,* chilies, tomato puree, and vegetable broth to the sauce. Season with the salt, if using. Cover and simmer for about 45 minutes to blend the flavors. Set aside to cool, uncovered.

*Transfer the sauce* to a blender and process just enough to break up the vegetables, so that the consistency is still slightly chunky. Set aside.

*Preheat the oven* to 350°F.

*To prepare the cabbage,* in a large bowl, combine the cabbage, salt, and lime juice, toss, and let stand for 30 minutes.

*To cook the chicken,* in a nonstick baking dish or ovenproof sauté pan just large enough to hold them, arrange the chicken breasts in a single layer. Drizzle with the lemon juice and broth and sprinkle with the oregano. Cover tightly and bake for 30 to 35 minutes, or until the juices run clear. Cool and cut into thin strips or shred by hand. (Leave the oven on.)

*To make the enchiladas*, in a large nonstick sauté pan, briefly warm the tortillas on both sides over medium-high heat. Lay on a work surface and using a pastry brush, coat one side of each with chili sauce. Spoon the black beans down the center of the tortillas and top with the Swiss chard, chicken, and feta cheese. Roll up each tortilla tightly and lay seam side down in a baking pan coated with vegetable oil spray. Brush with more chili sauce and warm for 10 to 15 minutes in the oven.

*Put the enchiladas* on warmed plates. Ladle about 3 tablespoons of chili sauce over each one and top each with a little of the yogurt. Spoon the cabbage next to the enchiladas. Garnish with the radishes and cilantro.

# Grilled Chicken Breasts with Barbecue Sauce

OVER THE YEARS, guests at the Golden Door have made it clear that sometimes they want good plain cooking. Here's an outstanding example of a simple American favorite, complete with barbecue sauce.

NOTE: The sauce can be stored in the refrigerator in a lidded container for up to 5 days.

2 teaspoons canola oil

1/2 cup diced onions
(2 ounces)

1 tablespoon minced garlic

1/4 cup cider vinegar

1/4 cup packed brown sugar

1 3/4 cups tomato puree

3/4 cup strong brewed coffee

1/2 cup Vegetable Broth
(page 280) or water

1/3 cup molasses

1 dried chili, such as ancho, softened in water, drained, and chopped

1 teaspoon chopped fresh rosemary

1/4 cinnamon stick

1 whole clove

1 bay leaf

4 boneless, skinless chicken breast halves, fat trimmed (1 pound)

1 to 2 teaspoons fresh lemon juice

Pinch of freshly ground black pepper

*Preheat the oven* to 375°F. Prepare a charcoal or gas grill or preheat a stove-top grill.

*In a small saucepan,* heat 1 teaspoon of the oil over medium heat. Sauté the onions and garlic for 2 to 3 minutes, until the onions are translucent. Add the vinegar and brown sugar and simmer, stirring, for 5 minutes, until the sugar dissolves.

*Stir in the tomato puree,* coffee, broth, molasses, chili, rosemary, cinnamon stick, clove, and bay leaf. Simmer for about 20 minutes, or until slightly thickened. Strain and set aside. Serve immediately or cover and refrigerate.

*Spray the grill* with vegetable oil spray. Rub the chicken breasts with the remaining 1 teaspoon oil and the lemon juice and sprinkle with the pepper. Grill the breasts just long enough to make diamond or square grill marks on both sides. Transfer to a shallow baking pan just large enough to contain the breasts. Bake for about 5 minutes, or until the juices run clear.

*Place a chicken breast* on each plate. Serve the sauce on the side.

# Chicken Breasts with Peanut-Ginger-Honey Sauce

**N**OTHING COULD BE EASIER than these chicken breasts served with an addictive peanut sauce that gives the simple chicken an Asian flair. When making the sauce, double the recipe so you can serve it with cold seafood or chicken salad—but be careful not to eat much more than recommended, as the calories add up quickly.

PER SERVING
(not including Peanut-Ginger-Honey Dressing or Sauce):

*323 calories*

*7 g total fat (20% of calories)*

*1 g saturated fat*

*67 mg cholesterol*

*30 g protein (37% of calories)*

*35 g carbohydrates*

*(43% of calories)*

*2 g fiber*

*220 mg sodium*

**MAKES 4 SERVINGS**

1 teaspoon minced fresh ginger

1/2 teaspoon Chinese toasted sesame oil

2 teaspoons low-sodium tamari or soy sauce

1 tablespoon lime juice

1 tablespoon cracked Szechwan peppercorns or Thai or Vietnamese chili paste

2 boneless, skinless chicken breast halves, fat trimmed and cut into 3/4-inch pieces (14 ounces)

2 teaspoons canola oil

1/2 red bell pepper, cut into 1/4-inch strips (2 ounces)

5 shiitake mushrooms, cleaned, trimmed, and thinly sliced (4 ounces)

1/4 cup Vegetable Broth (page 280) or water

1 cup broccoli florets (3 ounces)

16 snow peas (2 ounces)

8 baby carrots (4 ounces)

1 1/2 cups hot cooked brown rice

Peanut-Ginger-Honey Dressing or Sauce (page 90)

1/4 cup chopped fresh cilantro

*In a small glass or ceramic bowl,* whisk together the ginger, oil, tamari, lime juice, and peppercorns. Add the chicken, toss, cover, and refrigerate for at least 1 hour and no longer than 8 hours.

*In a large saucepan* or wok, heat the oil over medium-high heat. Add the chicken and any marinade and stir-fry for 3 to 4 minutes, until just slightly underdone. Add the bell pepper and mushrooms and stir-fry for another 2 to 3 minutes. Add the vegetable broth and scrape up any browned bits sticking to the pan.

*Meanwhile,* in a steaming basket set over boiling water, steam the broccoli, snow peas, and carrots just until fork-tender.

*Spoon the rice* onto warmed plates. Spoon the chicken and stir-fried vegetables over the rice and ladle 2 tablespoons of the sauce over each serving. Garnish with the steamed vegetables and cilantro.

# Chicken Stir-Fry with Sundried Tomatoes, Balsamic Vinegar, and Basil

**O**NCE ALL THE INGREDIENTS ARE PREPARED or measured, this becomes a quick one-pan meal that makes it an easy matter to bring the Golden Door into your own kitchen. Try it over pasta or creamy Arborio rice for a change of pace.

PER SERVING:

*275 calories*

*5 g total fat (16% of calories)*

*1 g saturated fat*

*48 mg cholesterol*

*21 g protein (30% of calories)*

*37 g carbohydrates*

*(53% of calories)*

*2 g fiber*

*68 mg sodium*

MAKES 4 SERVINGS

2 boneless, skinless chicken breast halves, fat trimmed and cut into ³/₄-inch pieces (10 ounces)

2 tablespoons thinly sliced soaked dry-packed sundried tomatoes (see Note)

1¹/₂ tablespoons balsamic vinegar

1 teaspoon minced garlic

¹/₂ teaspoon freshly ground black pepper

2 teaspoons olive oil

1 onion, diced (4 ounces)

2 large tomatoes, cored and diced (12 ounces)

2 medium-sized zucchini, sliced into ¹/₄-inch slices (14 to 16 ounces)

¹/₂ to ³/₄ cup Chicken Stock (page 282) or Vegetable Broth (page 280)

2 teaspoons arrowroot powder, dissolved in 2 tablespoons water

¹/₂ cup sliced fresh basil

16 snow peas (2 ounces)

1¹/₂ cups hot cooked basmati brown rice

*In a small glass or ceramic bowl,* combine the chicken, sundried tomatoes, vinegar, garlic, and pepper. Cover and refrigerate for at least 1 hour and for no longer than 8 hours.

*In a wok* or large sauté pan, heat the oil over medium-high heat. Add the chicken and any marinade and stir-fry for 3 to 4 minutes, until lightly browned. Add the onion and stir-fry for 2 to 3 minutes, until softened. Add the tomatoes and stir-fry for 2 to 3 minutes, until softened. Add the zucchini, toss well, and simmer, stirring, for 2 to 3 minutes. Stir in ¹/₂ cup of broth and the arrowroot mixture and stir until thickened; if necessary, add more chicken broth if the sauce seems too thick. Stir in the basil.

*Meanwhile,* in a steaming basket set over boiling water, steam the snow peas for 2 to 3 minutes, until crisp-tender.

*Spoon the rice* onto warmed plates and top with the chicken and stir-fried vegetables. Garnish with the snow peas.

*NOTE: To rehydrate dry-packed sundried tomatoes, soak them in warm water to cover for 15 to 20 minutes. Drain.*

# Chicken Tostadas with
# Anasazi Beans and Spa Guacamole

**A** FREQUENT REQUEST at the Golden Door is for Mexican food, and when we make this tostada for lunch, it's met with great enthusiasm. The recipe may look long and complex, but with a little effort, it can be done in about one hour. Save time and cook the beans a day ahead, or substitute canned black beans for the Anasazi beans.

PER SERVING
(not including Spa Guacamole):

*371 calories*

*5 g total fat (11% of calories)*

*2 g saturated fat*

*44 mg cholesterol*

*28 g protein (31% of calories)*

*54 g carbohydrates*

*(58% of calories)*

*4 g fiber*

*396 mg sodium*

**MAKES 5 SERVINGS**

*Beans*

³/₄ cup dried Anasazi beans, rinsed, or one 16-ounce can low-sodium black beans, drained and liquid reserved

Pinch of red pepper flakes

1 teaspoon dried oregano

2 teaspoons ground cumin

*Tostadas*

2 boneless, skinless chicken breast halves, fat trimmed (10 ounces)

1 teaspoon fresh lemon juice

2 tablespoons Vegetable Broth (page 280) or water

1 teaspoon dried oregano

Five 10-inch whole wheat tortillas (8³/₄ ounces)

2 large egg whites, lightly beaten

10 cups shredded Romaine or butter lettuce (8 ounces)

3 tomatoes, cored and diced (14 ounces)

1 red onion, diced (14 ounces)

3 tablespoons crumbled feta cheese (1 ounce) or low-fat mozzarella cheese (³/₄ ounce)

Spa Guacamole (page 34)

5 sprigs fresh cilantro

*To prepare the beans,* if using the dried beans, soak in cold water to cover for at least 8 hours, or overnight. Drain and rinse.

*Transfer the beans* to a saucepan and add 3 cups of water and the pepper flakes. Bring to a boil over high heat, reduce the heat, and simmer for 1¹/₂ hours, or until the beans are tender. Drain and set aside. (If using canned beans, add pepper flakes now.)

*Preheat the oven* to 350°F. Spray a baking sheet with vegetable oil spray.

*Transfer the beans* (cooked or canned) and some of the cooking liquid (or the liquid from the can) to a blender. Process until the beans are crushed but not pureed. Add the oregano and cumin and pulse just until mixed. Transfer to a bowl and set aside.

*In a nonstick baking pan* or ovenproof skillet just large enough to hold the chicken breasts, arrange them in a single layer. Drizzle with the lemon juice and broth and sprinkle with the oregano. Cover and bake for 30 to 35 minutes, or until the juices run clear when the meat is pierced with a fork or sharp knife. Let cool, then cut into thin strips or shred by hand.

*Brush both sides* of the tortillas with beaten egg whites and lay them on the baking sheet. Bake for about 15 minutes, or until they begin to crisp. Turn the tortillas, return to the oven, and crisp on the other side for 4 to 5 minutes.

*Spread the bean puree* evenly over the tortillas. Top with the shredded lettuce, tomatoes, onion, and then the chicken. Sprinkle with the feta cheese and top with the guacamole. Garnish with cilantro.

# Chinese-Style Egg Rolls with Chicken

**A**S WITH MOST ASIAN RECIPES, the ingredient list is long and so at first may seem daunting. But most of the ingredients are easy to find and the egg rolls can be prepared in advance, covered, and refrigerated until ready to bake. Try these crispy, crunchy rolls with the plum sauce I serve with the Vegetarian Wontons on page 24. Great!

PER SERVING
(not including
Orange Basmati Rice):

*355 calories*

*4 g total fat (10% of calories)*

*1 g saturated fat*

*39 mg cholesterol*

*25 g protein (28% of calories)*

*54 g carbohydrates*

*(61% of calories)*

*6 g fiber*

*827 mg sodium*

**MAKES 4 SERVINGS**

NOTE: *Slice the mushrooms and cabbage so that the pieces are about ¹/₄ inch thick.*

*Follow the package directions for rolling the egg roll wrappers around the filling.*

2 boneless, skinless chicken breast halves, fat trimmed (8 ounces)

¹/₄ teaspoon Chinese five-spice powder

¹/₂ teaspoon fresh lemon juice

1 teaspoon canola oil

2 teaspoons minced garlic

¹/₂ teaspoon minced fresh ginger

1 cup diagonally sliced celery (3¹/₂ ounces)

1 cup diagonally sliced carrots (3¹/₂ ounces)

1¹/₂ cups diagonally sliced zucchini (4 ounces)

³/₄ cup diagonally sliced red bell peppers (2 ounces)

1 cup sliced shiitake mushrooms (2 ounces; see Note)

³/₄ cup sliced Napa cabbage (1¹/₂ ounces; see Note)

²/₃ cup snow peas (1³/₄ ounces)

¹/₂ cup sliced scallions (including green tops; 1 ounce)

4 teaspoons low-sodium tamari or soy sauce

¹/₂ cup Vegetable Broth (page 280) or water, plus more if necessary

2 teaspoons arrowroot or cornstarch, dissolved in 2 tablespoons water

8 egg roll wrappers (6¹/₂ ounces)

1 large egg white, lightly beaten

8 large leaves Swiss chard, cut into large pieces (12 ounces)

¹/₄ teaspoon Chinese toasted sesame oil

¹/₄ teaspoon freshly ground black pepper, or to taste

Orange Basmati Rice (page 201)

*Preheat the oven to 350°F.*

*Lightly spray a nonstick baking pan just large enough to hold the chicken breasts with vegetable oil spray. Arrange the chicken in the pan in a single layer. Sprinkle with the five-spice powder and lemon juice. Cover*

tightly and bake for 25 to 30 minutes, or until the juices run clear when the meat is pierced with a fork or sharp knife. Cool, then cut into 8 slices. (Do not turn off the oven.)

*Meanwhile,* in a large sauté pan or wok, heat the oil over high heat. Add the garlic, ginger, celery, carrots, zucchini, and bell peppers and stir-fry for 2 to 3 minutes. Add the mushrooms and cabbage and stir-fry for 2 to 3 minutes. Toss in the snow peas and scallions. Add the tamari and then the vegetable broth. Slowly pour the dissolved arrowroot over the vegetables and bring to a simmer. Cook for 3 to 4 minutes longer, stirring, until thickened. Set aside to cool.

*Lay the egg roll wrappers* on a work surface and brush the edges with egg white. Spoon approximately 1/2 cup of the stir-fried vegetables onto each wrapper and lay 2 pieces of chicken on top. Fold each wrapper into a package (see Note).

*Spray a baking sheet* with vegetable oil spray. Lay the egg rolls, seam side down, on the pan and spray them with vegetable oil spray. Bake for 25 to 30 minutes, until lightly browned and crisp.

*Meanwhile,* in a nonstick sauté pan, cook the Swiss chard over medium heat, adding a few tablespoons of vegetable broth, if necessary. Drain off any excess liquid, and sprinkle with the sesame oil and black pepper.

*Arrange the egg rolls* on warmed plates and serve with the rice and Swiss chard.

# Baked Turkey with Parsnip-Carrot Sauce

**O**UR GUESTS OFTEN CHOOSE THIS TURKEY DISH when they crave down-home, comfort food. I heighten the comfort level by serving it with Sweet-and-Sour Red Cabbage (page 192) and a scoop of Leek-and-Garlic Mashed Potatoes (page 196).

One 3-pound boneless turkey breast

2 parsnips, cut into 2-inch lengths (8 ounces)

4 carrots, cut in half (1 pound)

1 onion, cut in half

2 sprigs fresh thyme

1 bay leaf

2 teaspoons freshly ground black pepper, or more to taste

About 1 cup Vegetable Broth (page 280) or water

1 teaspoon arrowroot or cornstarch

2 cups broccoli florets, steamed hot

¼ cup minced fresh flat-leaf parsley

*Preheat the oven* to 350°F.

*Put the turkey breast* in a deep baking pan just large enough to hold it. Arrange the parsnips, carrots, onion, thyme, and bay leaf around the turkey breast. Sprinkle with the pepper, cover with aluminum foil, and bake for about 1½ hours, until the juices run clear when the meat is pierced with a fork or sharp knife.

*Remove the turkey,* parsnips, carrots, and onion. Discard the bay leaf. Degrease the pan juices by skimming them with a ladle or blotting them with paper towels. Add enough broth to the pan juices to make 2 cups of liquid.

*In a blender* or food processor, blend the vegetables, broth, and arrowroot until smooth. Transfer to a small saucepan and heat until hot. Season with pepper. Keep warm.

*Remove the skin* from the turkey. Thinly slice the turkey breast and fan onto warmed plates. Ladle the sauce over the turkey and serve garnished with the broccoli florets and minced parsley.

## THE SECRET IN THE PANS

Many of our recipes call for partially cooking a dish on top of the stove and then finishing it off in a covered pan in the oven. Over the years, we have discovered this to be an effective way to cut back on fat and calories.

After the initial searing or sealing of foods on top of the stove, we add a small amount of liquid and then let the covered food finish cooking in a moderate oven. The liquid poaches the food so that it is more moist and tender. Oven time is often quite brief.

We buy nonstick pans with ovenproof, tight-fitting lids. If the pan is not covered snugly, food will dry out regardless of your best efforts. If you choose not to use the oven, reduce heat on the stove, cover your pan tightly with a lid, and cook several minutes longer. Juices remain within. Just add that touch of fresh herbs or a squeeze of lime as a final touch.

The right size pan is also very important. Cooking in a pan that allows foods to be "comfortably crowded" helps keep them moist. This is especially important when using so little fat. Too large a pan: food dries out. Too small a pan: food cooks unevenly. Have an array of pans so that one will be just right.

# Zucchini Stuffed with Turkey and Rice

**A**S LONG AS THE ZUCCHINI is about two inches thick, use any sort of zucchini you like: yellow bar, golden zucchini, the Lebanese tender pole variety, or the familiar green zucchini. Using larger, thick squash allows you to fill it easily and generously, which is important for a good hearty meal. Try this with summer's sweet corn on the cob.

$\frac{1}{3}$ cup uncooked brown rice

$\frac{1}{4}$ teaspoon fennel seeds

4 large zucchini, each about 2 inches thick (40 ounces)

8 ounces ground skinless turkey breast

1 teaspoon dried thyme

1 teaspoon kosher salt

$\frac{1}{4}$ teaspoon freshly ground black pepper, or more to taste

1 cup diced onions (4 ounces)

2 teaspoons minced garlic

1 cup sliced white mushrooms (3 ounces)

1 cup diced tomatoes (6 ounces)

12 cups loosely packed spinach leaves, chopped (10 ounces)

1 cup Marinara Sauce (page 284) or commercial marinara sauce

$\frac{1}{4}$ cup chopped fresh flat-leaf parsley

$\frac{1}{4}$ cup finely sliced fresh basil

1 to 1$\frac{1}{2}$ cups Vegetable Broth (page 280) or water

2 tablespoons freshly grated Asiago or Romano cheese (optional)

*In a saucepan,* combine the rice, fennel seeds, and 1$\frac{1}{4}$ cups of water and bring to a simmer over medium-high heat. Stir well, cover, and cook for 30 to 35 minutes, until most of the liquid is absorbed. Remove from the heat and let stand for 10 minutes. Fluff with a fork. Cover to keep warm.

*Preheat the oven* to 350°F.

*Trim the ends* of the zucchini and cut in half lengthwise. Using a small melon baller or small spoon, remove the pulp, being careful to leave a shell about $\frac{1}{4}$ inch thick. Chop the pulp and set aside.

*In a heavy nonstick saucepan,* combine the turkey, thyme, salt, and pepper and cook over medium heat, stirring continuously with a wooden spatula for even browning. (If the turkey begins to stick, add a little water.) Stir in the onions, garlic, and chopped squash pulp and cook for about 2 minutes. Stir in the mushrooms and tomatoes and simmer for 3 minutes. Add the spinach, rice, and ½ cup of the marinara sauce. Remove from the heat and stir in the parsley and basil.

*Spoon the filling* into the prepared zucchini shells, mounding it slightly. Place in a baking pan large enough to hold the zucchini in a single layer. Add enough vegetable broth to cover the bottom of the pan to a depth of about ½ inch. If desired, sprinkle pepper on the zucchini. Cover with foil and bake for about 25 minutes, or until the squash is softened.

*Meanwhile,* in a small saucepan, heat the remaining ½ cup marinara sauce until hot.

*Place* 2 filled zucchini boats on each plate and ladle the hot marinara sauce over them. Sprinkle the cheese, if desired, over all.

## Vegan-Style Stuffed Zucchini with Brown Rice and Pine Nuts

PER SERVING:

*268 calories*

*5 g total fat (16% of calories)*

*1 g saturated fat*

*0 mg cholesterol*

*9 g protein (14% of calories)*

*47 g carbohydrates*

*(70% of calories)*

*4 g fiber*

*64 mg sodium*

**MAKES 4 SERVINGS**

Omit the turkey and marinara sauce. Add 2 tablespoons toasted pine nuts and 1 tablespoon sweet paprika to the filling. Increase the mushrooms to 8 ounces (about 3 cups). Omit the parsley and increase the basil to ½ cup. Increase the tomatoes to 14 ounces and do not dice them; instead, slice them and lay them on top of the filled boats. Omit the cheese if desired.

# Turkey Patties on Garlic-Rosemary Buns

**O**UR GUESTS LOVE THESE TURKEY BURGERS, which are a weekly tradition. This is one of those meals that repeat visitors look forward to—and I hear about it if the turkey burgers are not on the weekly menu!

3/4 pound ground skinless turkey breast

1/4 pound ground skinless turkey thighs

1 tablespoon minced shallots

1 large egg white

1 tablespoon minced fresh flat-leaf parsley

1 teaspoon minced fresh tarragon

Freshly ground black pepper to taste

1/2 teaspoon canola oil

2 white onions, halved and thinly sliced (8 ounces)

1/8 teaspoon kosher salt (optional)

5 large Romaine or leaf lettuce leaves (3 ounces)

2 tomatoes, cored and sliced (9 ounces)

1 red onion, thinly sliced (4 ounces)

1 dill pickle, sliced (3 ounces)

5 Garlic-Rosemary Buns (page 215) or whole wheat buns

*Prepare a charcoal or gas grill* or preheat the broiler.

*In a bowl,* mix together the turkey, shallots, egg white, parsley, tarragon, and pepper. Form into 5 patties. Set aside.

*In a sauté pan,* heat the oil over medium to medium-high heat. Toss the white onions with the salt, if using, into the pan and sauté, turning with a large spatula, for 8 to 10 minutes, until the onions brown and soften. Set aside.

*Spray the grill* with vegetable oil spray. Grill the patties for 2 to 3 minutes on each side, turning to make diamond or square grill marks. To make sure that the turkey is thoroughly cooked, let them stand for 2 to 3 minutes after removing from the grill, or until the juices run clear. Divide the lettuce leaves, tomatoes, red onion, and dill pickle among the buns, layering them on the bottom halves of the buns. Top each with a turkey patty and grilled onions and then set the top of the bun over the onions.

# Turkey Scallop Sauté with Grainy Mustard Sauce

**T**HIS IS A GREAT FAVORITE at the Door. The turkey is served with a decidedly French-style mustard sauce, made with yogurt rather than cream but equally delicious. Take care not to overheat the yogurt—just warm it, or it may curdle.

PER SERVING
(not including
Broccoli Mashed Potatoes):

*209 calories*

*4 g total fat (19% of calories)*

*1 g saturated fat*

*55 mg cholesterol*

*27 g protein (51% of calories)*

*16 g carbohydrates*
*(30% of calories)*

*1 g fiber*

*165 mg sodium*

**MAKES 4 SERVINGS**

1 teaspoon olive oil

4 turkey breast cutlets
(14 ounces)

$\frac{1}{2}$ teaspoon dried basil

$\frac{1}{2}$ teaspoon freshly ground
black pepper

$\frac{1}{4}$ cup unbleached
all-purpose flour

8 baby carrots, cut lengthwise
in half (8 ounces)

$\frac{1}{2}$ cup diced onions
(2 ounces)

$1\frac{1}{2}$ to 2 tablespoons grainy
mustard

$\frac{1}{2}$ cup Chicken Stock
(page 282) or Vegetable Broth
(page 280)

1 teaspoon arrowroot,
dissolved in 2 tablespoons
water

$\frac{1}{4}$ cup nonfat plain yogurt

2 tablespoons finely sliced
fresh chives

Broccoli Mashed Potatoes
(page 197)

*In a nonstick sauté pan* just large enough to hold the cutlets, heat the olive oil over medium heat. Sprinkle the cutlets with the basil and pepper and dust lightly with the flour. Sauté for 2 to 3 minutes on each side. Cover and continue cooking for about 2 minutes, until cooked through. Transfer to a warm plate.

*In a steaming basket* set over boiling water, steam the carrots for 3 to 5 minutes, until fork-tender, and heat gently.

*Add the onions* to the pan and cook for 2 to 3 minutes until barely softened. Stir in the mustard, broth, and dissolved arrowroot until thickened.

*Return the turkey* to the pan, add the yogurt, shaking to distribute it in the sauce.

*Place the turkey* on warmed plates and ladle the sauce over it. Garnish with the carrots and a sprinkling of chives and serve with the mashed potatoes.

# Duck Breasts with Raspberry Sauce

**W**HILE DUCK IS RELATIVELY HIGH IN FAT, I love its rich flavor and cannot resist serving it now and then. I serve only three ounces, fanned on the plate so it looks attractive, and spoon a mound of Rice Trilogy with Almonds (page 198) next to it to contrast pleasingly with the taste and texture of the meat.

PER SERVING
(Not including Rice Trilogy with Almonds):

*291 calories*

*17 g total fat (52% of calories)*

*5 g saturated fat*

*46 mg cholesterol*

*12 g protein (17% of calories)*

*16 g carbohydrates*

*(22% of calories)*

*2 g fiber*

*105 mg sodium*

**MAKES 5 SERVINGS**

2½ tablespoons raspberry vinegar

2 tablespoons crushed raspberries, plus 15 whole raspberries (2 ounces), for garnish

1 tablespoon minced shallots

1 teaspoon dried basil

½ teaspoon freshly ground black pepper

One 1-pound duck breast, skin and silverskin removed and trimmed; reserve 1 ounce of skin and all meat scraps

1 teaspoon canola oil

½ cup diced onions (2 ounces)

½ teaspoon cracked black pepper

¾ cup Chicken Stock (page 282) or Vegetable Broth (page 280)

½ cup Marsala wine

1 tablespoon light brown sugar

1 teaspoon arrowroot, dissolved in 2 tablespoons water

¼ cup Raspberry Coulis (page 247)

15 baby turnips, unpeeled, stems trimmed to 1 inch (15 ounces)

1 cup green beans (5 ounces)

Rice Trilogy with Almonds (page 198)

5 sprigs fresh mint

*In a small bowl,* combine the vinegar, crushed raspberries, shallots, basil, and ground pepper and stir well. Lay the duck breast in a shallow baking pan and pour the marinade over it. Cover and refrigerate for at least 2 hours and up to 8 hours.

*Prepare a charcoal or gas grill* or preheat the broiler. Preheat the oven to 375°F.

*Transfer the duck* to a plate and reserve the marinade.

*In an ovenproof sauté pan,* heat the oil over medium heat. Add the reserved duck skin and trimmings, the onions, and cracked black pepper and cook for 4 to 5 minutes, until the meat is well browned. Add the reserved marinade, remove from the heat, and set the entire pan aside.

*Spray the grill* with vegetable oil spray. Grill the breast for 3 to 4 minutes on each side, turning to make diamond or square grill marks. (At this point, the duck breast should still be rare.) Transfer to the sauté pan with the trimmings and bake, uncovered, for 10 to 15 minutes, until medium-rare to medium. Transfer the breast to a warmed plate, leaving the trimmings and juices in the pan, and cover to keep warm.

*Return the pan* to the stove and set over medium heat. Add the broth and wine and simmer for 10 to 15 minutes, stirring to deglaze the pan, until the sauce is slightly reduced. Strain through a fine sieve and return to the pan. Skim off any visible fat on the surface of the sauce. Add the brown sugar, arrowroot mixture, and coulis and simmer for 2 minutes longer, or until slightly thickened.

*Meanwhile,* in a steaming basket set over boiling water, steam the turnips for 8 to 9 minutes until crisp-tender. Drain. Steam the beans for 4 to 5 minutes until crisp-tender. Drain.

*Spoon the rice* off-center onto warmed plates. Slice the duck breast into sixteen $1/4$-inch diagonal slices and fan 4 each on one side of each serving of rice. Ladle 2 tablespoons of sauce over the duck. Arrange the steamed turnips and beans around the rice and garnish with the whole raspberries and sprigs of mint.

# Pintade with Apples and Calvados

**G**UINEA FOWL, OR PINTADE, has the lowest fat content of all poultry and is delicious when prepared with apples and Calvados. Ask the butcher to order guinea fowl for you. You can make this sauce, or simply deglaze the sauté pan with sweet white wine and chicken broth. Rock Cornish hens or chicken can be substituted.

PER SERVING:

*223 calories*

*7 g total fat (29% of calories)*

*0 g saturated fat*

*0 mg cholesterol*

*23 g protein (41% of calories)*

*12 g carbohydrates*

*(22% of calories)*

*0 g fiber*

*13 mg sodium*

**MAKES 6 SERVINGS**

3 whole guinea fowl breasts with wings attached (20 ounces)

¼ cup sweet white wine, such as Riesling or sauterne

1 tablespoon balsamic vinegar

2 tablespoons coarsely chopped shallots

1 teaspoon crushed juniper berries

¼ teaspoon freshly ground black pepper

2 to 3 Fuji or Rome apples, cored and sliced into ¼-inch-thick rounds (8 ounces)

1 teaspoon canola oil

2 tablespoons Calvados

¾ cup Chicken Stock (page 282) or Vegetable Broth (page 280)

2 teaspoons arrowroot (optional)

¼ cup chopped fresh chervil, scallions, or flat-leaf parsley

¼ cup canned whole-berry cranberry sauce

*To prepare the fowl,* remove the wings from the breasts and discard. Place the breasts, skin side up, in a shallow baking pan. Combine the wine, vinegar, shallots, juniper berries, and pepper, mix well, and pour over the breasts. Cover and refrigerate for at least 2 hours, or overnight.

*Preheat the oven* to 350°F.

*Spray a large ovenproof nonstick sauté pan* with vegetable oil spray and heat over medium heat. Cook the apple slices for 1 to 2 minutes on each side, until lightly browned. Remove the pan from the heat and set aside.

*In another nonstick sauté pan,* heat the oil over medium heat. Lift the breasts from the marinade, reserving the marinade, and sauté the breasts, skin side down, for 2 to 3 minutes, until lightly browned. Turn and brown the other side. Lay the sautéed breasts, skin side up, on top of the apples and set the pan you used to cook the pintade aside.

*Sprinkle the breasts* with the Calvados, cover loosely with foil, and bake for about 15 minutes, or until the juices run clear when the meat is pierced with a fork or sharp knife. Set aside to cool slightly. Reduce the oven heat to 250°F. Remove the skin from the breasts and discard. Return the breasts covered to the oven to keep warm.

*To prepare the sauce,* drain the fat from the pan used to sauté the breasts. Add the reserved marinade and stir to deglaze the pan. Add the broth and simmer for 5 to 6 minutes, until reduced to about ½ cup. Thicken with the arrowroot, if desired. Strain and set aside.

*Slice the breasts* and fan them on warmed plates. Top with the apple slices and ladle about 2 tablespoons of sauce on top of each serving. Sprinkle with the chopped chervil and garnish with the cranberry sauce, placed in the center of the apple slices.

# Roasted Cornish Game Hens with Wild Rice and Almonds

**T**HE SHALLOT MARMALADE SAUCE makes all the difference in this simple dish, and the orange slices and star anise contribute a heady aroma during cooking. Be sure to use a pan just large enough to hold the hens so that they emerge nice and juicy—not dry.

*Game hens*

Four 1-pound Rock Cornish game hens, skinned

1 orange, sliced crosswise into 8 slices

1 whole star anise

1 bay leaf

¼ teaspoon freshly ground black pepper

*Sauce*

1 teaspoon olive oil

3 shallots, diced (1½ ounces)

2 tablespoons diced dried apricots

1 tablespoon brown sugar

Pinch of fresh or dried rosemary

1 tablespoon sherry vinegar

½ cup Chicken Stock (page 282) or Vegetable Broth

(page 280), plus more if necessary

2 tablespoons dry white wine (optional)

1 teaspoon cornstarch, dissolved in 1 tablespoon water

Kosher salt to taste

8 baby turnips, scrubbed and cut into ½-inch slices (8 ounces)

4 baby carrots (2 ounces)

20 to 24 green beans (2 ounces)

1½ cups hot cooked wild rice

⅓ cup toasted sliced almonds

1 teaspoon chopped blanched orange zest (see Note)

4 sprigs fresh chervil or flat-leaf parsley

*Preheat the oven* to 375°F.

*To prepare the hens,* split them in half lengthwise. Remove the wings and backbones and discard. Trim and discard all excess fat.

*In a shallow baking pan* just large enough to hold the game hens, layer the orange slices and set the star anise and bay leaf on top. Arrange the game hens on top of the oranges and sprinkle with the pepper. Bake for 40 minutes, or until the juices run clear when the thigh is pierced with a fork or sharp knife.

*Remove the skin* and rib bones from the hens. Using a sharp knife, make a ½-inch-deep cut in the joint between the drumstick and thigh and then split the leg at the joint. Assemble each breast half with each leg, piecing the halves together like two interlocking puzzle pieces. Cover and keep warm.

*Skim off the fat* from the baking pan and reserve the cooking juices for the sauce.

*To make the sauce,* in a small sauté pan, heat the olive oil over low heat. Sauté the shallots for 5 to 7 minutes, or until lightly browned. Add the apricots, brown sugar, and rosemary and cook for about 10 minutes longer, until the shallots caramelize and turn a rich, dark brown. Deglaze the pan with the vinegar, add the broth and the wine, if desired, and cook for 4 to 5 minutes, until slightly reduced. Add the reserved cooking juices. Add the cornstarch mixture and stir until the sauce thickens, then adjust the consistency with additional broth if necessary. Season to taste with salt.

*Meanwhile,* in a steaming basket set over boiling water, steam the turnips for about 5 to 8 minutes, until crisp-tender. Drain. Steam the carrots for 3 to 5 minutes, until crisp-tender, then steam the green beans for 2 to 3 minutes, until crisp-tender. Drain.

*Mix the wild rice* with the almonds and spoon onto warmed plates. Place the hens on top. Ladle 2 tablespoons of sauce over each serving. Arrange the turnips, carrots, and beans next to the hens and sprinkle with the orange zest. Garnish with the chervil.

NOTE: *To blanch orange zest, submerge it in boiling water for about 1 minute. Drain and pat dry.*

# Vegetables and Grains

WHEN I DEVELOP A DISH, I think of the entire meal's concept and rarely think about separating the elements that will be served together. But for this book, I have segregated some of our more popular side dishes so that you can mix and match them at home with simple preparations such as broiled chicken or grilled fish. These are among my favorites, and you will find almost every one served with at least one main-course recipe in this book.

# Sweet-and-Sour Red Cabbage

PER SERVING:

*81 calories*

*0 g total fat (4% of calories)*

*0 g saturated fat*

*0 mg cholesterol*

*1 g protein (6% of calories)*

*18 g carbohydrates*

*(90% of calories)*

*1 g fiber*

*599 mg sodium*

**MAKES 8 SERVINGS**

½ cup diced white onions (2 ounces)

⅔ cup cider vinegar or red wine vinegar

½ cup unsweetened apple juice

⅓ cup Cabernet Sauvignon or red Burgundy (optional; see Note)

½ cup packed light brown sugar

1 bay leaf

2 whole cloves

One 1¼-pound red cabbage, trimmed, quartered, cored, and sliced into ¼-inch slices

½ cup Vegetable Broth (page 280) or water, plus more if necessary

2 tart green apples, peeled, cored, and cut into ⅛-inch slices (8 ounces)

Kosher salt to taste (optional)

½ teaspoon freshly ground black pepper

NOTE: *If not using the wine, increase the amount of broth or water by ⅓ cup.*

*In a nonreactive saucepan,* combine the onions, vinegar, apple juice, the wine, if using, brown sugar, bay leaf, and cloves and bring to a boil over high heat. Add the cabbage and broth, reduce the heat, and simmer, partially covered, for 30 minutes.

*Add the apples* and simmer, uncovered, for about 20 minutes longer. Remove from the heat and let stand for 15 to 20 minutes. Discard the bay leaf and the cloves. Season with the salt, if using, and pepper, add more broth if necessary, and serve.

# Lemon-Grass Spicy Vegetables

**W**HEN THE *NEW YORK TIMES* ran this Golden Door recipe in the fall of 1994. The only caveat was, "Find the ingredients. The rest is easy." Thankfully, it's quite easy to find the ingredients nowadays. I have also simplified the recipe somewhat from the original.

2 stalks lemon grass (see Note)

1 tablespoon minced fresh ginger

2 shallots, minced (1½ ounces)

1 teaspoon minced garlic

2 teaspoons Thai or Vietnamese chili paste

2 tablespoons fresh lime juice

4 teaspoons sugar

¼ cup low-fat coconut milk

¼ cup Vegetable Broth (page 280) or water

2 teaspoons low-sodium tamari or soy sauce

1 teaspoon toasted sesame oil

1 teaspoon canola oil

2 carrots, coarsely grated (8 ounces)

1 rib celery, thinly sliced on the diagonal (4 ounces)

4 shiitake mushrooms, cleaned, stemmed, and thinly sliced (4 ounces)

1 cup thinly sliced scallions (3 ounces)

½ cup broccoli florets, coarsely chopped (2 ounces)

1½ cups hot cooked long-grain brown rice

*NOTE: The most flavorful part of the lemon grass is the root end, so be sure not to trim too much of it. Lemon grass is sold in Asian markets and some specialty shops. To save time, make the lemon grass mixture in advance. It keeps in the refrigerator for up to 5 days.*

*Trim the roots* and the tough outer leaves from the lemon grass stalk. Thinly slice the root end and chop into small pieces.

*In a small bowl,* combine the lemon grass, ginger, shallots, garlic, chili paste, lime juice, and sugar. Stir and set aside.

*In a bowl,* combine the coconut milk, broth, tamari, and sesame oil. Stir to mix well.

*In a sauté pan* or wok, heat the canola oil over medium-high heat. Add the lemon grass mixture and stir-fry for about 1 minute. Add the carrots, celery, mushrooms, scallions, and broccoli and stir-fry for about 1 minute longer. Reduce the heat to medium-low and add the coconut milk mixture. Cook for 4 to 6 minutes longer, or until the vegetables are crisp-tender.

*Spoon the rice* onto 4 warmed plates and top with the vegetable stir-fry.

# Caramelized Red Onions

PER SERVING:

107 calories

1 g total fat (12% of calories)

0 g saturated fat

0 mg cholesterol

2 g protein (9% of calories)

21 g carbohydrates

(79% of calories)

1 g fiber

7 mg sodium

MAKES 4 SERVINGS

COOKING RED ONIONS BRINGS OUT their natural sweetness, which is balanced by the vinegar.

1 teaspoon olive oil

3 large red onions, thinly sliced (28 ounces)

1 tablespoon pure maple syrup or light brown sugar

1 tablespoon balsamic vinegar

2 teaspoons dried basil

2 tablespoons Vegetable Broth (page 280) or water

*In a nonstick sauté pan,* heat the olive oil over high heat. Add the onions and stir constantly for about 10 minutes, adjusting the heat so the onions do not burn, until deep golden brown, caramelized, and soft.

*Stir in the maple syrup,* balsamic vinegar, and basil and serve.

# Potato-Parsnip Puree

PER SERVING:

202 calories

2 g total fat (8% of calories)

0 g saturated fat

0 mg cholesterol

4 g protein (8% of calories)

43 g carbohydrates

(85% of calories)

4 g fiber

21 mg sodium

MAKES 4 SERVINGS

1 teaspoon canola oil

½ cup diced onions (2 ounces)

2 large Yellow Finnish or russet potatoes, peeled and cut into 1-inch pieces (1 pound)

4 large parsnips, peeled and cut into 1-inch pieces (16 ounces)

½ teaspoon kosher salt (optional)

*In a saucepan,* heat the oil over medium heat. Add the onions and sauté for 2 to 3 minutes, until translucent. Add the potatoes, parsnips, the salt, if using, and enough water to cover by 1 to 2 inches. Bring to a boil over high heat, cover, reduce the heat, and simmer for about 15 minutes, until the potatoes and parsnips are tender. Cook for 5 minutes longer, uncovered, to reduce the cooking liquid slightly. Drain and reserve the cooking liquid.

*Using a potato masher* or sturdy whisk, mash the potatoes and parsnips. Add some of the reserved cooking liquid as necessary to make the vegetables creamy. Serve hot.

# Winter Vegetable Mashed Potatoes

PER SERVING:

*152 calories*

*0 g total fat (3% of calories)*

*0 g saturated fat*

*0 mg cholesterol*

*3 g protein (9% of calories)*

*33 g carbohydrates*

*(88% of calories)*

*3 g fiber*

*617 mg sodium*

**MAKES 4 SERVINGS**

1 leek (white part only) cut into 1-inch slices (3 ounces)

2 large Yellow Finnish or russet potatoes, peeled and cut into 1-inch cubes (1 pound)

1 parsnip, peeled and cut into 1-inch pieces (4 ounces)

1 carrot, peeled and cut into 1-inch pieces (4 ounces)

1 cup chopped savoy cabbage (2½ ounces)

1 teaspoon dried thyme

1 teaspoon kosher salt, or to taste

¼ to ½ teaspoon freshly ground black pepper

*In a saucepan,* combine the leek, potatoes, parsnip, carrot, cabbage, thyme, salt, and pepper and add enough water to barely cover. Bring to a boil, partially covered, over high heat. Reduce the heat and simmer, covered, for 10 minutes. Uncover and simmer for 10 to 15 minutes longer, until the vegetables are fork-tender and almost all the cooking liquid has evaporated.

*Using a potato masher* or sturdy whisk, mash the vegetables until only small pieces remain. Serve hot.

# Leek-and-Garlic Mashed Potatoes

PER SERVING:

*111 calories*

*1 g total fat (7% of calories)*

*0 g saturated fat*

*0 mg cholesterol*

*3 g protein (11% of calories)*

*22 g carbohydrates*

*(81% of calories)*

*2 g fiber*

*25 mg sodium*

**MAKES 8 SERVINGS**

1 teaspoon canola oil

3 leeks (white part only), cut into ½-inch pieces (9 ounces)

1 tablespoon minced garlic

3 large Yellow Finnish or russet potatoes, peeled and quartered (1½ pounds)

1 bay leaf

1 teaspoon kosher salt (optional)

¼ teaspoon freshly ground black pepper

½ cup nonfat plain yogurt (optional)

*In a saucepan,* heat the oil over medium heat. Add the leeks and garlic and sauté for 3 to 4 minutes until softened. Add the potatoes, bay leaf, the salt, if using, and pepper. Add water to just cover the vegetables. Bring to a boil, partially covered, over high heat. Reduce the heat and simmer, covered, for 10 minutes. Uncover and simmer for 10 to 15 minutes longer, until the potatoes are fork-tender. Drain and reserve the cooking liquid. Discard the bay leaf.

*Using a potato masher* or sturdy whisk, mash the leek-potato mixture until smooth. Add enough of the reserved cooking liquid for creamy, mashed-potato consistency. For a creamier texture, add the yogurt and stir gently. Serve immediately.

# Broccoli Mashed Potatoes

PER SERVING:

*179 calories*

*2 g total fat (11% of calories)*

*0 g saturated fat*

*1 mg cholesterol*

*6 g protein (14% of calories)*

*33 g carbohydrates*

*(75% of calories)*

*3 g fiber*

*711 mg sodium*

**MAKES 4 SERVINGS**

1 teaspoon canola oil

½ cup diced onions
(2 ounces)

12 ounces broccoli, peeled,
trimmed, and cut into 1-inch
pieces

3 small Yellow Finnish or
russet potatoes, peeled and
cut into 1-inch cubes
(14 ounces)

3 cups Vegetable Broth
(page 280) or water

1 teaspoon kosher salt
(optional)

½ cup commercial dried
Italian bread crumbs

*In a saucepan,* heat the oil over medium heat. Add the onions and sauté for 2 to 3 minutes, until translucent. Add the broccoli and potatoes, cover with the broth, and add the salt, if desired. Simmer, partially covered, for about 30 minutes, or until the potatoes are fork-tender. Raise the heat to medium-high and cook for 2 to 3 minutes longer, until the liquid reduces slightly. Drain.

*Use a potato masher* or sturdy whisk to mash the vegetables until smooth. Transfer to a small baking dish and sprinkle with bread crumbs. Serve immediately.

# Rice Trilogy with Almonds

**W**HILE I WAS WORKING IN THE SOUTH OF FRANCE, we often prepared rice with almonds, a nut I absolutely love. At the Door we use a mixture of long-grain brown rice, wild rice, and basmati rice, a blend that is available in health and gourmet food stores. When you find it, buy several packages and store in sealed containers in the refrigerator or freezer. Or, of course, you can make your own blend, as I have done here.

¼ cup uncooked long-grain brown rice

¼ cup uncooked wild rice, rinsed

¼ cup brown basmati rice

1 bay leaf

1 whole star anise

1½ ounces sliced almonds

½ cup chopped fresh flat-leaf parsley

*Preheat the oven* to 350°F.

*In a large saucepan,* combine the rices, bay leaf, and star anise. Add 1⅔ cups of water, stir well, and bring to a boil over high heat. Reduce the heat and simmer, covered, for 30 to 35 minutes, until all the liquid is absorbed.

*Meanwhile,* spread the almonds in a single layer on a baking sheet and roast for 8 to 10 minutes, shaking the pan several times to prevent burning, until lightly browned and fragrant. Transfer to a plate to stop the cooking.

*Remove the rice* from the heat and let stand for 10 minutes. Remove the bay leaf and star anise. Add the almonds and parsley and fluff with a fork until mixed. Serve.

# Spanish Rice

1 teaspoon canola oil

½ cup diced onions
(2 ounces)

¾ cup uncooked brown
basmati rice

2 tomatoes, cored and diced
(9 ounces)

1 tablespoon chili powder

1¾ to 2 cups Vegetable Broth
(page 280) or water

¾ cup fresh or frozen peas,
blanched (4 ounces)

*In a saucepan,* heat the oil over medium heat. Add the onions and sauté for about 2 minutes. Add the rice and sauté for 2 to 3 minutes, until the rice looks opaque.

*Add the tomatoes,* chili powder, and 1¾ cups of broth and bring to a boil over high heat. Reduce the heat and simmer, covered, for about 35 minutes, until all the liquid is absorbed. Watch the rice during cooking and add more broth to prevent sticking if necessary. Stir in the peas and serve.

## Spanish Rice with Corn

Omit the peas and add 1 generous cup blanched corn kernels (from 1 ear).

# Green Rice

PER SERVING:

*200 calories*

*2 g total fat (8% of calories)*

*0 g saturated fat*

*0 mg cholesterol*

*6 g protein (11% of calories)*

*41 g carbohydrates*

*(81% of calories)*

*2 g fiber*

*40 mg sodium*

**MAKES 4 SERVINGS**

1 cup uncooked long-grain brown rice

2¼ cups Vegetable Broth (page 280) or water

1 bay leaf

2 cups shredded spinach leaves (2 ounces)

½ cup finely sliced scallions (2 ounces)

1 cup chopped fresh flat-leaf parsley

¼ cup chopped fresh basil

1 tablespoon chopped fresh tarragon

⅛ teaspoon freshly grated nutmeg

*In a saucepan,* combine the rice, broth, and bay leaf and bring to a boil over high heat. Reduce the heat and simmer, covered, for about 35 minutes, until all the liquid is absorbed. Set aside.

*In another saucepan,* stir the spinach over medium heat until it begins to wilt. Mix into the rice. Fold in the scallions, parsley, basil, tarragon, and nutmeg just until mixed; the herbs should stay green and fresh (i.e., uncooked).

# Deborah's Basmati Rice

**PER SERVING:**

*169 calories*

*1 g total fat (7% of calories)*

*0 g saturated fat*

*0 mg cholesterol*

*4 g protein (9% of calories)*

*36 g carbohydrates*

*(84% of calories)*

*1 g fiber*

*6 mg sodium*

**MAKES 4 SERVINGS**

³/₄ cup uncooked brown basmati rice

¹/₂ teaspoon fennel seeds

2 cups Vegetable Broth (page 280) or water

1 cup corn kernels (from 1 ear)

¹/₂ red bell pepper, diced

¹/₃ cup thinly sliced scallions (1¹/₂ ounces)

*In a saucepan,* combine the rice, fennel seeds, and 1³/₄ cups of the broth and bring to a boil over medium-high heat. Reduce the heat and simmer, covered, for about 30 minutes until the liquid evaporates. Remove from the heat and let stand for 5 minutes. Fluff with a fork, cover to keep warm, and set aside.

*In a small sauté pan,* combine the corn, red bell pepper, and the remaining ¹/₄ cup broth and simmer for 2 to 3 minutes. Mix into the rice with the scallions.

# Orange Basmati Rice

**PER SERVING:**

*149 calories*

*1 g total fat (7% of calories)*

*0 g saturated fat*

*0 mg cholesterol*

*3 g protein (8% of calories)*

*32 g carbohydrates*

*(85% of calories)*

*1 g fiber*

*3 mg sodium*

**MAKES 4 SERVINGS**

³/₄ cup uncooked brown basmati rice

1 cup Vegetable Broth (page 280) or water

³/₄ cup fresh orange juice

¹/₂ teaspoon fennel seeds

*In a saucepan,* combine the rice, broth, orange juice, and fennel seeds and bring to a boil over high heat. Reduce the heat and simmer, covered, for about 30 minutes, until all the liquid is absorbed.

*Let the rice stand* off the heat for about 5 minutes. Fluff with a fork and serve.

# Wild Rice Pilaf with Pineapple and Ginger

**T**HE DISTINCT FLAVOR OF THIS WILD RICE DISH is provided by the star anise combined with the gingery sweet-and-sour pineapple. Star anise is found in Asian and Indian markets and specialty gourmet shops.

PER SERVING:

*125 calories*

*1 g total fat (9% of calories)*

*0 g saturated fat*

*0 mg cholesterol*

*4 g protein (12% of calories)*

*23 g carbohydrates*

*(73% of calories)*

*1 g fiber*

*276 mg sodium*

**MAKES 6 SERVINGS**

³⁄₄ cup uncooked wild rice, rinsed

3½ cups Vegetable Broth (page 280) or water

1 whole star anise

1 bay leaf

1 teaspoon canola oil

2 teaspoons minced fresh ginger

1 cup diced pineapple (¹⁄₄ pineapple)

1 teaspoon Thai or Vietnamese chili paste

¹⁄₄ cup seasoned rice vinegar

¹⁄₄ cup mirin (sweet rice wine)

¹⁄₄ cup unsweetened pineapple juice

1 tablespoon low-sodium tamari or soy sauce

³⁄₄ cup diced celery, blanched (6 ounces)

¹⁄₄ cup thinly sliced scallions (1 ounce)

2 teaspoons finely chopped Japanese pickled ginger

*In a saucepan,* combine the rice, broth, star anise, and bay leaf and bring to a boil over high heat. Reduce the heat and simmer, partially covered, for about 45 minutes, or until all the liquid is absorbed. Discard the star anise and bay leaf and transfer the rice to a bowl. Set aside to cool.

*In a nonstick sauté pan,* heat the oil over medium heat. Add the ginger and pineapple and sauté for about 10 minutes, stirring occasionally, until the pineapple releases its juice. Add the chili paste, vinegar, mirin, and pineapple juice. Simmer, uncovered, for 5 to 6 minutes, until the liquid is reduced by half. Remove from the heat and stir in the tamari. Set aside to cool.

*Toss the cooled pineapple mixture* into the rice. Fold in the celery, scallions, and pickled ginger and serve immediately, or cover and refrigerate until ready to serve.

# Quinoa with Parsley

PER SERVING:

125 calories

2 g total fat (14% of calories)

0 g saturated fat

0 mg cholesterol

4 g protein (14% of calories)

23 g carbohydrates
(72% of calories)

2 g fiber

9 mg sodium

**MAKES 4 SERVINGS**

1½ cups Vegetable Broth
(page 280) or water

½ teaspoon kosher salt
(optional)

¾ cup quinoa, rinsed under
cool running water and
drained

1 bay leaf

⅓ cup chopped fresh flat-leaf
parsley

*In a saucepan,* bring the broth to a boil over high heat. Add the salt, if using, quinoa, and bay leaf, reduce the heat, cover, and simmer for 20 minutes. Remove from the heat and let stand for 10 minutes.

*Remove the bay leaf* and fluff the quinoa with a fork while you add the parsley.

## THE GOODNESS OF GRAINS

One question I hear over and over from guests is about grains: we are told to eat more grains, they say, but how exactly should we do this?

We are lucky to be living in a time when many grains are available that as recently as a generation ago were nearly lost and certainly forgotten by most of the population. Now we can go beyond rice and oatmeal to grains such as quinoa, kamut, amaranth, barley, and millet, available at health food stores and many larger markets. I especially like quinoa, an ancient mild-tasting grain that originated in the mountains of Peru. I use it often in recipes, and I urge you to try it and others, too.

Rice is one of the most versatile grains and luckily it is available to the average shopper in forms other than long-grain white rice. Try brown rice, basmati, jasmine, arborio, and Spanish- or Asian-style medium-grain white rice. The subtleties of flavor and texture are endlessly delightful.

# Breads, Muffins, and Pizzas

BREAD IS A DELICIOUS, fiber-rich complex carbohydrate that nourishes and satisfies as few other foods do. I make a number of quick breads and yeast breads for our guests and always send a hearty loaf home with them at the end of their week's visit, which I suggest they freeze. I have also included our pizza dough in this chapter, because as good as it is with the pizza recipes in the book, it's also a great base for your own pizza toppings.

# Butternut Squash and Cranberry Bread

**B**ECAUSE IT'S LESS WATERY and sweeter than pumpkin, I prefer baking or cooking with butternut squash whenever I can. Our guests love this moist, sweet bread because it tastes almost like dessert. Serve it with the Nonfat Yogurt Cheese on page 290 and perhaps some lemony applesauce. Delicious.

PER SERVING:

*137 calories*

*2 g total fat (12% of calories)*

*0 g saturated fat*

*13 mg cholesterol*

*3 g protein (10% of calories)*

*27 g carbohydrates*

*(78% of calories)*

*1 g fiber*

*134 mg sodium*

MAKES 16 SERVINGS

1 small butternut squash (8 ounces) or 1 cup canned unsweetened pumpkin puree

1½ cups unbleached all-purpose flour

1 teaspoon baking powder

½ teaspoon baking soda

2 teaspoons ground cinnamon

1 cup whole wheat flour

½ teaspoon salt

½ cup light brown sugar

½ cup nonfat plain yogurt or buttermilk

¼ cup frozen orange juice concentrate, thawed

1 large egg, lightly beaten

1 tablespoon canola oil

1 tablespoon grated orange zest

¾ cup sweetened dried cranberries

*Preheat the oven* to 350°F.

*Pierce the skin* of the squash in several places with a metal skewer. Place on a baking sheet and bake for about 1 hour, until soft. (Do not turn off the oven.) Halve the squash, scoop out the seeds, and scrape out the pulp from the neck of the squash. Mash the pulp and measure out 1 cup. Discard the rest of the pulp, or save it for another use.

*Spray* an 8½-by-4-inch loaf pan with vegetable oil spray.

*Sift together* the all-purpose flour, baking powder, baking soda, and cinnamon into a large bowl. Add the whole wheat flour and salt and whisk to blend.

*In a blender* or food processor, combine the mashed squash, brown sugar, yogurt, orange juice concentrate, egg, and oil and process until smooth. Add the orange zest and pulse to combine.

*Make a well* in the dry ingredients, add the wet ingredients, and stir gently but thoroughly just until no specks of flour remain. Do not overmix. Gently stir in the cranberries and scrape the batter into the prepared pan.

*Bake* for about 50 minutes, or until a toothpick inserted in the center of the bread comes out clean. Cool in the pan for about 5 minutes; turn out onto a wire rack and cool completely. Cut into thin slices to serve.

*N*OTE: *If you prefer, you can cook the squash in the microwave. Put it in a microwave-safe baking dish, cover with plastic wrap, and microwave at High (100 percent) power for about 15 minutes, until soft. The flesh from the neck of the squash is more tender and less stringy than the rest.*

# Cranberry-Anise Oat Bread

**B**ECAUSE I LIKE TO EXPERIMENT with spices and other flavorings, I was delighted by the pleasantly piquant flavor of licorice the anise seeds contributed to this cranberry-and-walnut-studded bread. It's a refreshing change. If you prefer, use fennel seeds for an even bolder flavor.

¾ cup unbleached all-purpose flour

1 teaspoon baking powder

½ teaspoon baking soda

1¼ cups whole wheat flour

½ teaspoon salt (optional)

2 teaspoons anise seeds or fennel seeds, ground or crushed (see Note)

¼ cup light brown sugar

1 ripe banana, cut into chunks (3½ ounces)

1¼ cups low-fat buttermilk

1 large egg

2 large egg whites

2 tablespoons fresh lemon juice

1 tablespoon grated lemon zest

¾ cup old-fashioned rolled oats

¾ cup unsweetened dried cranberries or 1½ cups halved fresh cranberries

½ cup chopped walnuts

*Preheat the oven* to 350°F. Spray an 8½-by-4-inch loaf pan with vegetable oil spray.

*Sift together* the all-purpose flour, baking powder, and baking soda into a large bowl. Add the whole wheat flour, the salt, if desired, and anise seeds and whisk to blend.

*In a blender* or food processor, combine the brown sugar, banana, buttermilk, egg, egg whites, and lemon juice and process until smooth. Add the lemon zest and pulse to mix. Add the oats and pulse several times to break up the oats.

*Make a well* in the dry ingredients, add the wet ingredients, and stir gently but thoroughly just until no specks of flour remain. Do not overmix. Stir in the cranberries and walnuts and pour the batter into the prepared pan.

*Bake* for 55 minutes to 1 hour, or until the bread is golden brown and pulls away from the sides of the pan, and a toothpick inserted in the center comes out clean. Cool in the pan for about 5 minutes. Turn out onto a wire rack and cool for a few minutes before cutting into slices for serving.

NOTE: *You can grind the seeds in a spice grinder or mortar and pestle; or use the flat side of a large knife to crush the seeds against a cutting board.*

# Banana-Date Bread

THIS RECIPE has become a Golden Door favorite. I have been particularly careful to include it inthis book, because if I did not, our loyal friends would be very upset indeed—and who could blame them? For the sweetest, most flavorful result, use very ripe bananas.

PER SERVING:

*166 calories*

*2 g total fat (10% of calories)*

*0 g saturated fat*

*14 mg cholesterol*

*4 g protein (10% of calories)*

*33 g carbohydrates*

*(80% of calories)*

*1 g fiber*

*108 mg sodium*

MAKES 16 SERVINGS

1½ cups unbleached all-purpose flour

1 teaspoon baking powder

1 teaspoon baking soda

2 teaspoons ground cinnamon

1 teaspoon ground allspice

1¼ cups whole wheat flour

½ teaspoon salt (optional)

1 large egg

1 large egg white

1 tablespoon canola oil

½ cup light brown sugar

2 very ripe bananas, cut into chunks (7 ounces)

1½ cups low-fat buttermilk

1 teaspoon pure vanilla extract

1 cup chopped pitted dates

*Preheat the oven* to 350°F. Spray an 8½-by-4-inch loaf pan with vegetable oil spray.

*Sift together* the all-purpose flour, baking powder, baking soda, cinnamon, and allspice into a large bowl. Add the whole wheat flour and the salt, if using, and whisk to blend.

*In a blender* or food processor, combine the egg, egg white, oil, brown sugar, bananas, buttermilk, and vanilla and process until smooth.

*Make a well* in the dry ingredients, add the wet ingredients, and stir gently but thoroughly just until no specks of flour remain. Do not overmix. Add the dates and stir gently to combine. Pour into the prepared pan.

*Bake* for 55 to 60 minutes, or until a toothpick inserted in the center comes out clean. Cool in the pan for about 5 minutes; turn out onto a wire rack and cool completely. Cut into thin slices to serve.

# Dried Cherry Banana Bread

**T**HE TEXTURE OF THIS BREAD is just a little crunchy because of the cornmeal, and it's not too sweet, two characteristics I find especially appealing.

1 cup dried cherries (see Note)

1 cup unbleached all-purpose flour

1 teaspoon baking powder

1/2 teaspoon baking soda

2 teaspoons ground cinnamon

1/2 teaspoon ground allspice

1 1/4 cups whole wheat flour

1/4 cup yellow cornmeal, preferably coarsely ground

1/2 teaspoon salt (optional)

2 ripe bananas, cut into chunks (7 ounces)

1/2 cup light brown sugar

1 large egg

1 large egg white

2 tablespoons canola oil

1 1/2 cups low-fat buttermilk

2 tablespoons grated orange zest

*In a small bowl,* soak the cherries in warm water to cover for about 30 minutes, until softened.

*Preheat the oven* to 350°F. Spray an 8 1/2-by-4-inch loaf pan with vegetable oil spray.

*Sift together* the all-purpose flour, baking powder, baking soda, cinnamon, and allspice into a large bowl. Add the whole wheat flour, cornmeal, and the salt, if desired, and whisk to blend.

*In a blender* or food processor, combine the bananas, brown sugar, egg, egg white, oil, and buttermilk and process until smooth. Add the orange zest and pulse just until combined.

*Make a well* in the dry ingredients, add the wet ingredients, and stir gently but thoroughly just until no specks of flour remain. Do not overmix. Drain the cherries and stir them into the batter. Scrape into the prepared pan.

*Bake* for about 55 minutes, or until a toothpick inserted in the center of the bread comes out clean, the top is golden brown, and the sides pull away slightly from the pan. Cool in the pan for about 5 minutes; turn out onto a wire rack and cool for a few minutes before slicing for serving.

*NOTE: Dried cherries are becoming increasingly available in specialty stores and are also sold through a number of mail-order catalogs dealing in fine foods. You can substitute dried cranberries, currants, raisins, prunes, figs, or dates for the dried cherries—but if you do, omit the step for soaking the dried fruit.*

# Zucchini Spa Bread

**T**HIS QUICK BREAD—pleasingly moist from the zucchini—is also desirably hearty because of the wheat bran. At the Golden Door, we like to serve this for breakfast. It contributes to a satisfying meal after the brisk early morning mountain hike so many of our guests enjoy.

½ cup unbleached all-purpose flour

1 teaspoon baking powder

½ teaspoon baking soda

2 teaspoons ground cinnamon

¼ teaspoon ground cloves

1¼ cups whole wheat flour

¼ cup wheat bran

½ teaspoon salt

1 large egg

1 large egg white

2 tablespoons canola oil

⅓ cup honey

½ cup low-fat buttermilk

1 teaspoon pure vanilla extract

1 ripe banana, cut into chunks (3½ ounces)

1 cup grated zucchini (5 ounces)

⅓ cup chopped nuts, such as almonds, walnuts, or pecans

¾ cup chopped pitted dates

*Preheat the oven* to 350°F. Spray an 8½-by-4-inch loaf pan with vegetable oil spray.

*Sift together* the all-purpose flour, baking powder, baking soda, cinnamon, and cloves into a large bowl. Add the whole wheat flour, bran, and salt and whisk to blend.

*In a blender* or food processor, combine the egg, egg white, oil, honey, buttermilk, vanilla, and banana and process until smooth.

*Make a well* in the dry ingredients, add the wet ingredients, and stir gently but thoroughly just until no specks of flour remain. Add the zucchini, nuts, and dates and stir just to blend. Do not overmix. Scrape into the prepared pan.

*Bake* for 55 to 60 minutes, or until a toothpick inserted in the center comes out clean. Let the bread cool in the pan for 10 minutes; turn out onto a wire rack and cool completely. Cut into thin slices to serve.

NOTE: *To make muffins, fill 12 standard-sized muffin cups about two-thirds full. Bake for 25 to 30 minutes, until lightly browned and a toothpick inserted in the center comes out clean. Turn out onto wire racks to cool.*

## THE CHANGE IN SEVEN DAYS

The Golden Door believes in a minimum one-week stay for many reasons, among them camaraderie, renewed fitness, learning new exercise and stretching programs, and indulging in plenty of relaxation and pampering!

The Door's weeklong program is analogous to a set of stairs. You move from one level to the next, identifying and feeling new muscles, learning what stretches work best for you, gaining new understanding of your body. With each new day, you come to feel the close relationship between mind, body, and spirit. The workouts are educational without being pedantic; even the most experienced fitness devotees are surprised at how much they learn beginning on day one.

And, unlike the workouts you do at home, the Door's gentle, everyday exercise regimen is complemented by massages, herbal wraps, body rubs, and other relaxing luxuries, which minimize sore muscles. Imagine exercise and movement without those "I'm going to regret this tomorrow" consequences.

Equally important is the shift in eating habits and awareness that gets a strong start in just seven days. At the Golden Door the menu and portion sizes are tailored to each guest's wants and expectations —and carefully matched to activity levels.

No guest "goes hungry." Indeed, many tell us we serve just the right amount—or slightly more—food than they can eat. One of the great luxuries here, of course, is to eat without guilt and anxiety . . . to be satisfied . . . to be thrilled by tastes and preparations comparable to the most extraordinary of cuisines.

Without fail, the body rewards each guest with a newfound wellspring of energy. *Vitality* is a word that takes on true meaning.

# Corn Bread Muffins

**T**HESE SAVORY MUFFINS, with a spicy kick from the minced jalapeño peppers, are brunch or luncheon fare. Leave out the jalapeños and shallots if you want to bake these for breakfast.

PER MUFFIN:

*111 calories*

*1 g total fat (11% of calories)*

*0 g saturated fat*

*18 mg cholesterol*

*4 g protein (15% of calories)*

*20 g carbohydrates*

*(73% of calories)*

*0 g fiber*

*270 mg sodium*

**MAKES 12 MUFFINS**

1 teaspoon canola oil

1 tablespoon minced shallots

1 tablespoon minced jalapeño peppers, stemmed and seeded

1 cup yellow cornmeal

¾ cup whole wheat flour

1 teaspoon baking powder

½ teaspoon baking soda

½ teaspoon salt

1 large egg

2 large egg whites

1 tablespoon light brown sugar

1 cup low-fat buttermilk

1 cup canned cream-style corn

2 tablespoons freshly grated Pecorino Romano or Parmesan cheese (optional)

*Preheat the oven* to 350°F. Spray a 12-cup standard-sized muffin tin with vegetable oil spray.

*In a small sauté pan,* heat the oil over medium heat. Add the shallots and jalapeños and sauté for about 3 minutes, until the shallots are translucent. Set aside to cool.

*In a large bowl,* stir together the cornmeal, whole wheat flour, baking powder, baking soda, and salt. In another bowl, combine the egg, egg whites, brown sugar, buttermilk, corn, and the cheese, if desired, and whisk well. Stir in the shallot-jalapeño mixture. Make a well in the dry ingredients, add the wet ingredients, and stir gently but thoroughly just until no specks of flour remain. Spoon the batter into the prepared muffin cups, filling them about two-thirds full.

*Bake* for 25 to 30 minutes, until the muffins are a rich golden brown and a toothpick inserted in the center of one comes out clean. Turn out onto a wire rack and serve warm.

NOTE: *To make corn bread, pour the batter into an 8-by-8-inch baking pan and bake for 35 to 40 minutes, until lightly browned and a toothpick inserted in the center comes out clean. Cool in the pan on a wire rack. Cut into 12 squares.*

# Blueberry Bran Muffins

**T**HESE MUFFINS HAVE BECOME A SIGNATURE of the Door. The kitchen staff makes these just about every day—and can do so with their eyes closed! We tuck them into sacks for munching on early morning hikes and offer them to guests who need a pick-me-up later in the day.

NOTE: *You can vary these muffins by substituting other seasonal fruits such as strawberries or cranberries for the blueberries or by using dried fruit such as dates or prunes.*

1 teaspoon ground cinnamon

$1/2$ teaspoon ground ginger

$1/2$ teaspoon baking powder

$1/2$ teaspoon baking soda

$1^1/4$ cups whole wheat flour

$1/2$ cup wheat bran

$1/4$ cup wheat germ

$1/2$ teaspoon salt

3 large egg whites

1 tablespoon canola oil

$1/4$ cup pure maple syrup or honey

1 cup low-fat buttermilk or plain yogurt or apple juice

1 ripe banana, cut into chunks ($3^1/2$ ounces)

$1/2$ cup blueberries

*Preheat the oven* to 350°F. Spray a 12-cup standard-sized muffin tin with vegetable oil spray.

*Sift together* the cinnamon, ginger, baking powder, and baking soda into a large bowl. Stir in the wheat flour, wheat bran, wheat germ, and salt.

*In a blender* or food processor, combine the egg whites, oil, maple syrup, buttermilk, and banana and process until smooth.

*Make a well* in the dry ingredients, add the wet ingredients, and stir gently but thoroughly just until no specks of flour remain. Gently fold in the blueberries. Pour the batter into the muffin cups, filling them about two-thirds full.

*Bake* for 30 to 35 minutes, until the tops of the muffins are lightly browned and a toothpick inserted in the center of one comes out clean. Turn out onto a wire rack and serve warm, or let cool.

# Focaccia

**T**HIS FULL-FLAVORED BREAD originated in Italy and has become a standard at the Door because it is so splendidly versatile. It can be formed into the traditional flat bread for grilled sandwiches, shaped into buns for burgers, or even rolled into long narrow French-style baguettes or skinny bread sticks.

1 tablespoon olive oil

1 tablespoon minced garlic

2 tablespoons minced fresh rosemary

1 tablespoon active dry yeast (one ¼-ounce envelope)

1 teaspoon sugar or honey

1¼ cups lukewarm water

1½ teaspoons salt

1¾ cups unbleached all-purpose flour, plus more for dusting

1 cup whole wheat flour

2 tablespoons cornmeal

Filling (see Note)

*In a small nonstick sauté pan,* heat the olive oil over medium heat. Sauté the garlic and rosemary for 2 to 3 minutes, until the garlic is translucent. Set aside.

*In the bowl of an electric mixer* fitted with a dough hook, dissolve the yeast and sugar in the water. Add the garlic-rosemary mixture.

*In another bowl,* combine 1 teaspoon of the salt and the flours and whisk to blend. With the mixer running, add the flours, 1 cup at a time, mixing until the dough pulls away from the sides of the bowl. Continue mixing until the dough is smooth and elastic. Transfer the dough to an oiled bowl, cover, and let rise in a warm area for 30 to 40 minutes, or until doubled in volume.

*Preheat the oven* to 375°F. Spray a baking sheet with vegetable oil spray and sprinkle with the cornmeal.

*Turn the dough out* onto a floured board and knead for about 5 minutes. Using a rolling pin, form the dough into a 10-by-12-inch rectangle. Transfer to the baking sheet. Spray the dough with vegetable oil spray and sprinkle with the remaining ½ teaspoon salt. Let rise for 15 to 20 minutes.

*Bake* for 25 to 30 minutes, until crisp and golden brown. About 5 minutes before removing the focaccia from the oven, spray again with vegetable oil spray. Turn out on a wire rack and let cool.

*Cut the bread* into 8 rectangles. Using a serrated knife, slice each horizontally and fill with a chosen filling, such as grilled vegetables or grated cheese (see Note).

## Garlic-Rosemary Buns

Divide the kneaded dough into 8 pieces. With lightly floured hands, roll each piece into a 2½- to 3-inch ball. Set on the baking sheet about 1 inch apart and let the balls rest for about 5 minutes. Flatten each with your palm and let rise for about 10 minutes. Bake at 350°F for 25 to 30 minutes, until lightly browned and crusty. Cool on wire racks.

## Garlic-Rosemary Baguettes

Divide the kneaded dough into 3 pieces. Shape each into a 10-inch-long baguette by rolling with your palms on a lightly floured surface. Set on the baking sheet. Sprinkle with cornmeal and set aside to rise for 30 to 40 minutes, or until doubled in volume. Bake at 350°F for about 40 minutes, until crisp and lightly browned. Cool on wire racks.

# Pizza Dough

USE THIS RECIPE FOR THE CARAMELIZED RED ONION PIZZA on page 116, or when making a pizza with your own topping. It's a delicious basic pizza dough that bakes beautifully.

1 tablespoon active dry yeast (one ¼-ounce package)

1 teaspoon sugar or honey

1¼ cups lukewarm water

1 cup whole wheat flour

1⅔ cups unbleached all-purpose flour, plus more for dusting

1 teaspoon olive oil

2 teaspoons salt

2 tablespoons fine cornmeal or semolina flour

*In the bowl of an electric mixer* fitted with the dough hook, dissolve the yeast and sugar in the water.

*With the mixer running,* add the flours, olive oil, and salt. Mix until the dough forms a ball, pulls away from the sides of the bowl, and is smooth and elastic. Transfer to an oiled mixing bowl, cover, and let rise in a warm area for about 20 minutes, or until the dough has doubled in volume.

*Spray* a 19-inch pizza pan with vegetable oil spray and sprinkle with the cornmeal.

*Turn the dough out* onto a lightly floured work surface and knead for about 5 minutes. Using a rolling pin, roll the dough to a 18- to 19-inch circle. Transfer to the prepared pizza pan. Bake as instructed in the recipe.

NOTE: *Alternatively, the pizza dough can be divided into 6 pieces and rolled out to make 6 individual pizzas.*

# Old-Fashioned Tecate Bread

**T**HIS RECIPE ORIGINATED AT OUR SISTER SPA, Rancho La Puerta, in Tecate, Baja California, Mexico. When Ignacio Cerda Leon, the baker at the ranch, came to the Golden Door in the 1970s, he introduced me to this wonderful complex bread. It is great toasted by itself or with a topping. The bread freezes well; for two loaves, double the recipe.

PER SERVING:

*121 calories*

*2 g total fat (17% of calories)*

*0 g saturated fat*

*0 mg cholesterol*

*4 g protein (12% of calories)*

*21 g carbohydrates*

*(71% of calories)*

*1 g fiber*

*238 mg sodium*

**MAKES 15 SERVINGS**

1 tablespoon active dry yeast (one ¼-ounce package)

1 tablespoon honey

1¼ cups lukewarm water

2 tablespoons canola oil

2 tablespoons dark molasses

1½ teaspoons salt

½ cup wheat bran

3 to 3¼ cups whole wheat flour, plus more for dusting

*In the bowl of an electric mixer* fitted with a dough hook, dissolve the yeast and honey in the water. Add the oil and molasses.

*With the mixer running,* add the salt, bran, and 3 cups of flour. Continue mixing until the dough is smooth and elastic and pulls away from the sides of the bowl. Add more flour if necessary.

*Transfer the dough* to a bowl dusted with flour, cover, and set aside in a warm area. Let rise for 30 to 40 minutes, or until doubled in volume.

*Preheat the oven* to 350°F. Lightly spray a 9½-by-4½-inch loaf pan with vegetable oil spray.

*Turn the dough out* onto a lightly floured board and knead vigorously for 7 to 8 minutes, until smooth. Form into a loaf and put in the prepared pan. Cover and let rise again for 20 to 30 minutes, until nearly doubled.

*Bake* for about 50 minutes, or until the bread is browned on top and the bottom is firm. Turn out of the pan and cool on a wire rack.

# Poppy-Seed Bran Bread

THIS BREAD EXEMPLIFIES the absolute goodness of baking. It's filled with healthful and good-tasting ingredients, is soul-satisfying to make, and it's even better to eat. Whether it's consumed fresh from the oven or toasted, it's comfort food at its best—and the crunchiness of the seeds only adds to the pleasure.

PER SERVING:

*144 calories*

*4 g total fat (28% of calories)*

*0 g saturated fat*

*0 mg cholesterol*

*4 g protein (12% of calories)*

*22 g carbohydrates*

*(60% of calories)*

*1 g fiber*

*239 mg sodium*

**MAKES 15 SERVINGS**

1 tablespoon active dry yeast (one ¼-ounce package)

1 tablespoon honey

1¼ cups lukewarm water

2 tablespoons canola oil

2 tablespoons dark molasses

1½ teaspoons salt

½ cup wheat bran

½ cup poppy seeds

2½ to 3 cups whole wheat flour, plus more for dusting

*In the bowl of an electric mixer* fitted with a dough hook, dissolve the yeast and honey in the water. Add the oil and molasses.

*With the mixer running,* add the salt, bran, poppy seeds, and 2½ cups of flour. Continue mixing until the dough is smooth and elastic and pulls away from the sides of the bowl. Add more flour if necessary.

*Transfer the dough* to a bowl dusted with flour, cover, set aside in a warm area, and let rise for 30 to 40 minutes, or until doubled in volume.

*Preheat the oven* to 350°F. Lightly spray a 9½-by-4½-inch loaf pan with vegetable oil spray.

*Turn the dough out* onto a lightly floured board and knead vigorously for 7 to 8 minutes, until smooth. Form into a loaf and put in the prepared pan. Cover and let rise again for 20 to 30 minutes.

*Bake* for about 50 minutes, or until the bread is browned on top and the bottom is firm. Turn out of the pan and cool on a wire rack.

# Sunflower-Seed Bran Bread

**A**FREQUENT GUEST AT THE GOLDEN DOOR always requests two of these loaves to take home with her. The unsliced bread, well wrapped in plastic wrap, keeps well in the freezer for several months. To make two loaves, double the recipe.

1 tablespoon active dry yeast (one ¼-ounce package)

1 tablespoon honey

1¼ cups lukewarm water

2 tablespoons canola oil

2 tablespoons dark molasses

1½ teaspoons salt

½ cup wheat bran

½ cup sunflower seeds

2½ to 3 cups whole wheat flour, plus more for dusting

*In the bowl of an electric mixer* fitted with a dough hook, dissolve the yeast and honey in the water. Add the oil and molasses.

*With the mixer running,* add the salt, bran, sunflower seeds, and 2½ cups of flour. Continue mixing until the dough is smooth and elastic and pulls away from the sides of the bowl. Add more flour if necessary.

*Transfer the dough* to a bowl dusted with flour, cover, set aside in a warm area, and let rise for 30 to 40 minutes, or until doubled in volume.

*Preheat the oven* to 350°F. Lightly spray a 9½-by-4½-inch loaf pan with vegetable oil spray.

*Turn the dough out* onto a lightly floured board and knead vigorously for 7 to 8 minutes, until smooth. Form into a loaf and put in the prepared pan. Cover and let rise again for 20 to 30 minutes.

*Bake* for about 50 minutes, or until the bread is browned on top and the bottom is firm. Turn out of the pan and cool on a wire rack.

# Fruit Desserts

WITHOUT A DOUBT, there are times when a piece of perfectly ripe fruit is the best dessert there is, but at the Golden Door, our guests crave something more than an apple or a pear for dessert. Our fruit desserts—cobblers, crumbles, puddings, sorbets, and compotes—are terrific. We have the advantage of picking the fruit from our own organic orchards and gardens, which thrive on our sunny California mountainside. And when I need to, it's never difficult to find glorious seasonal fruit from local organic farmers. When deciding which dessert to make, begin with the fruit, selecting what is in season in your region and making sure it's at the peak of ripeness. You can't go wrong.

# Apricot Cobbler with Berries

**T**HE TOPPING FOR THIS SUMMER COBBLER is a tender, moist génoise cake batter instead of the biscuit dough topping most often associated with cobblers. Choose the ripest, sweetest fruits for your cobbler; if the apricots are a little tart, add a bit more brown sugar. For a perfect génoise, spoon any excess juice from the fruit before baking.

PER SERVING:

*200 calories*

*2 g total fat (9% of calories)*

*0 g saturated fat*

*53 mg cholesterol*

*5 g protein (10% of calories)*

*40 g carbohydrates*

*(81% of calories)*

*1 g fiber*

*35 mg sodium*

**MAKES 8 SERVINGS**

*Fruit*

2 pounds apricots, pitted and halved

1 pint blueberries, blackberries, or raspberries

½ cup unsweetened apple juice

¼ cup light brown sugar, or more to taste

*Génoise topping*

2 large eggs, at room temperature

2 large egg whites, at room temperature

½ cup granulated sugar

1 teaspoon orange liqueur

2 teaspoons grated orange zest

½ cup unbleached all-purpose flour

Raspberry Sorbet or Strawberry Sorbet (page 244, optional)

*To cook the fruit,* in a small saucepan, combine the apricots, berries, apple juice, and brown sugar and cook, covered, over medium heat, stirring occasionally, for 10 to 15 minutes, or until the fruit softens. Transfer to an 8-by-8-inch baking dish and set aside to cool: if there is so much liquid with the fruit that you can easily remove ¼ cup or more, spoon off the excess juice from the fruit and discard. The fruit should be juicy and moist but not swimming in liquid.

*Preheat the oven* to 350°F.

*In the bowl of an electric mixer* placed over a bowl of hot water, whisk the eggs, egg whites, sugar, orange liqueur, and orange zest until frothy. Remove the bowl from the hot water.

*Using the electric mixer* set on medium-high, beat the mixture for about 5 minutes, until it triples in volume. Sift half the flour over the egg mixture and fold it in carefully. Repeat with the remaining flour. Pour the batter over the cooled apricot-berry mixture and spread with a rubber spatula to cover the fruit almost completely.

*Bake* for about 1 hour, until the génoise is a rich golden brown on top and the sides pull away from the pan. Cool to room temperature on a wire rack and serve with sorbet, if desired.

## OUR ANCIENT BELL TOLLS MEAL HOURS

Most large temples in Japan have a temple bell for tolling the time of day and night. This traditional usage has its origin in Buddhism. Ananda, a disciple of Buddha, struck a bell to call Bhikkus and Upavasathas to services, while, according to a certain Buddhist sutra, the striking of a bell exorcises evil. In the old days of Edo, capital of the Shogunate government, a Zojo-ji Temple Bell boomed regularly at a certain time in the afternoon.

Two decades ago, we discovered our very own Josneji Bell. Two eighteenth-century Japanese craftsmen, Tsuji Yataro and Fujiwara Naotane, both from Mie Prefecture, cast it almost three hundred years ago.

The sound created when we strike this massive instrument embodies a tone symbolic of the purity within each of us. The first ring symbolizes purification of one's mind and body before beginning a particular activity, such as eating well.

The ensuing continuous ring—which can linger hauntingly for several minutes—is equally significant, for it symbolizes the continued health, happiness, goodwill, prosperity, and peace of all people gathered within earshot, as well as throughout the world.

# Apricot Soufflé

**T**HIS ETHEREAL SOUFFLÉ IS AS MYSTERIOUS as soufflés always are, and as such is always a winner with our guests. It relies on dried apricot puree instead of yolks and cream, and while it is light and airy, it delivers intense fruit flavor. If you prefer using fresh apricots, see the variation that follows.

1 cup dried apricots
(5 ounces)

1 tablespoon orange liqueur

1 teaspoon grated orange zest

6 large egg whites, at room temperature

¼ teaspoon cream of tartar

Pinch of salt

2 to 3 tablespoons fructose
(to taste)

½ cup Raspberry Coulis
(page 247; optional)

*In a small saucepan,* combine the apricots with 2 cups of water. Cover the pan and simmer over medium-low heat for about 25 minutes, until the apricots soften and plump. Uncover and cool.

*Transfer the apricots* and about half the cooking liquid to a food processor and process until the consistency of smooth, thick applesauce. Add the orange liqueur and orange zest and pulse just to mix. Transfer to a large bowl.

*Preheat the oven* to 350°F. Spray eight 8-ounce soufflé dishes with vegetable oil spray, taking care to coat the rim of each dish so that the soufflés will rise properly.

*In the bowl of an electric mixer,* combine the egg whites, cream of tartar, and salt and beat on medium-high speed until soft peaks form. Add the fructose and beat until the whites are stiff but not dry. Fold the beaten whites into the fruit puree.

*If desired,* spoon 1 tablespoon of the raspberry coulis into the bottom of each soufflé dish. Spoon the apricot mixture into the dishes to fill them and level with a spatula or kitchen knife. Place the dishes on a baking sheet and bake for 25 to 30 minutes, until the soufflés rise above the level of the dishes and are golden brown on top; do not open the oven door during baking. Serve immediately.

## Fresh Apricot Soufflé

PER SERVING
(with fresh apricots):

*87 calories*

*0 g total fat (3% of calories)*

*0 g saturated fat*

*0 mg cholesterol*

*5 g protein (21% of calories)*

*16 g carbohydrates*

*(74% of calories)*

*0 g fiber*

*131 mg sodium*

**MAKES 6 SERVINGS**

Make the fruit puree by cooking 1 pound apricots, pitted and halved, with ½ cup unsweetened apple juice for about 15 minutes, until soft. Cool and puree with 1 teaspoon orange liqueur and the 1 teaspoon orange zest in a blender or food processor. Proceed with the recipe as directed, but increase the amount of fructose to 3 to 4 tablespoons.

# Phyllo-Dough Apple Strudel

**W**HEN I PLACE THIS WARM, GOLDEN-BROWN STRUDEL on the table, everyone smiles. Made with phyllo dough and spritzes of vegetable oil spray instead of slatherings of melted butter, it is as delicious and soothing as any grandmother's strudel.

PER SERVING:

*157 calories*

*0 g total fat (2% of calories)*

*0 g saturated fat*

*0 mg cholesterol*

*1 g protein (1% of calories)*

*38 g carbohydrates*

*(96% of calories)*

*1 g fiber*

*49 mg sodium*

**MAKES 6 SERVINGS**

5 Golden Delicious apples, peeled, cored, and sliced (20 ounces)

2 teaspoons ground cinnamon

Pinch of ground cloves

¼ cup raisins or dried cranberries

½ cup brown sugar

Five 12-by-17-inch sheets phyllo dough (2⅔ ounces)

Confectioners' sugar for sprinkling

*Coat a large nonstick sauté pan* with vegetable oil spray and sauté the apples with the cinnamon, cloves, raisins, and brown sugar over medium heat for 8 to 10 minutes, stirring frequently, until the apples begin to soften. Transfer to a bowl to cool.

*Preheat the oven* to 350°F. Spray a baking sheet with vegetable oil spray.

*Place 1 sheet of phyllo on a work surface,* with a long side toward you, and spray it with vegetable oil spray. Stack the remaining phyllo, spraying each sheet. Spoon the apple filling in a long row across the center of the dough. Starting with the long side facing you, roll the dough up around the filling to enclose it. Tuck in the ends and transfer to the baking sheet, seam side down.

*Lightly spray the top* of the roll with vegetable oil spray. Bake for 35 to 40 minutes, until the pastry is golden brown. Sprinkle with confectioners' sugar, cut into slices, and serve warm.

# Baked Apples with Papaya Sauce

**B**AKED APPLES ARE EASY TO MAKE and taste great, but too often are over-looked, even during apple season. These will make anyone change their dessert habits. We serve these spiced baked apples with a gingery papaya sauce—a healthy alternative to the English custom of pouring custard around baked apples.

PER SERVING:

*132 calories*

*1 g total fat (4% of calories)*

*0 g saturated fat*

*0 mg cholesterol*

*1 g protein (2% of calories)*

*31 g carbohydrates*

*(94% of calories)*

*1 g fiber*

*5 mg sodium*

**MAKES 4 SERVINGS**

*Apples*

4 Golden Delicious apples, cored, to make a cavity (1 pound)

4 teaspoons raisins or currants

4 teaspoons honey

$\frac{1}{2}$ teaspoon ground cinnamon

$\frac{1}{2}$ cup unsweetened apple juice

*Sauce*

1 papaya, peeled and seeded (6 ounces)

1 teaspoon fresh lime juice

1 teaspoon minced candied ginger

4 sprigs fresh mint

Fresh berries

*Preheat the oven* to 350°F.

*Trim the blossom ends* of the apples so that they sit upright. Arrange in a baking dish just large enough to hold them, cored side up. Put the raisins into the cavities, drizzle with the honey, and sprinkle with the cinnamon. Pour the apple juice around the apples.

*Cover loosely* with foil and bake for 50 to 60 minutes, or until the apples are tender when pierced with a fork. Set the pan on a wire rack to cool. Transfer the cooking juices to a blender or food processor.

*To make the sauce,* add the papaya, lime juice, and ginger to the blender or food processor and blend until smooth.

*Serve the apples* with the sauce spooned over them. Garnish with the mint sprigs and berries.

# Apple-Lime Parfait with Exotic Fruit

PRESENTATION IS SO IMPORTANT at the Golden Door because satisfying the visual sense goes a long way to satisfying the other senses too. This light, pretty dessert is lusciously fresh and smooth and if its reception at the dinner table is any indication, it appeals to all five senses!

PER SERVING:

*103 calories*

*3 g total fat (30% of calories)*

*1 g saturated fat*

*0 mg cholesterol*

*5 g protein (19% of calories)*

*13 g carbohydrates*

*(49% of calories)*

*1 g fiber*

*5 mg sodium*

**MAKES 4 SERVINGS**

NOTE: *Agar, sometimes called Japanese gelatin, is a tasteless dried seaweed used widely in Asia as a setting agent. It can be purchased in Asian markets in the form of blocks, flakes, powder, or strands.*

1 kiwi, peeled, halved, and thinly sliced (2 ounces)

½ mango, peeled and thinly sliced (4 ounces)

½ cup raspberries (2½ ounces)

6 tablespoons frozen apple juice concentrate, thawed

1 tablespoon fresh lime juice

1½ teaspoons orange liqueur or light rum

½ teaspoon flaked dried agar (see Note)

7 ounces soft tofu, crumbled

1 teaspoon grated lime zest

1½ tablespoons granola

*Make one layer of kiwi,* one layer of mango, and one layer of raspberries in the bottom of each of 4 parfait or champagne flutes. Reserve the remaining fruit, setting aside 4 of the most perfect raspberries for garnish.

*In a blender* or food processor, combine the apple juice concentrate, lime juice, and orange liqueur. Sprinkle the agar flakes over the liquid and let stand for 5 minutes to soften. Pulse to break up the agar flakes. Add the tofu and process until smooth and creamy. Add the lime zest and pulse once or twice to blend. Immediately finish assembling the parfaits so that the agar does not harden. Spoon a layer of the tofu filling over the fruit in the parfait glasses. Continue layering the fruit and tofu filling, ending with tofu. Sprinkle with the granola and garnish with the reserved raspberries. Chill until ready to serve.

# Exotic Fruit Salad with Mint and Gingersnap Crumble

**H**ERE IS MY FAVORITE FRUIT DISH. Perhaps this is because it reminds me of Paris, where often, after a five-course dinner, we would end the meal with just such a fresh fruit salad steeped in subtly spiced syrup.

PER SERVING:

*138 calories*

*1 g total fat (6% of calories)*

*0 g saturated fat*

*0 mg cholesterol*

*2 g protein (5% of calories)*

*31 g carbohydrates*

*(89% of calories)*

*2 g fiber*

*9 mg sodium*

**MAKES 4 SERVINGS**

*Syrup*

1 cup frozen white grape juice concentrate, thawed

½ cup water

1 tablespoon grated lime zest

½ vanilla bean, split

1 whole star anise

1 whole clove

2 sprigs fresh mint

1 tablespoon fresh lime juice

*Fruit*

1 mango, peeled, pitted, and thinly sliced (5 ounces)

2 kiwi, peeled and sliced (5 ounces)

2 peaches, peeled, pitted, and sliced (5 ounces)

¼ pineapple, peeled, cored, and thinly sliced (5 ounces)

2 cups blueberries, blackberries, or raspberries (10 ounces)

1 cup crumbled gingersnaps, from Gingersnap Cookies (page 269) or store-bought gingersnaps

*To make the syrup,* in a small saucepan, combine the grape juice, water, lime zest, vanilla bean, star anise, clove, and mint. Bring to a boil over high heat, reduce the heat to medium, and simmer, uncovered, for about 10 minutes, until reduced by one third. Add the lime juice and strain through a sieve into a bowl or cup. Cool.

*To prepare the fruit,* put the mango, kiwi, peaches, pineapple, and blueberries in a nonreactive bowl and pour the syrup over it. Stir gently, cover, and refrigerate for at least 8 hours, or overnight.

*Spoon the fruit* and syrup into chilled bowls and sprinkle with the gingersnap crumbs.

# Lemon Crepes with Poached Bananas

**B**ECAUSE WE ALWAYS HAD CREPES at family gatherings when I was growing up in Belgium, I learned to flip them over a hot stove at an early age. Later, when I worked in fine restaurants, I learned to make them very thin, as these are. The batter uses one egg, and making batter with anything less is not practical. Therefore, you will have more than enough; use the excess for breakfast the next day.

*Crepe batter*

$3/4$ cup 1% low-fat milk

1 large egg

$1/2$ teaspoon salt (optional)

$1/2$ teaspoon canola oil

$1/2$ teaspoon pure vanilla extract

$1/2$ teaspoon grated lemon zest

$1/4$ cup unbleached all-purpose flour

$1/4$ cup whole wheat flour

*Sauce*

$1/2$ cup frozen orange juice concentrate, thawed

$1/4$ cup water

1 tablespoon honey

1 teaspoon orange liqueur

*Garnish*

2 tablespoons julienned orange zest

*Bananas*

2 bananas (7 ounces)

$1/2$ cup unsweetened apple juice

$1/2$ teaspoon ground cinnamon

*To make the crepes,* in a blender, combine the milk, egg, the salt, if using, oil, vanilla, and lemon zest and pulse to mix. Add the flours and blend until smooth. Transfer to a bowl and let stand at room temperature for at least 1 hour but no longer than 2 hours.

*Generously spray a 6-inch crepe pan* with vegetable oil spray. Set over medium-high heat and when hot, wipe out any excess oil with a paper towel. Spoon about $1\frac{1}{3}$ tablespoons of batter into the pan and rotate the pan to spread it evenly over the bottom. Cook for 1 to 2 minutes on one side, until the crepe is nicely browned. Turn the crepe with a spatula and cook it briefly on the other side. Lift from the pan and set on a plate. Repeat to make 8 crepes, stacking the crepes on the plate with a sheet of waxed paper between each one. (Refrigerate the remaining batter for another use.) Set aside at room temperature until ready to serve.

*To make the sauce,* in a nonreactive saucepan, combine the orange juice concentrate, water, and honey. Simmer, uncovered, for about 10 minutes over medium heat, until reduced by half. Stir in the liqueur and set aside.

*To prepare the garnish,* fill a small saucepan halfway with water and bring to a boil over high heat. Add the orange zest and simmer for about 3 minutes, until softened. Drain, refresh under cool running water, and set aside.

*To prepare the bananas,* slice each banana lengthwise into four pieces and then cut each piece in half. Arrange the slices in a sauté pan just large enough to hold them, add the apple juice, sprinkle with the cinnamon, and bring to a boil over high heat. Reduce the heat to low, cover, and poach for 4 to 5 minutes, until softened.

*To assemble the crepes,* arrange one crepe browned side down on each dessert plate. Spoon a banana slice and a bit of poaching liquid onto one quarter of each crepe. Fold in half, then in quarters, enclosing the filling.

*Reheat the sauce if necessary,* drizzle over the crepes, and garnish with the orange zest.

# Figs with Walnut Ambrosia

**W**HEN FIGS ARE IN SEASON in California, this simple dessert never fails to delight and charm our guests. A former chef described it as "one of the best of the Golden Door's treats." I agree.

PER SERVING:

*178 calories*

*6 g total fat (29% of calories)*

*2 g saturated fat*

*13 mg cholesterol*

*6 g protein (14% of calories)*

*25 g carbohydrates*

*(55% of calories)*

*1 g fiber*

*53 mg sodium*

**MAKES 6 SERVINGS**

NOTE: *If figs are unavailable, this dessert is also delicious made with peeled and halved ripe peaches.*

*See page 65 for a list of edible flowers. To make a chiffonade, slice the flowers into very thin strips. This is most easily accomplished by rolling the blooms into cylinders and then slicing them.*

3 tablespoons coarsely chopped walnuts

1 cup low-fat ricotta cheese

1 tablespoon honey

2 teaspoons grated lemon zest

2 teaspoons orange liqueur

6 ripe figs
(12 ounces; see Note)

18 orange segments
(from 2 oranges; 10 ounces)

½ cup blueberries

Chiffonade of edible flowers
(see Note; optional)

*In a small skillet,* toast the walnuts over medium heat for 4 to 5 minutes, until fragrant and a shade darker. Transfer to a bowl and stir in the ricotta, honey, lemon zest, and liqueur.

*Cut each fig* in half. Spoon the filling into the natural cavities of the figs and arrange 2 halves on each dessert plate. Partially insert 3 orange segments into the ricotta mixture on fig half. Garnish with the berries and the edible flowers, if desired.

# Phyllo-Dough Fruit Cups with Strawberry Coulis

**E**VERYONE LOVES THESE delicate, pretty cups filled with colorful fresh fruit and berries.

PER SERVING:

*98 calories*

*0 g total fat (3% of calories)*

*0 g saturated fat*

*0 mg cholesterol*

*1 g protein (3% of calories)*

*22 g carbohydrates*

*(91% of calories)*

*1 g fiber*

*40 mg sodium*

**MAKES 6 SERVINGS**

Four 11-by-17-inch sheets phyllo dough (2¼ ounces)

1 cup raspberries (5 ounces)

¾ cup blueberries (4 ounces)

2 kiwi, peeled and diced (4 ounces)

Strawberry Coulis (page 246)

*Preheat the oven* to 350°F. Spray 12 standard-sized muffin cups with vegetable oil spray.

*Place 1 sheet of phyllo on a work surface.* Cut the sheet into 6 squares (make one cut lengthwise down the center and then two cuts, evenly spaced, crosswise). Spray with vegetable oil spray. Stack 4 pieces, turning the second and fourth pieces to create an eight-pointed star. Carefully transfer the stacked phyllo to a muffin cup, lightly pressing it into the sides. Repeat the process to make 6 cups. (Use every other muffin cup to allow space for the edges of each phyllo cup to brown evenly.)

*Bake* for about 20 minutes, until the top edges are lightly browned. Remove the baked cups and cool completely on a wire rack. (The phyllo cups can be stored in a dry, cool place, loosely covered, for several hours.)

*Combine the raspberries,* blueberries, and kiwi in a bowl and toss gently to combine.

*To serve,* place a phyllo cup on each dessert plate. Spoon the fruit into the cups and drizzle with the coulis.

# Plum and Apple Compote with Passion Fruit Meringue

**V**ARY THE FRUIT IN THIS RECIPE according to your preference, the season, and the fruit's ripeness. Other summer fruits such as nectarines, cherries, strawberries, or peaches are excellent choices. The possibilities go on as long as a lazy summer day.

PER SERVING:

*126 calories*

*1 g total fat (5% of calories)*

*0 g saturated fat*

*0 mg cholesterol*

*2 g protein (7% of calories)*

*28 g carbohydrates*

*(89% of calories)*

*1 g fiber*

*81 mg sodium*

**MAKES 8 SERVINGS**

### Compote

8 red plums, pitted and cut into large pieces (24 ounces)

2 apples, peeled, cored, and cut into large pieces (8 ounces)

¼ cup unsweetened apple juice

¾ cup light brown sugar, or more if necessary (see Note)

½ cinnamon stick

### Garnish

2 tablespoons julienned orange zest

### Meringue

3 large egg whites, at room temperature

¼ teaspoon cream of tartar

Pinch of salt

¼ cup frozen passion fruit concentrate, thawed (see Note)

1 teaspoon orange liqueur (optional)

Confectioners' sugar for sprinkling

*To make the compote,* in a medium-sized nonreactive saucepan, combine the plums, apples, apple juice, brown sugar, and cinnamon stick and bring to a boil over high heat, stirring. Reduce the heat to medium-low, cover, and simmer for 10 to 15 minutes, until the fruit softens. Uncover, raise the heat to medium, and simmer, stirring to break up the fruit, for 3 to 4 minutes, until the juices are slightly thickened. Discard the cinnamon stick. Divide the fruit among 8 small shallow ovenproof ramekins or custard cups. Set aside.

*Preheat the oven* to 350°F.

*To prepare the garnish,* fill a small saucepan halfway with water and bring to a boil over high heat. Add the orange zest and simmer for about 3 minutes, until softened. Drain, refresh under cool running water, and set aside.

*To make the meringue,* in the bowl of an electric mixer, combine the egg whites, cream of tartar, and salt and with the mixer on medium-high

NOTE: *Add more sugar to the fruit if it needs extra sweetener. You can buy passion fruit juice concentrate in some specialty shops.*

speed, beat the whites to soft peaks. With the mixer running, gradually add the passion fruit concentrate and beat until thick and smooth. Beat in the orange liqueur, if desired.

*Spoon the meringue* over the fruit compote and set the ramekins on a baking sheet. Bake for 20 to 25 minutes, or until the meringue is golden brown.

*To serve,* dust the meringue with confectioners' sugar and garnish with the orange zest.

# Rhubarb, Apple, and Strawberry Compote with Orange Meringue

**W**HEN I WAS GROWING UP in Europe, my parents had a large rhubarb patch in the garden. My mother stewed the rhubarb for a compote, and to this day I relish its sweet-tart taste. Try it once and you, too, may form a life-long attachment. This recipe is very similar to the Plum and Apple Compote with Passion Fruit Meringue on page 234. By comparing the recipes, you can see how easy it is to vary the fruit and the flavoring for the meringue.

PER SERVING:

*113 calories*

*0 g total fat (3% of calories)*

*0 g saturated fat*

*0 mg cholesterol*

*2 g protein (8% of calories)*

*25 g carbohydrates*

*(89% of calories)*

*1 g fiber*

*83 mg sodium*

**MAKES 8 SERVINGS**

*Compote*

6 cups chopped trimmed rhubarb (24 ounces)

2 apples, peeled, cored, and thinly sliced (8 ounces)

1 cup hulled strawberries (6 ounces)

1/2 cup unsweetened apple juice

3/4 cup light brown sugar

1/2 cinnamon stick

*Meringue*

3 large egg whites, at room temperature

1/4 teaspoon cream of tartar

Pinch of salt

1/4 cup orange juice concentrate, thawed

1 teaspoon orange liqueur (optional)

Confectioners' sugar for dusting

8 raspberries

*To make the compote,* in a medium-sized nonreactive saucepan, combine the rhubarb, apples, strawberries, apple juice, brown sugar, and cinnamon stick. Bring to a boil over high heat, stirring. Reduce the heat to medium-low and cook, covered, for 10 to 15 minutes, until the rhubarb begins to soften. Uncover, raise the heat to medium, and continue to cook, stirring, for 3 to 4 minutes, until the fruit breaks down and the juices are slightly thickened. Remove the cinnamon stick. Divide the fruit among 8 small shallow ovenproof ramekins or custard cups.

*Preheat the oven* to 350°F.

*To make the meringue,* in the bowl of an electric mixer, combine the egg whites, cream of tartar, and salt and with the mixer on medium-high speed, beat the whites to soft peaks. With the mixer running, gradually add the orange juice concentrate and beat until thick and smooth. Beat in the orange liqueur, if desired.

*Spoon the meringue* evenly over the fruit compote and place the ramekins on a baking sheet. Do not mound high. Bake for 20 to 25 minutes, until the meringue is golden brown. Make sure the meringue is well cooked.

*To serve,* dust the meringue with confectioners' sugar and garnish each serving with a raspberry.

# Apple Pizza

**T**UCKED AWAY NEAR THE RAILWAY STATION in Beaulieu in the South of France was a little pizza restaurant I loved to visit when I lived there. If you ordered in advance, the chef would make an apple pizza very similar to this one. I am thrilled that I have been able to re-create the recipe. Although you need only half the pizza dough recipe, I suggest making the entire amount and freezing the rest for another pizza later in the month.

1 tablespoon fine cornmeal or semolina flour

½ recipe Pizza Dough (page 216)

4 Golden Delicious apples, peeled, cored, and halved (1 pound)

¼ cup granulated sugar

1 teaspoon ground cinnamon

¼ cup sugar-free apricot preserves

1 tablespoon orange liqueur or apple juice

*Preheat the oven* to 375°F. Spray a 13- to 14-inch pizza pan or a baking sheet with vegetable oil spray and sprinkle with the cornmeal or semolina flour.

*On a lightly floured surface,* using a lightly floured rolling pin, roll the dough into a 14-inch diameter circle. Transfer to the prepared pan.

*Using a sharp knife,* slice the apple halves crosswise into thin slices. Fan the slices on the dough, starting at the edge and ringing the perimeter. Work toward the center, fanning the apples in smaller and smaller circles until the entire circle is covered. The layer of apples should be as thick, or thicker than, the crust.

*In a small bowl,* combine the sugar and cinnamon. Sprinkle evenly over the apples. Bake for 20 to 25 minutes, until the crust is golden brown.

*In a small saucepan,* combine the preserves and liqueur and cook over low heat, stirring, until the preserves dissolve. Brush over the apples to glaze them and immediately cut into wedges for serving.

# Orange-Poached Peaches

TREE-RIPENED PEACHES, picked at their peak of juiciness and sweetness, are perfect for this recipe. Look for them at farmers' markets in the summertime or, better yet, pick them at an nearby orchard. I like to serve these with the Gingersnap Cookies on page 269.

1 tablespoon julienned orange zest

4 peaches (20 ounces)

Juice of 1 orange (½ cup)

1 cup peach nectar or unsweetened apple juice

1 tablespoon cornstarch, dissolved in 3 tablespoons water

1 tablespoon orange liqueur

½ cup blueberries or other seasonal berries (2½ ounces)

*Fill a small saucepan* halfway with water and bring to a boil over high heat. Add the orange zest and simmer for about 3 minutes, until softened. Drain, refresh under cool running water, and set aside.

*Fill a large saucepan* about halfway with water and bring to a boil over high heat. Blanch the peaches for 40 to 50 seconds and then, using a slotted spoon, gently lift them from the water. Transfer to a colander and cool under cold running water. Peel, halve, and pit the peaches.

*In a small nonreactive saucepan,* combine the peaches with the orange juice and nectar. Bring to a simmer over medium heat and cook for about 10 minutes, or until the peaches begin to soften. Using a slotted spoon, transfer the peaches to a bowl. Set aside.

*Stir the cornstarch mixture* into the cooking liquid and simmer, stirring occasionally, until the sauce is thickened. Remove from the heat and stir in the liqueur.

*Arrange 2 peach halves* on each plate and spoon the sauce over them. Garnish with the orange zest and berries.

NOTE: *You can substitute Bartlett pears for the peaches.*

# Banana-Strawberry Napoleons

**T**HIS IS ONE OF THE MOST POPULAR desserts at the Golden Door. Admittedly, it is labor-intensive but because some steps, including baking the phyllo layers, can be done ahead of time, it is not terribly difficult. For this, you will need butter-flavored vegetable oil spray. When assembled and decorated, the napoleons make a smashing presentation.

PER SERVING:

*130 calories*

*7 g total fat (47% of calories)*

*4 g saturated fat*

*22 mg cholesterol*

*3 g protein (10% of calories)*

*14 g carbohydrates*

*(43% of calories)*

*0 g fiber*

*132 mg sodium*

**MAKES 8 SERVINGS**

Three 12-by-17-inch sheets phyllo dough (1⅓ ounces)

1 tablespoon granulated sugar

*Banana filling*

1 ripe banana (3½ ounces)

1½ teaspoons fresh lime juice

1½ teaspoons orange liqueur

¼ teaspoon pure vanilla extract

1 cup reduced-fat cream cheese, softened

¼ cup sifted confectioners' sugar, plus more for sprinkling

8 strawberries, thinly sliced

1 cup Strawberry Coulis (page 246; optional)

Fudge Sweet chocolate sauce (see Note)

*Preheat the oven* to 400°F. Line a baking sheet with parchment paper.

*Place 1 sheet of phyllo on a work surface.* Spray with butter-flavored vegetable oil spray and sprinkle with 1 teaspoon of the sugar. Place the remaining 2 sheets phyllo directly over the first, spraying each one with vegetable oil spray and sprinkling with sugar. Cut the phyllo stack into sixteen 4-by-2¾-inch rectangles, trimming the phyllo if necessary. Discard any scraps.

*Transfer the rectangles* to the prepared baking sheet and bake for 3 to 5 minutes, until crisp and golden brown. Check frequently during baking, as thin phyllo burns easily. Lift the entire sheet of parchment off the baking sheet, transfer to a large wire rack and cool. (The phyllo can be baked several hours ahead and ╌╌ ╌╌cu, loosely wrapped, in a dry place until ready to serve.)

*Shortly before serving,* make the filling: In the bowl of an electric mixer, mash the banana to a puree. Add the lime juice, orange liqueur, and

*Note: Fudge Sweet is a nonfat chocolate Dutch topping that I use quite often. It is available in some specialty stores and can be ordered from Wax Orchards, 22744 Wax Orchards Road, S.W., Vashon, Washington, 98070 (206–463–9735).*

vanilla. With the electric mixer set on medium speed, beat the mixture until smooth. Beat in the softened cream cheese and confectioners' sugar until smooth.

*To assemble the napoleons,* place 8 phyllo rectangles on dessert plates. Spoon approximately ¼ cup of the banana cream onto each pastry and layer with the sliced strawberries. Top with the remaining phyllo rectangles.

*If desired, pool 1 tablespoon* of coulis off-center on each plate. Decorate the tops of the napoleons with a swirl of Fudge Sweet and a liberal sprinkling of confectioners' sugar.

# Green Apple–Lime–Candied Ginger Sorbet

**T**HE CANDIED GINGER gives this pretty pale green sorbet an elegant kick of flavor.

PER SERVING:

*45 calories*

*0 g total fat (5% of calories)*

*0 g saturated fat*

*0 mg cholesterol*

*0 g protein (2% of calories)*

*10 g carbohydrates*
*(93% of calories)*

*1 g fiber*

*5 mg sodium*

**MAKES 8 SERVINGS**

*NOTE: The sorbet can be kept in the freezer for several days. Let it sit at room temperature for up to an hour (depending on its hardness) before serving. It should be pleasingly soft but not watery.*

4 tart green apples
(16 ounces)

2 cups unsweetened apple juice

1 tablespoon fresh lime juice

1 tablespoon minced candied ginger

4 sprigs fresh mint

*Peel, core, and thinly slice* 3 of the apples. Set the other aside to use as garnish.

*In a blender* or food processor, combine the apples, apple juice, and lime juice and process until smooth. Add the ginger and pulse just to mix.

*Transfer to an ice cream maker* and freeze according to the manufacturer's directions.

*Thinly slice the remaining apple.* Spoon the sorbet into chilled bowls and garnish with the apple slices and mint sprigs.

# Mango-Banana Sorbet

**T**HESE TWO TROPICAL FRUITS BLEND together to make a sweet, rich sorbet.

PER SERVING:

*87 calories*

*0 g total fat (3% of calories)*

*0 g saturated fat*

*0 mg cholesterol*

*0 g protein (2% of calories)*

*20 g carbohydrates*
*(93% of calories)*

*0 g fiber*

*2 mg sodium*

**MAKES 8 SERVINGS**

NOTE: *The sorbet can be kept in the freezer for several days. Let it sit at room temperature for up to an hour (depending on its hardness) before serv-ing. It should be pleas-ingly soft but not watery.*

*You can substitute 2 peeled and pitted peaches for the mango.*

1 mango, peeled, pitted, and cut into pieces (8 ounces)

1 banana, sliced (3½ ounces)

2½ cups fresh orange juice (5 to 7 oranges)

1 tablespoon fresh lime juice

2 to 3 tablespoons honey

*In a blender* or food processor, combine the mango, banana, orange juice, lime juice, and honey and process until smooth.

*Transfer to an ice cream maker* and freeze according to the manufacturer's directions.

*Spoon the sorbet* into chilled bowls.

# Raspberry Sorbet

**B**ERRY SORBETS ARE AMONG EVERYONE'S FAVORITES. I selected raspberry sorbet as the master recipe because so many people name it as their favorite. Strawberries make a delightful variation.

PER SERVING:

*49 calories*

*0 g total fat (5% of calories)*

*0 g saturated fat*

*0 mg cholesterol*

*0 g protein (4% of calories)*

*11 g carbohydrates*

*(86% of calories)*

*1 g fiber*

*1 mg sodium*

**MAKES 6 SERVINGS**

*NOTE: The sorbet can be kept in the freezer for several days. Let it sit at room temperature for up to an hour before serving.*

2 cups fresh or unsweetened frozen raspberries (10 ounces)

2 tablespoons fructose

½ cup unsweetened apple juice or unsweetened white grape juice

2 teaspoons orange liqueur or raspberry liqueur

*In a blender* or food processor, combine the raspberries, fructose, and apple juice and process briefly. Take care not to crush the raspberry seeds to maintain the sorbet's bright color.

*Strain through a fine sieve* to remove the seeds. Stir in the liqueur, transfer to an ice cream maker, and freeze according to the manufacturer's directions.

*Spoon the sorbet* into chilled bowls.

PER SERVING:

*39 calories*

*0 g total fat (4% of calories)*

*0 g saturated fat*

*0 mg cholesterol*

*0 g protein (3% of calories)*

*8 g carbohydrates*

*(86% of calories)*

*0 g fiber*

*2 mg sodium*

**MAKES 6 SERVINGS**

## Strawberry Sorbet

Replace the raspberries with fresh or unsweetened frozen strawberries. Flavor the sorbet with the orange liqueur (not raspberry liqueur).

# Yam-Banana Sorbet

**T**HE FLAVOR COMBINATION may sound highly unusual for sorbet, but I have found that most of our guests are enchanted by this rich-tasting dessert.

PER SERVING:

*132 calories*

*0 g total fat (3% of calories)*

*0 g saturated fat*

*0 mg cholesterol*

*1 g protein (4% of calories)*

*31 g carbohydrates*

*(94% of calories)*

*1 g fiber*

*18 mg sodium*

**MAKES 8 SERVINGS**

NOTE: *When I call for yams, I mean the tubers with dark skin and bright orange flesh. These actually are a type of sweet potato.*

*The sorbet can be kept in the freezer for several days. Let it sit at room temperature for up to an hour (depending on its hardness) before serving. It should be pleasingly soft but not watery.*

2 yams, well scrubbed (12 ounces; see Note)

1 banana (3½ ounces)

2½ cups fresh orange juice (about 5 to 7 oranges)

¼ cup honey

1 tablespoon fresh lemon juice

1½ teaspoons ground cinnamon

⅛ teaspoon ground cloves

Fresh berries (optional)

*Fill a saucepan* with enough cold water to cover the yams by 1 to 2 inches. Bring to a boil, reduce the heat, and cook in gently boiling water over medium-high heat for about 30 minutes, until fork-tender. Drain and cool. Peel the yams and cut into small chunks. (This should measure about 1½ cups.)

*In a blender* or food processor, combine the yams, banana, orange juice, honey, lemon juice, cinnamon, and cloves and process until smooth and light.

*Transfer to an ice cream maker* and freeze according to the manufacturer's directions.

*Spoon the sorbet* into chilled bowls. Garnish with fresh berries, if desired.

# Strawberry Coulis

**T**HIS UNCOOKED FRUIT SAUCE is the perfect accompaniment to any number of desserts. Serve it with sorbets, cookies, or small slices of cake.

PER TABLESPOON:

*10 calories*

*0 g total fat (5% of calories)*

*0 g saturated fat*

*0 mg cholesterol*

*0 g protein (4% of calories)*

*2 g carbohydrates*

*(91% of calories)*

*0 g fiber*

*0 mg sodium*

**MAKES ABOUT
1¹/₂ CUPS**

NOTE: *Fructose is sold at many supermarkets and in most health food stores.*

*This coulis and the variations that follow will keep in the refrigerator for up to 3 days.*

2 cups fresh strawberries, hulled, or thawed frozen strawberries (12 ounces)

2 tablespoons fructose (see Note)

2 tablespoons unsweetened apple juice, plus more if necessary

2 teaspoons orange liqueur (optional)

*In a food processor* or blender, combine the strawberries, fructose, and apple juice. Process just until the mixture smooths out; do not overprocess or the strawberries will discolor. Add more apple juice if the mixture is too thick.

*Strain through a fine sieve* into a nonreactive bowl, pressing gently on the fruit to extract as much liquid as possible. Stir in the liqueur, if using. Cover and refrigerate until ready to serve.

## Raspberry Coulis

Replace the strawberries with fresh or unsweetened frozen raspberries. Flavor the coulis with orange or raspberry liqueur, if desired.

PER TABLESPOON: *13 calories, 0 g total fat (6% of calories), 0 g saturated fat, 0 mg cholesterol, 0 g protein (4% of calories), 3 g carbohydrates (90% of calories), 0 g fiber, 0 mg sodium*

## Mango Coulis

Replace the strawberries with 2 mangoes, peeled and pitted (12 ounces), and the apple juice with ½ cup fresh orange juice. Use 1 tablespoon fructose and, if desired, 1 tablespoon orange liqueur. Do not strain.

PER TABLESPOON: *13 calories, 0 g total fat (3% of calories), 0 g saturated fat, 0 mg cholesterol, 0 g protein (3% of calories), 3 g carbohydrates (94% of calories), 0 g fiber, 0 mg sodium*

## Blueberry Coulis

Replace the strawberries with fresh or unsweetened frozen blueberries and flavor the coulis with crème de cassis, if desired, instead of orange liqueur.

PER TABLESPOON: *14 calories, 0 g total fat (4% of calories), 0 g saturated fat, 0 mg cholesterol, 0 g protein (3% of calories), 3 g carbohydrates (94% of calories), 0 g fiber, 1 mg sodium*

## Blackberry Coulis

Replace the strawberries with fresh or unsweetened frozen blackberries and flavor the coulis with crème de cassis, if desired, instead of orange liqueur.

PER TABLESPOON: *12 calories, 0 g total fat (4% of calories), 0 g saturated fat, 0 mg cholesterol, 0 g protein (3% of calories), 3 g carbohydrates (93% of calories), 0 g fiber, 0 mg sodium*

# Cakes, Cookies, and Custards

NEITHER OUR GUESTS NOR I can live on fruit desserts alone, and therefore I have developed a number of other confections to satisfy a variety of "sweet tooths." The secret to enjoying desserts is to use the very best ingredients available and to eat them in moderation. While it's rare to find butter or rich cheeses used in the Golden Door kitchen, there is always some on hand for baking. These desserts are really special.

# Orange-Carrot Cake

MORE THAN TWENTY YEARS AGO, I made carrot cake at the Kona Kai Club in San Diego that was moist and rich, just the way a carrot cake should be. But to achieve that texture, I used lots of oil. I have since learned to make a cake that is just as wonderful but has very little fat.

1 cup unbleached all-purpose flour

1 teaspoon baking powder

½ teaspoon baking soda

1 teaspoon ground cinnamon

½ teaspoon ground cloves

½ cup whole wheat flour

½ cup unsweetened dried cranberries

¾ cup fresh orange juice

1 large egg yolk

¼ cup canola oil

½ cup nonfat plain yogurt

⅓ cup light brown sugar

2 tablespoons pure maple syrup

1 tablespoon orange liqueur

1 teaspoon pure vanilla extract

1½ cups grated carrots (3 carrots; 12 ounces)

1 teaspoon grated orange zest

3 large egg whites, at room temperature

¼ teaspoon cream of tartar

*Preheat the oven* to 350°F. Spray a 10-inch nonstick springform pan with vegetable oil spray.

*Sift together* the all-purpose flour, baking powder, baking soda, cinnamon, and cloves into a large bowl. Add the whole wheat flour and whisk just to mix.

*In a small saucepan,* combine the cranberries and orange juice and simmer over low heat for 5 to 6 minutes, or until nearly all the juice is absorbed. Cool.

*Transfer the cranberries* and their liquid to a large bowl and add the egg yolk, oil, yogurt, brown sugar, maple syrup, liqueur, vanilla, carrots, and orange zest. Using a wooden spoon, stir to mix.

*Make a well* in the center of the dry ingredients and add the liquid ingredients. Gently stir just until combined. Do not overmix.

*In the bowl of an electric mixer* set on medium-high speed, beat the egg whites and cream of tartar until foamy. Increase the speed to high and beat until soft peaks form. Fold the egg whites into the batter just until incorporated; there may be a few specks of white still showing. Scrape into the pan and spread evenly.

*Bake* in the center of the oven for 50 to 55 minutes, or until the cake springs back when lightly touched in the center. Cool in the pan on a wire rack for about 10 minutes. Release the sides of the pan and remove from the cake. Let the cake cool completely before serving.

# Chocolate-Prune Cake

**C**HOCOLATE IS A SUBLIME INGREDIENT and one we do not neglect at the Golden Door. The secret to this rich, moist cake is replacing the usual butter with prune puree. This is a great chocolate dessert.

PER SERVING:

*169 calories*

*1 g total fat (4% of calories)*

*0 g saturated fat*

*0 mg cholesterol*

*3 g protein (7% of calories)*

*37 g carbohydrates*

*(61% of calories)*

*1 g fiber*

*107 mg sodium*

**MAKES 16 SERVINGS**

1½ cups pitted prunes

1½ cups water

1¼ cups unbleached all-purpose flour

½ cup nonalkalized cocoa powder (see Note)

1 teaspoon baking powder

1 teaspoon baking soda

1 cup granulated sugar

1 teaspoon coffee liqueur

1 teaspoon chocolate extract

⅔ cup water

4 large egg whites, at room temperature

3 bananas, thinly sliced (10½ ounces)

2 cups raspberries (10 ounces)

*In a saucepan,* combine the prunes with the first quantity of water, bring to a simmer over medium-high heat, and cook for 20 to 25 minutes, until softened. Set aside to cool. When cool, transfer the prunes and about two thirds of the cooking liquid to a food processor and process until pureed. Strain through a sieve and set aside. (There should be about 1½ cups.)

*Preheat the oven* to 350°F. Spray a 10-inch nonstick springform pan with vegetable oil spray.

*Sift together* the all-purpose flour, cocoa, baking powder, and baking soda into a large bowl.

*In another bowl,* whisk together the sugar, liqueur, chocolate extract, ½ cup of the prune puree, and the second quantity of water. Using a rubber spatula, mix into the dry ingredients until incorporated.

*In the bowl of an electric mixer* set on medium-high speed, beat the egg whites until foamy. Increase the speed to high and beat until soft peaks form. Fold the egg whites into the batter just until incorporated. There may be a few specks of white still showing. Scrape into the pan and spread evenly.

*Bake* in the center of the oven for 25 to 30 minutes, or until the cake springs back when lightly touched in the center. Cool in the pan on a wire rack for about 10 minutes. Release the sides of the pan and remove from the cake. Let the cake cool completely.

*Using a serrated knife,* cut the cake horizontally into two even layers. Set the bottom layer on a plate and spread ½ cup of the remaining prune puree over it. Arrange the banana slices over the puree and top with the other layer of cake. Spread the remaining puree over the top of the cake. Arrange the raspberries in a circle around the circumference of the cake, about 1 inch from the edge and serve.

# Festive Fruitcake

**I** HAVE HAD THE PLEASURE of being the guest chef aboard a Cunard cruise ship on which the Golden Door runs a luxury spa program for interested passengers. During a holiday cruise, I made this cake to rave reviews. Like all fruitcakes, it requires a fair amount of preparation and, once baked, tastes best after it has been allowed to mellow for a period of time. Unlike most, this one needs only a few days in the refrigerator.

PER SERVING:

*157 calories*

*4 g total fat (21% of calories)*

*0 g saturated fat*

*13 mg cholesterol*

*3 g protein (6% of calories)*

*29 g carbohydrates*

*(73% of calories)*

*1 g fiber*

*84 mg sodium*

**MAKES 16 SERVINGS**

¾ cup unbleached all-purpose flour

1 teaspoon baking powder

1 teaspoon baking soda

1 teaspoon ground cinnamon

¼ teaspoon freshly grated nutmeg

¼ teaspoon ground allspice

½ cup whole wheat flour

1 large egg

1 large egg white

¼ cup light brown sugar

2 tablespoons canola oil

¼ cup light molasses

1 banana (3½ ounces)

One 20-ounce can crushed pineapple in juice, drained (8 ounces after draining)

1 tablespoon finely chopped orange zest

½ cup raisins (3 ounces)

⅓ cup unsweetened dried cranberries (2½ ounces)

½ cup chopped pitted dates or prunes (3 ounces)

⅓ cup chopped walnuts or pecans (1 ounce)

*Preheat the oven* to 350°F. Spray an 8½-by-4-inch loaf pan with vegetable oil spray.

*Sift together* the all-purpose flour, baking powder, baking soda, cinnamon, nutmeg, and allspice into a large bowl. Add the whole wheat flour and whisk just to mix.

*In a blender* or food processor, blend the egg, egg white, brown sugar, oil, molasses, and banana until smooth. Transfer to a bowl and stir in the pineapple and orange zest.

*Make a well* in the center of the dry ingredients, add the liquid ingredients, and mix just until incorporated. Add the raisins, cranberries, dates, and nuts and stir until well mixed. Do not overmix. Scrape the batter into the pan and spread evenly. Tap the pan on the countertop several times to rid the batter of any air bubbles.

*Set the loaf pan* in a larger pan and add enough hot water to come about 1 inch up the sides of the pan. Bake in the center of the oven for 55 to 60 minutes, or until a toothpick inserted in the center of the cake comes out clean. Turn out the cake onto a wire rack and cool completely. When cool, wrap well in plastic and foil and refrigerate for at least 1 day and up to 3 days before serving.

## SWEETNESS AND LIGHT

At the Golden Door, I rely on fruit juices and fruit juice concentrates to sweeten many dishes. When juices are not sufficient, I use fructose or fruit sugar. However, I am not opposed to using granulated sugar when appropriate, and also call for brown sugar, honey, and confectioners' sugar.

I encourage guests to drink herbal tea, iced tea, and coffee without adding sweeteners, artificial or real. Breaking the sweetener habit makes these beverages taste more refreshing than ever.

# Spiced Apple Cake

**W**HENEVER I SERVE THIS CAKE, it's a sure hit. It's hard to believe it's so low in fat and calories, but I rely on a banana rather than butter for moistness—a trick I employ time and again in my baking. I particularly like to bake this in the fall and winter, when the spices fill the kitchen with an intoxicating aroma.

**PER SERVING:**

*164 calories*

*3 g total fat (17% of calories)*

*0 g saturated fat*

*18 mg cholesterol*

*4 g protein (10% of calories)*

*30 g carbohydrates*

*(72% of calories)*

*1 g fiber*

*77 mg sodium*

**MAKES 12 SERVINGS**

1 cup unbleached all-purpose flour

½ teaspoon baking powder

½ teaspoon baking soda

1 teaspoon ground cinnamon

½ teaspoon ground allspice

¼ teaspoon ground cloves

½ teaspoon salt (optional)

¾ cup whole wheat flour

1 large egg

2 large egg whites

1 banana (3½ ounces)

¼ cup light brown sugar

½ cup low-fat buttermilk

2 tablespoons canola oil

¼ cup strong brewed coffee

2 teaspoons coffee liqueur

1 teaspoon pure vanilla extract

2 tart green apples, peeled, cored, and thinly sliced (8 ounces; see Note)

⅓ cup apricot preserves

*Preheat the oven* to 350°F. Spray an 8-by-8-inch baking pan with vegetable oil spray.

*Sift together* the all-purpose flour, baking powder, baking soda, cinnamon, allspice, cloves, and the salt, if using, into a large bowl. Add the whole wheat flour and whisk just to mix.

*In a blender* or food processor, blend the egg, egg whites, banana, brown sugar, buttermilk, oil, coffee, coffee liqueur, and vanilla until smooth.

*Make a well* in the center of the dry ingredients and add the apples. Gently toss them with the dry ingredients until coated. Add the liquid ingredients and mix just until combined. Do not overmix. Scrape the batter into the prepared pan and spread evenly.

*Bake* in the center of the oven for 40 to 45 minutes, or until a knife or a toothpick inserted in the center of the cake comes out clean. Cool in the pan on a wire rack for 10 minutes. Invert the cake onto the rack.

*In a small saucepan,* heat the jam over low heat until liquefied. Brush over the warm cake and then let the cake cool completely before serving.

*NOTE: Do not be tempted to cut the apples far ahead of time and soak them in acidulated water (lemon water) to keep them from browning—the fruit will absorb some of the water and make the cake taste doughy.*

# Cheesecake

**C**HEESECAKE! The cry goes up from our guests, who are thrilled when we serve this. We often feature it on our Sunday dinner menu, the first meal many of our guests have. After a long day of travel, it leaves them feeling satisfied and well cared for—the ideal way, we think, to welcome them.

PER SERVING:

*134 calories*

*4 g total fat (26% of calories)*

*2 g saturated fat*

*37 mg cholesterol*

*9 g protein (27% of calories)*

*16 g carbohydrates*

*(46% of calories)*

*0 g fiber*

*215 mg sodium*

**MAKES 8 SERVINGS**

*Crust*

4 whole graham crackers, broken into pieces (1¾ ounces), or ¾ cup All-Bran cereal

*Filling*

1 cup low-fat ricotta cheese

1 cup 1% low-fat cottage cheese

¼ cup nonfat plain yogurt

1 large egg

1 large egg white

2 teaspoons fresh lemon juice

1 teaspoon pure vanilla extract

⅓ cup confectioners' sugar

3 tablespoons cornstarch, sifted

1 teaspoon grated lemon zest

1 cup Strawberry Coulis (page 246) or Blueberry Coulis (page 247), fresh fruit, or mint sprigs

*To make the crust,* preheat the oven to 350°F. Spray an 8-by-8-inch square baking dish or 9-inch pie pan with vegetable oil spray.

*In a food processor,* pulse the graham crackers into coarse crumbs. Transfer to the baking dish and spread the crumbs over the bottom and up the sides.

*To prepare the filling,* in a food processor or blender, combine the ricotta cheese, cottage cheese, yogurt, egg, egg white, lemon juice, vanilla, confectioners' sugar, and cornstarch and process until smooth. Add the zest and pulse two or three times, just until mixed. Slowly pour the filling into the prepared dish and smooth the top with a rubber spatula.

*Set the dish in a larger pan* and add enough hot water to come about halfway up the sides of the dish. Bake in the center of the oven for 25 to 35 minutes, until the filling is set and firm. Let the cheesecake cool completely in the pan on a wire rack.

*To serve,* cut the cheesecake into squares or wedges and serve with the coulis, fresh fruit, or mint.

# Apple-Lime Tofu Cheesecake

**N**O DAIRY PRODUCTS ARE REQUIRED to make this smooth, rich, satiny, and ultimately satisfying "cheesecake"—just soft, silky tofu bound with egg whites, enriched with a whole egg, and sweetened with honey. We serve this with mango sauce and decorate it with fresh bananas and berries.

*Crust*

4 whole graham crackers, broken into pieces (1¾ ounces)

*Filling*

14 ounces soft tofu, crumbled (see Note)

½ cup honey

¼ cup unsweetened apple juice

1 large egg

2 large egg whites

2 tablespoons fresh lime juice

1 tablespoon rum or orange liqueur (optional)

2 teaspoons grated lime zest

*Sauce*

2 mangoes (1 pound)

1 cup fresh orange juice

2 tablespoons fresh lime juice

8 sprigs fresh mint

*To make the crust,* preheat the oven to 350°F. Spray an 8-by-8-inch square baking dish or 9-inch pie pan with vegetable oil spray.

*In a food processor,* pulse the graham crackers into coarse crumbs. Transfer to the baking dish and spread the crumbs over the bottom and up the sides.

*To prepare the filling,* in a food processor or blender, combine the tofu, honey, apple juice, egg, egg whites, lime juice, and rum, if desired, and process until smooth. Add the zest and pulse two or three times, just until mixed. Slowly pour the filling into the prepared dish and smooth the top with a rubber spatula.

*Set the dish in a larger pan* and add enough hot water to come about halfway up the sides of the dish. Bake in the center of the oven for 35 to 40 minutes, until the filling is set and a toothpick inserted in the center comes out clean. Let the cheesecake cool completely in the pan on a wire rack.

*NOTE: Be sure to buy soft, or silken, tofu—not firm tofu. The soft tofu gives the best texture and will blend nicely with the egg and egg whites.*

*Just before serving the cheesecake,* make the sauce: peel and pit the mangoes and put the flesh of the fruit in a food processor or blender. Add the orange juice and lime juice and process until smooth.

*To serve,* cut the cheesecake into squares or wedges and serve with the mango sauce alongside. Garnish each serving with a sprig of mint.

# Butternut Squash–Maple Flan

**I** LOVE THE MILD YET DISTINCTIVE FLAVOR of butternut squash and cook with it whenever I can. Most people only think of it for the main part of the meal, but it happily makes the crossover to desserts, just as sweet potatoes, yams, and pumpkins (fresh or canned) have done before it. In fact, any of those can be substituted for the squash, if you prefer. Whichever you choose, you will be pleased with this silky, light, and deliciously sweet flan. For a touch of whimsy, I serve the custards with cranberry sauce. The simpler variation for Maple Flan that follows offers a nice little surprise: sliced peaches in the bottom of the ramekins.

1 butternut squash (1 pound)

1 teaspoon ground cinnamon

½ teaspoon ground allspice

⅛ teaspoon ground cloves

3 cups 1% low-fat milk

6 tablespoons pure maple syrup

2 large eggs, at room temperature

3 large egg whites, at room temperature

1 teaspoon pure vanilla extract

½ cup fresh or canned whole-berry cranberry sauce or fresh fruit

NOTE: *If you would rather cook the butternut squash in the microwave, microwave at High (100 percent) power for 15 to 20 minutes.*

*The flesh from the neck of the squash is more tender and less stringy than the rest.*

*Preheat the oven* to 350°F.

*Using a small sharp knife or fork,* pierce the squash in several places. Put in a baking pan just large enough to hold it. Bake for 45 to 50 minutes, until fork-tender. Cool. (Leave the oven on.)

*When cool,* peel the neck of the squash (see Note) and puree the flesh in a food processor. (There should be about 1 cup puree.) Transfer to a large bowl and whisk in the cinnamon, allspice, and cloves. Set aside. (Reserve the rest of the squash for another use.)

*In a saucepan,* combine the milk and maple syrup and bring almost to a boil over medium-high heat. Remove from the heat.

*In a bowl,* whisk together the eggs, egg whites, and vanilla. In a thin steady stream, pour the hot milk mixture into the egg mixture, whisking vigorously to prevent the eggs from cooking, or scrambling. Skim and discard the froth. Pour the milk mixture into the squash puree and stir to mix.

*Spoon* into eight 1-cup ramekins or custard cups; the flan mixture will not fill the cups to the top. Set the ramekins in a roasting pan and add enough hot water to come about a third of the way up their sides. Bake in the center of the oven for about 50 minutes, or until firm and set and the tops are light golden brown. Let the ramekins cool on a wire rack to room temperature.

*Serve the flans* garnished with the cranberry sauce or fresh fruit.

## Maple Flan

PER SERVING:

*120 calories*

*3 g total fat (21% of calories)*

*1 g saturated fat*

*75 mg cholesterol*

*7 g protein (23% of calories)*

*17 g carbohydrates*

*(57% of calories)*

*0 g fiber*

*92 mg sodium*

**MAKES 6 SERVINGS**

Omit the butternut squash, cinnamon, allspice, and cloves. Decrease the milk to 2½ cups and the maple syrup to ¼ cup, and use only 2 large egg whites. Decrease the amount of vanilla extract to ½ teaspoon. Slice 2 fresh peaches into 12 slices (or use sliced frozen or canned peaches) and lay 2 slices each in the bottom of six ¾-cup ramekins or custard cups. Fill the cups with the flan mixture and sprinkle each with a little freshly grated nutmeg. Garnish with sliced kiwi, strawberries, or other fresh fruit.

# Brownies

**T**O CUT THE FAT and boost the flavor, I substitute a banana for butter in these moist, sweet brownies. Try to eat these brownies the same day they are baked (it probably won't be a problem in most households!). If you cannot, wrap them, or any leftovers, well to prevent them from drying out.

PER BROWNIE:

*122 calories*

*1 g total fat (5% of calories)*

*0 g saturated fat*

*0 mg cholesterol*

*3 g protein (10% of calories)*

*26 g carbohydrates*

*(84% of calories)*

*1 g fiber*

*215 mg sodium*

**MAKES 12 BROWNIES**

³/₄ cup unbleached all-purpose flour

¹/₂ cup nonalkalized cocoa powder (see Note)

1 teaspoon baking powder

¹/₂ teaspoon baking soda

1 banana (3¹/₂ ounces)

³/₄ cup light brown sugar

¹/₂ cup unsweetened apple juice

1 teaspoon pure vanilla extract

¹/₂ teaspoon chocolate extract

4 large egg whites, at room temperature

¹/₂ teaspoon salt

¹/₄ cup Fudge Sweet Chocolate Sauce

Orange wedges and blueberries

*Preheat the oven* to 350°F. Spray a nonstick 8-by-8-inch baking pan with vegetable oil spray.

*In a bowl,* combine the flour, cocoa, baking powder, and baking soda and whisk to mix.

*In a blender* or food processor, combine the banana, brown sugar, apple juice, and vanilla and chocolate extracts and process until smooth. Using a rubber spatula, fold into the dry ingredients.

*In the bowl of an electric mixer* set on medium-high speed, beat the egg whites and salt until foamy. Increase the speed to high and beat until soft peaks form. Fold half the egg whites into the batter. When incorporated, fold in the remaining whites just until incorporated. There may be a few specks of white still showing. Scrape into the pan and spread evenly.

*Bake* in the center of the oven for 30 to 35 minutes, or until the brownie springs back when gently pressed in the center. Cool in the pan on a wire rack.

*Cut the brownie* into 12 squares and serve drizzled with the Fudge Sweet. Garnish each square with orange wedges and blueberries.

NOTE: *Nonalkalized cocoa powder is also called natural cocoa powder. It tastes bolder than alkalized cocoa powder.*

# Chocolate Madeleines

A MADELEINE IS A SHELL-SHAPED CONFECTION that is a lovely marriage of small cake and cookie. For true madeleines, you need madeleine molds, which are sold at nearly all cookware stores. However, any mold that holds a quarter cup of batter will work, although the results won't be immediately recognizable as madeleines. But, just as a rose by any other name smells as sweet, so does a madeleine in any other shape taste as sweet. At the Door, we serve heart-shaped madeleines.

PER MADELEINE:

*113 calories*

*1 g total fat (8% of calories)*

*0 g saturated fat*

*21 mg cholesterol*

*3 g protein (9% of calories)*

*23 g carbohydrates*
*(81% of calories)*

*0 g fiber*

*217 mg sodium*

**MAKES 10 MADELEINES**

³⁄₄ cup unbleached all-purpose flour

¹⁄₄ cup alkalized cocoa powder (see Note)

³⁄₄ teaspoon baking soda

¹⁄₂ teaspoon salt

¹⁄₃ cup Fudge Sweet Chocolate Sauce

2 tablespoons frozen orange juice concentrate, thawed

¹⁄₄ cup strong brewed coffee

2 teaspoons coffee liqueur

1 large egg, at room temperature

1 large egg white, at room temperature

¹⁄₃ cup granulated sugar

¹⁄₂ teaspoon pure vanilla extract

¹⁄₂ teaspoon chocolate extract

*Preheat the oven* to 350°F. Spray 10 madeleine molds with vegetable oil spray.

*Sift together* the flour, cocoa, baking soda, and salt, then sift again into a large bowl.

*In a small bowl,* combine the Fudge Sweet, orange juice concentrate, coffee, and liqueur. Mix well and set aside.

*In the bowl of an electric mixer,* combine the egg, egg white, sugar, and vanilla and chocolate extracts and beat on high speed until the mixture doubles in volume. Reduce the speed to low and gradually add the Fudge Sweet mixture, beating just until incorporated; with mixer at low speed, gradually add the dry ingredients. Stop the mixer and scrape the sides of the bowl often during the process. Do not overmix.

NOTE: *Alkalized cocoa powder is also called Dutch-processed cocoa.*

*Spoon the batter* into the madeleine molds, filling each about one-third full. Set the molds on a baking sheet and bake for 15 to 20 minutes, until firm. Invert onto a wire rack and cool. Serve with the coulis, if desired.

# Apricot and Currant Biscotti

**B**ISCOTTI ARE EXTREMELY POPULAR these days, having become familiar fixtures at the coffee bars that have sprung up just about everywhere. They are great cookies, wonderful dunked into the hot coffee or eaten alongside. Originally from Italy, they get their name from their baking method: they are "twice baked."

PER BISCOTTI:

*67 calories*

*1 g total fat (17% of calories)*

*0 g saturated fat*

*13 mg cholesterol*

*2 g protein (12% of calories)*

*12 g carbohydrates*

*(71% of calories)*

*0 g fiber*

*34 mg sodium*

**MAKES 34 BISCOTTI**

1½ cups unbleached all-purpose flour

1 teaspoon baking powder

½ teaspoon baking soda

½ teaspoon salt (optional)

¾ cup whole wheat flour

½ cup dried apricots, finely diced (3½ ounces)

¾ cup currants

2 teaspoons orange liqueur

1½ teaspoons apricot nectar or unsweetened apple juice

2 teaspoons ground anise

2 teaspoons grated orange zest

¾ cup light brown sugar

¼ cup slivered almonds (optional)

2 tablespoons canola oil

2 large eggs

4 large egg whites

½ teaspoon ground cinnamon

*Preheat the oven* to 350°F. Spray a baking sheet with vegetable oil spray.

*Sift together* the all-purpose flour, baking powder, baking soda, and the salt, if using, into a large bowl. Whisk in the whole wheat flour.

*In another bowl,* combine the apricots, currants, liqueur, apricot nectar, anise, orange zest, brown sugar, the almonds, if using, and oil. Toss to mix. Beat the eggs and 3 of the egg whites, add to the apricot mixture, and stir until the mixture is moist.

*Make a well* in the center of the dry ingredients and add the apricot mixture. Stir until the dough is well mixed; it will be sticky.

*Turn the dough out* onto a liberally floured work surface and, with floured hands, form into 2 balls. Using your hands, roll each into a cylinder about 12 inches long and 2 inches in diameter. Transfer the cylinders to the baking sheet and flatten slightly.

*In a small bowl*, whisk the remaining egg white. Brush the cylinders with the egg white and sprinkle with the cinnamon.

*Bake* for 20 to 25 minutes, until browned on the top and bottom. (Do not turn off the oven.) Transfer the cylinders to a cutting board and while still warm, slice on the diagonal into ½-inch slices.

*Lay the slices on the baking sheet* and bake for about 10 minutes, until the bottoms are browned. Turn and bake for 10 minutes longer, until lightly browned on both sides. Take care not to overbake, or the biscotti will be too hard.

*Cool the cookies* on a wire rack. Serve immediately, or store in an airtight container.

# Oatmeal Cookies

**T**HESE COOKIES ARE SO POPULAR with our guests that their fame has spread far and wide. A few bakeries in San Francisco reproduce them, and we know that guests from as far away as Japan and Morocco have carried samples home to share with their families. For best results, be sure the eggs are at room temperature.

**PER COOKIE:**

*48 calories*

*1 g total fat (13% of calories)*

*0 g saturated fat*

*12 mg cholesterol*

*2 g protein (15% of calories)*

*9 g carbohydrates*

*(72% of calories)*

*0 g fiber*

*51 mg sodium*

**MAKES 36 COOKIES**

2 large eggs, at room temperature

3 large egg whites, at room temperature

1 teaspoon pure vanilla extract

1 teaspoon ground cinnamon

$^{1}/_{2}$ teaspoon salt

1 teaspoon baking powder

$^{1}/_{2}$ cup granulated sugar

$^{1}/_{4}$ cup light brown sugar

2$^{3}/_{4}$ cups old-fashioned rolled oats

$^{1}/_{3}$ cup whole wheat flour

*Preheat the oven* to 350°F. Spray 2 baking sheets with vegetable oil spray.

*In the bowl of an electric mixer,* combine the eggs, egg whites, vanilla, cinnamon, salt, baking powder, and both sugars. Beat at high speed until doubled in volume and the mixture forms a ribbon when the beaters are raised. Using a rubber spatula, fold in the oats and flour.

*Drop tablespoon-sized mounds of dough* onto the baking sheets, leaving about an inch between each one. Bake for 15 to 20 minutes, until the cookies are lightly browned. Immediately lift the cookies from the baking sheets and cool on wire racks.

## A CLASS IN THE KITCHEN

The Golden Door's kitchen is professional in scale and its equipment is like that found in any small restaurant but it has a homey feel thanks in part to its huge butcher-block island. Here we line up a row of tall director's chairs in the evening once a week and present our popular cooking class.

Over a brief hour and a half, we try to give guests who are relatively new to low-fat cooking an introduction to our techniques, equipment, and recipes. We also try to interest those guests who are accomplished home cooks in their own right.

One tradition is a final tasting of oatmeal cookies hot from the oven. No one, unless they've watched us make them, can believe that these cookies are as low in fat as they are!

The classes and guests' many requests for recipes gave birth to this cookbook. We sincerely hope that every guest, every week, can take as much of the Door home with them as possible; what better way than a new knowledge of healthful cooking?

# Orange Sunburst Cookies

THESE COOKIES ARE THE CREATION OF Pat Henry, our hostess at the Golden Door. Pat's hobby is baking, as her numerous prizes from Pillsbury baking contests attest. These are a real treat, with a noticeable touch of sunny orange. We serve these with a tiny scoop of sorbet and fresh fruit.

PER COOKIE:

*46 calories*

*2 g total fat (30% of calories)*

*0 g saturated fat*

*7 mg cholesterol*

*1 g protein (10% of calories)*

*7 g carbohydrates*

*(60% of calories)*

*0 g fiber*

*33 mg sodium*

**MAKES 32 COOKIES**

NOTE: *Put the bran cereal between two sheets of waxed paper and crush it with a rolling pin. Or, put the cereal in a self-sealing plastic bag, smooth it out on the countertop, and crush the cereal with a rolling pin.*

¾ cup unbleached all-purpose flour

1 teaspoon baking powder

¼ teaspoon baking soda

½ cup whole wheat flour

½ cup crushed bran cereal (see Note)

⅛ teaspoon freshly grated nutmeg

1 large egg

1 large egg white

½ cup light brown sugar

3 tablespoons canola oil

3 tablespoons nonfat plain yogurt

3 tablespoons frozen orange juice concentrate, thawed

1 tablespoon finely chopped orange zest

*Preheat the oven* to 350°F. Spray 2 baking sheets with vegetable oil spray.

*Sift together* the all-purpose flour, baking powder, and baking soda into a large bowl. Add the whole wheat flour, bran cereal, and nutmeg and whisk just to mix.

*In the bowl of an electric mixer,* combine the egg, egg white, brown sugar, oil, yogurt, orange juice concentrate, and zest. Beat at medium-high speed until smooth and creamy. Using a rubber spatula, fold in the dry ingredients.

*Drop tablespoon-sized mounds of dough* onto the baking sheets, leaving about an inch between each one. Bake for 10 to 12 minutes, until the cookies are lightly browned. Immediately lift the cookies from the baking sheets and cool on wire racks.

# Gingersnap Cookies

**M**OST GINGERSNAP COOKIES HAVE FAR MORE SUGAR and fat than mine do, but these are still marvelous cookies and a great favorite with our guests. Take care not to bake them too long, or the spices might taste bitter.

1½ cups plus 2 tablespoons unbleached all-purpose flour

½ teaspoon baking soda

1 teaspoon ground cinnamon

1 teaspoon ground ginger

¼ teaspoon ground cloves

½ cup whole wheat flour

¼ cup light brown sugar

¼ cup canola oil

¼ cup dark molasses

2 large egg whites

½ teaspoon salt (optional)

*Preheat the oven* to 350°F. Spray 2 baking sheets with vegetable oil spray.

*Sift together* the all-purpose flour, the baking soda, cinnamon, ginger, and cloves into a large bowl. Add the whole wheat flour and whisk just to mix.

*In the bowl of an electric mixer,* combine the brown sugar, oil, molasses, egg whites, and the salt, if using. Beat at medium-high speed until smooth and creamy. Using a rubber spatula, fold in the dry ingredients; the dough will be stiff.

*Roll small pieces of the dough* between floured palms to form 1-inch-diameter balls. Place the balls about 4 inches apart on the baking sheets. (You may have to make these in two batches.) Flatten each ball with a fork to make a crisscross pattern. Bake for 10 to 12 minutes, until the cookies are lightly browned. Immediately lift the cookies from the baking sheets and cool on wire racks.

# Beverages

UPON HEARING THAT I WAS WORKING ON A BOOK, guests inevitably asked if I was planning to include our famous Potassium Broth—the hot vegetable drink that we serve mid-morning by the pool. I wouldn't dream of omitting such a Golden Door classic! I have also included fruit smoothies, which our guests enjoy in the late afternoon, and a few other favorites.

# Original Golden Door Potassium Broth

PER SERVING:

*19 calories*

*0 g total fat (12% of calories)*

*0 g saturated fat*

*0 mg cholesterol*

*1 g protein (14% of calories)*

*4 g carbohydrates*

*(74% of calories)*

*0 g fiber*

*7 mg sodium*

**MAKES 12 (4¹/₂-OUNCE) SERVINGS**

I CONSIDERED GIVING THIS GOLDEN DOOR FAVORITE a name more enticing than the work-a-day one we have always used. But Potassium Broth is how our guests know this warm, reviving beverage, and so it remains. Potassium, available in fruits and vegetables, is an important mineral that needs replenishing after energetic workouts, when much is lost (as much as 500 to 600 milligrams after two or three hours of strenuous exercise). This is why we serve this mid-morning by the pool after our guests have hiked, weight-trained, and participated in aerobics classes. They need it! And they love it.

Even if you haven't worked out for several hours, the broth is a great energy boost as well as a source of potassium. I suggest making it with the left-over vegetables in your refrigerator—this way nothing goes to waste. At the Door, we serve the broth hot, with extra red pepper flakes for those guests who like to sprinkle them on top.

12 to 14 plum tomatoes, quartered (2 pounds) or one 28-ounce can crushed plum tomatoes (see Note)

4 cups chopped vegetable trimmings, such as celery ribs and leaves, onions, carrots, cabbage, bell peppers, and parsley stems

2 cloves garlic, crushed

1 teaspoon dried basil or 1 tablespoon chopped fresh basil leaves

1 teaspoon red pepper flakes (optional)

*NOTE: While we make this with fresh tomatoes whenever possible, you can, in a pinch, substitute one 46-ounce can of low-sodium tomato juice or V-8 Juice.*

*In a stockpot* or large saucepan, combine the tomatoes, vegetable trimmings, basil, pepper flakes, if using, and 10 cups of water and bring to a boil over high heat. Reduce the heat and simmer, uncovered, for about 45 minutes until the flavors blend.

*Strain the broth* through a sieve, gently pressing on the solids to extract as much flavor as possible. Discard the solids. Serve hot.

## THE FAMOUS POTASSIUM BROTH BREAK

By 9 A.M. the Golden Door's fitness day has begun in earnest. Depending on a guest's individual schedule, she may be involved in a weight training class, a circuit training session, or aerobics. Within an hour or two, she will definitely be hungry.

We counter this hunger with a healthful snack break at 11 A.M. We offer the guests, as they gather in the Wisteria Lounge and on the decks around the swimming pool, baskets of fresh fruits and vegetables picked that morning in our organic orchards and gardens. Often guests are surprised at how good a fresh strawberry followed by a spear of asparagus can taste! This intermingling of fruits and vegetables—if they're perfectly ripe and fresh—is wonderful. When doing this at home, be sure to cut the vegetables just before serving and squeeze lemon or lime juice over them. This gives them a piquant edge, assuring that your taste buds won't be a bit bored.

We also bring out several pitchers of Potassium Broth—a slightly spicy vegetable broth kept simmering on our stove throughout the day. A small raku cup of broth, along with the fruit and veggies, is the perfect pick-me-up.

# Relaxing Chamomile Drink

PER SERVING:

12 calories

0 g total fat (12% of calories)

0 g saturated fat

0 mg cholesterol

0 g protein (10% of calories)

2 g carbohydrates

(77% of calories)

0 g fiber

7 mg sodium

**MAKES 4 SERVINGS**

**T**HIS HOT BREW IS MADE WITH CHAMOMILE tea and so is especially soothing. Some of our guests drink this all day long.

| | |
|---|---|
| 2½ cups water | 1 clove |
| 1½ cups unsweetened unfiltered apple juice | One ¼-inch slice fresh ginger, about 1 inch wide |
| 2 tea bags chamomile tea | ½ orange, thinly sliced |
| 1 small cinnamon stick | |

*In a small saucepan,* combine the water and juice and bring to a simmer over medium-high heat. Add the tea bags, cinnamon, clove, and ginger and simmer gently for about 10 minutes.

*Strain into a teapot* and serve immediately garnished with orange slices.

# Energizer

PER SERVING:

160 calories

2 g total fat (11% of calories)

1 g saturated fat

5 mg cholesterol

6 g protein (16% of calories)

29 g carbohydrates

(73% of calories)

0 g fiber

62 mg sodium

**MAKES 2 SERVINGS**

NOTE: *You can substitute nonfat yogurt for the low-fat.*

**A** CREAMY-SMOOTH BLENDER DRINK, this one is specifically designed to perk you up at any time of day.

| | |
|---|---|
| ¾ cup fresh orange juice | 4 to 5 pitted dates, cut into pieces |
| ¾ cup low-fat plain yogurt | 1 tablespoon wheat germ |
| 1 banana (3½ ounces) | |

*In a blender,* combine the orange juice, yogurt, banana, dates, and wheat germ and process until smooth. Serve immediately.

## LEMONADE AND ICED HERBAL TEA

Our guests drink fluids all day long. Pure, fresh water is most important, but we serve cold lemonade and iced tea with lunch, which is served by the pool, and also always have them available in the Wisteria Lounge. The combination of the California sun and plenty of exercise prompts guests to quench their thirst often, and we find these beverages are in great demand.

We make lemonade without sugar. I have not supplied a recipe because it's a simple formula of one part fresh lemon juice to eight parts water. Add ice and enjoy!

Iced tea at the Door is made with herbal tea. Guests particularly like the berry-flavored teas, such as raspberry, currant, and blackberry. Again, the ratio is eight to one: a cup of brewed tea to eight cups of cold water, plus ice. Both these drinks are easy to make at home and keep in the refrigerator for pleasant drinking any time. And because they contain neither caffeine nor sugar, they are really nothing more than flavored water—and therefore nothing but good for you.

When serving these, treat yourself by using tall, pretty glasses and then garnish each drink with a slice of lemon, lime, or orange, a sprig of mint, or even a fanned strawberry or a few fresh raspberries. As with food, paying attention to how the beverage is served makes a difference.

# Banana-Strawberry Smoothie

PER SERVING:

*131 calories*

*1 g total fat (4% of calories)*

*0 g saturated fat*

*2 mg cholesterol*

*7 g protein (22% of calories)*

*24 g carbohydrates*

*(73% of calories)*

*1 g fiber*

*88 mg sodium*

**MAKES 4 SERVINGS**

**L**ET YOUR IMAGINATION AND TASTE BUDS GUIDE YOU to vary the fruit in this smoothie. For example, raspberries or peaches would be delicious in place of the strawberries.

| | |
|---|---|
| 1½ cups hulled strawberries (7½ ounces) | 2 cups nonfat plain yogurt |
| 2 bananas (7 ounces) | |

*In a blender,* combine the strawberries, bananas, and yogurt and process until smooth. Serve immediately.

# Almond Milk

PER SERVING:

*99 calories*

*4 g total fat (38% of calories)*

*1 g saturated fat*

*0 mg cholesterol*

*2 g protein (8% of calories)*

*13 g carbohydrates*

*(54% of calories)*

*0 g fiber*

*1 mg sodium*

**MAKES 2 SERVINGS**

**T**HIS WAS AN INTEGRAL AND POPULAR PART of the liquid diet we served back in the 1970s. Although we no longer advocate liquid diets, we appreciate the gentle soothing properties of almond milk, as well as its lovely flavor. In Europe, it's often used as a replacement for cow's milk, particularly for babies with lactose intolerance.

| | |
|---|---|
| ½ ounce blanched almonds (about 12 almonds) | ¼ teaspoon pure vanilla extract |
| 1 banana (3½ ounces) | 2 pinches freshly grated nutmeg |
| ¾ cup water | |

*In a blender,* combine the almonds, banana, water, vanilla, and nutmeg with 2 ice cubes. Process until smooth and serve immediately.

## WATER, WATER!

How much water should you drink? The answer is simple: as much as you can! Most nutritionists, exercise physiologists, and doctors recommend a minimum of eight glasses a day. This is because, even without strenuous exercise, the body needs to replenish itself with several quarts of water every day. When we exercise, we need even more. The body extracts water from foods such as vegetables and fruit and from juices, herb teas, and milk. However, caffeinated beverages such as coffee, tea, and colas and alcoholic drinks are not efficient sources of water, because they act as diuretics.

At the Golden Door, we make sure water is available at all times. A carafe of fresh filtered water is found in every bedroom, and water coolers are located near the doorways of our gym and exercise rooms. Our guests readily admit that having water so accessible makes it easy to consume enough, but once they go home, some have to make an effort to keep it up.

Do not wait to be thirsty to drink water. We suggest drinking an eight-ounce glass before every meal, which automatically ensures three glasses a day. Keep a bottle of water in the refrigerator or on your desk for frequent sipping. Carry water with you when you travel in the car, ride your bike, take a walk, or visit the gym. Water refreshes and revives, increases alertness, and diminishes fatigue.

If the tap water in your town is pure and tastes good, drink it. However, if you don't like the taste or have any questions as to its purity, buy bottled water or sign on with a company that provides spring water for home or office coolers. Bottled water can be still or carbonated, flavored or not. (Be wary of the sodium content in some brands of seltzer.) You don't have to buy the most expensive brand— drink the water that tastes best to you. But drink plenty of it!

# Golden Door Pantry Recipes

ON WEDNESDAY EVENINGS, I give a cooking class for our guests, which is always a very well attended event, I am happy to report. Our guests often are surprised that there are so few bottles, boxes, and jars in the kitchen. Instead, they see baskets of fresh vegetables and fruit on the shelves of our large walk-in cold room, and bowls and sacks of grains and legumes fill the kitchen shelves. I make nearly everything I cook with, beginning with stocks and continuing through sauces and mayonnaises. This way, I am sure the flavors will be clean and fresh, that nothing is overloaded with salt or sugar, or tastes stale or packaged. In this section, I include some of the staple recipes I use again and again in my cooking and with the recipes in this book.

# Vegetable Broth

**W**HEN I STARTED COOKING spa food about twenty years ago, I learned the value of using homemade vegetable broth to prevent foods from drying out during cooking. Of course, it's essential for soups and for cooking grains and legumes too. I also use this in place of chicken or fish stock when I want a milder, fresher flavor and a purely vegetarian meal. I use this frequently in the recipes in this book and although I usually say you can use water instead, I urge you to use vegetable broth whenever possible. It adds good flavor and is extremely easy to make.

**PER CUP:**

*24 calories*

*0 g total fat (6% of calories)*

*0 g saturated fat*

*0 mg cholesterol*

*1 g protein (12% of calories)*

*5 g carbohydrates*

*(83% of calories)*

*1 g fiber*

*417 mg sodium*

**MAKES 6 TO 7 CUPS**

NOTE: *Vegetable broth has no fat and so does not require skimming during cooking, as other stocks do. Freeze the broth in 1-cup containers for easy use.*

1 leek (white and green parts), coarsely chopped (5 ounces)

2 ribs celery, coarsely chopped (6 ounces)

1 carrot, coarsely chopped (4 ounces)

1 small onion, studded with 4 to 5 cloves (3 ounces)

2 to 3 large cabbage leaves (2 ounces)

4 sprigs fresh flat-leaf parsley

2 sprigs fresh basil (optional)

1 sprig fresh thyme

1 bay leaf

1 teaspoon kosher salt, or to taste

1 teaspoon cracked black pepper, or to taste

10 cups water

*In a stockpot,* combine the leek, celery, carrot, onion, cabbage leaves, parsley, the basil, if using, thyme, bay leaf, salt, and pepper. Add the water and bring to a boil over high heat. Reduce the heat and simmer, uncovered, for about 1½ hours, until reduced to 6 to 7 cups.

*Strain the stock* through a fine sieve or a colander lined with a double thickness of cheesecloth. Press gently on the solids, and then discard them. Return the liquid to the pot.

*Plunge the pot into a large bowl* or sinkful of ice cubes and water to cool. Use immediately, or refrigerate in a tightly lidded container for 3 to 4 days or freeze for up to 1 month.

## BROTH POWER

We keep a pot of vegetable broth simmering at the ready. From this, we ladle a tablespoon or two to add moisture to cooking food without adding fat and calories. You can also use low-fat chicken broth or even water for the same purpose, but we prefer the clean, subtle flavor of vegetable broth.

Most of our soups, rice, grains, and sauces are made with this good easy-to-make vegetable broth.

# Chicken Stock

**A**T THE GOLDEN DOOR, we use stock in much of our cooking to moisturize and flavor all sorts of food. We make our own chicken, fish, and vegetable stocks and I suggest you do the same. The flavor and body are always better—and if you make a large amount and freeze it in small quantities, it is as convenient as canned. However, when a recipe calls for chicken stock, you can, if pressed for time, substitute low-sodium canned broth. Be sure to spoon off any fat floating on top of the canned broth.

PER CUP:

*12 calories*

*0 g total fat (5% of calories)*

*0 g saturated fat*

*0 mg cholesterol*

*1 g protein (11% of calories)*

*3 g carbohydrates*

*(84% of calories)*

*0 g fiber*

*9 mg sodium*

**MAKES 7 TO 8 CUPS**

NOTE: *Freeze the stock in 1-cup containers for easy use.*

2½ pounds chicken bones, cut into 3-inch pieces, rinsed

12 cups water

1 onion (4 ounces), dotted with 4 to 5 cloves

1 small carrot, coarsely chopped (2 ounces)

1 small rib celery, coarsely chopped (2 ounces)

2 to 3 sprigs fresh flat-leaf parsley

1 clove garlic, crushed

1 bay leaf

¼ teaspoon black peppercorns

¼ teaspoon dried thyme

Kosher salt to taste (optional)

*In a nonaluminum stockpot,* combine the bones and water and bring to a boil over high heat. Reduce the heat and simmer, uncovered, for 2 hours, skimming the fat from the surface as it rises.

*Add the onion,* carrot, celery, parsley, garlic, bay leaf, peppercorns, thyme, and the salt, if desired. Simmer for 1 to 2 hours longer, until the stock is flavorful and has developed color and body.

*Strain the stock* through a fine sieve or a colander lined with a double thickness of cheesecloth. Press gently on the solids, and then discard them. Return the liquid to the pot.

*Plunge the pot into a large bowl* or sinkful of ice cubes and water to cool. When cool, skim the fat and foam from the surface of the stock. (Fat and impurities affect the flavor of the stock.)

*Use immediately,* or refrigerate in a tightly lidded container for 2 to 3 days or freeze for up to 1 month.

# Fish Stock

**H**OMEMADE FISH STOCK IS EASY and quick to make. There really is no commercially available substitute.

PER CUP:

*33 calories*

*0 g total fat (6% of calories)*

*0 g saturated fat*

*0 mg cholesterol*

*1 g protein (10% of calories)*

*7 g carbohydrates*

*(81% of calories)*

*1 g fiber*

*36 mg sodium*

MAKES 5 TO 6 CUPS

1 to 1¼ pounds nonoily fish bones, including heads and tails, rinsed (see Note)

2 ribs celery, coarsely chopped (6 ounces)

1 carrot, coarsely chopped (4 ounces)

1 leek (white and green parts), coarsely chopped (5 ounces), or 1 onion, chopped (5 ounces)

2 bay leaves

2 sprigs fresh thyme

4 to 5 sprigs fresh flat-leaf parsley

1 cup dry white wine or water

7 cups water

*In a nonaluminum stockpot,* combine the fish bones, celery, carrot, leek, bay leaves, thyme, parsley, and wine. Add the water and bring to a boil over high heat. Reduce the heat and simmer, uncovered, for about 45 minutes, skimming the fat from the surface as it rises. Do not stir the stock.

*Strain the stock* through a fine sieve or a colander lined with a double thickness of cheesecloth. Press gently on the solids, and then discard them. Return the liquid to the pot.

*Plunge the pot into a large bowl* or sinkful of ice cubes and water to cool. When cool, skim the fat and foam from the surface of the stock. (Fat and impurities affect the flavor of the stock.)

*Use immediately,* or refrigerate in a tightly lidded container for 3 to 4 days or freeze for up to 1 month.

*NOTE: Nonoily fish, such as sea bass, sole, and halibut, make a cleaner-tasting and less fatty stock than oily fish such as tuna and salmon.*

# Marinara Sauce

**T**HIS BASIC TOMATO SAUCE HAS NUMEROUS USES. I use it again and again—and so will you.

*NOTE: This can be stored in the refrigerator in a lidded container for up to 4 days.*

1 teaspoon olive oil

3/4 cup diced onions (3 ounces)

4 cloves garlic, minced

2 pounds fresh plum tomatoes, peeled, seeded, and diced, or canned plum tomatoes, seeded and diced

1 cup tomato puree

2 teaspoons minced fresh thyme

1 tablespoon minced fresh oregano

1 bay leaf

1 teaspoon granulated sugar (optional)

1 cup slivered fresh basil

Freshly ground black pepper

*In a skillet,* heat the oil over medium heat. Add the onions and garlic and sauté for about 5 minutes, until the onions soften.

*Add the tomatoes,* tomato puree, thyme, oregano, bay leaf, and the sugar, if desired. Cook, stirring occasionally, for about 45 minutes, until thick. Remove and discard the bay leaf, add the basil, and season to taste with pepper.

# Two-Pepper Coulis

**I** USE THIS OFTEN FOR PRESENTATION, drizzling a little on a plate to provide color, moisture, texture, and flavor.

PER SERVING:

*29 calories*

*1 g total fat (40% of calories)*

*0 g saturated fat*

*0 mg cholesterol*

*1 g protein (7% of calories)*

*4 g carbohydrates*

*(53% of calories)*

*0 g fiber*

*1 mg sodium*

**MAKES 4 SERVINGS**

2 roasted red bell peppers, peeled, seeded, and chopped (see page 99; 8 ounces)

2 teaspoons olive oil

2 pinches cayenne pepper

2 roasted yellow bell peppers, peeled, seeded, and chopped (see page 99; 8 ounces)

*In a blender* or food processor, combine the red peppers, 1 teaspoon of the olive oil, a pinch of cayenne, and 1 tablespoon of water. Process until smooth, adding more water if necessary for a smooth consistency. Transfer to a small bowl and set aside.

*In the clean blender* or food processor, combine the yellow peppers, the remaining 1 teaspoon oil and pinch of cayenne, and 1 tablespoon of water. Process until smooth, adding more water if necessary for a smooth consistency. Transfer to a small bowl.

*Serve the red pepper coulis* separately from the yellow pepper coulis, or serve them side by side.

# Spa Pesto

**T**HERE IS VERY LITTLE FAT in this pesto, but lots of flavor and texture. Use the freshest basil you can find—preferably picked from your own garden.

PER TABLESPOON:

*11 calories*

*0 g total fat (26% of calories)*

*0 g saturated fat*

*0 mg cholesterol*

*1 g protein (28% of calories)*

*1 g carbohydrates*

*(46% of calories)*

*0 g fiber*

*9 mg sodium*

**MAKES ABOUT 1 CUP**

1 tablespoon pine nuts (¼ ounce)

1 teaspoon minced garlic

¾ cup nonfat plain yogurt

¼ teaspoon freshly ground black pepper

¾ cup packed fresh basil leaves

*In a nonstick sauté pan,* cook the pine nuts over medium-high heat for 2 to 3 minutes, until lightly browned; shake the pan to prevent sticking and burning. Transfer to a plate to cool.

*In a blender,* combine the pine nuts, garlic, yogurt, and pepper and blend until smooth. Add the basil and pulse just to break up the leaves. Do not overprocess, or the pesto will look uniformly green. Serve immediately, or cover and refrigerate for up to 3 days. Stir well before serving.

# Salsa Mexicana

**L**IVING SO CLOSE TO MEXICO, I am happily influenced by the cooking of that country. This salsa is easy to make but its secret is impeccably fresh ingredients diced so that its texture is as pleasing as its flavor. For a tasty variation, add a cup of corn, fresh pomegranate seeds, or finely diced papaya. If you prefer less heat, scrape the pulp as well as the seeds from the chili.

4 tomatoes, stemmed and diced (1¼ pounds)

½ cup finely diced red onions (2½ ounces)

1 red serrano chili or jalapeño pepper, seeded and minced (½ ounce)

2 tablespoons coarsely chopped fresh cilantro

½ teaspoon dried oregano

1 tablespoon fresh lime juice

½ teaspoon salt

½ teaspoon freshly ground black pepper

*In a bowl,* combine the tomatoes, onions, chili, cilantro, oregano, lime juice, salt, and pepper. Stir gently to mix, cover, and refrigerate for at least 1 hour. Stir gently and serve.

# Tomatillo Chili Sauce

**T**HIS CHILI SAUCE HAS A USEFUL PLACE in low-fat cooking, especially when paired with simple grilled chicken and seafood, which might need a flavor boost. I also like to serve it with black bean enchiladas or grain enchiladas, as well as with the Rancho La Puerta Whole Wheat Tortilla Lasagne on page 126.

**PER TABLESPOON:**

*15 calories*

*0 g total fat (15% of calories)*

*0 g saturated fat*

*0 mg cholesterol*

*1 g protein (15% of calories)*

*3 g carbohydrates*

*(70% of calories)*

*0 g fiber*

*5 mg sodium*

**MAKES ABOUT 2 CUPS**

*Note: The sauce will keep in the refrigerator for 1 week.*

1 teaspoon canola oil

½ cup diced onions (2 ounces)

2 teaspoons minced garlic

1 carrot, diced (4 ounces)

1 serrano chili, seeded and minced

1½ pounds tomatillos, husked, rinsed, shelled, and chopped

8 ounces roasted Anaheim chilies (page 99) or canned Anaheim chilies

1 tablespoon ground cumin

1 teaspoon kosher salt (optional)

½ cup Vegetable Broth (page 280) or water

2 tablespoons chopped fresh cilantro

*In a saucepan,* heat the oil over medium heat. Add the onions, garlic, carrot, and serrano chili and sauté for 4 to 5 minutes, until the vegetables begin to soften.

*Add the tomatillos,* Anaheim chilies, cumin, and the salt, if using, and stir to mix. Cover and simmer for about 15 minutes, until the tomatillos begin to soften. Add the broth and simmer, uncovered, for 5 to 10 minutes longer, until the tomatillos are very soft.

*Transfer the mixture* to a blender or food processor, add the cilantro, and process just until mixed. Take care not to crush the tomatillo seeds. Serve immediately, or cover and refrigerate until ready to serve.

# Silken Tofu Mayonnaise

**S**OFT, OR SILKEN TOFU, is the base for this flavorful mayonnaise substitute.

PER TABLESPOON:

*11 calories*

*1 g total fat (48% of calories)*

*0 g saturated fat*

*0 mg cholesterol*

*1 g protein (36% of calories)*

*0 g carbohydrates*

*(16% of calories)*

*0 g fiber*

*15 mg sodium*

**MAKES ABOUT
1²/₃ CUPS**

*Note: The mayonnaise will keep in the refrigerator for 1 week.*

1 tablespoon minced shallots

1 tablespoon Dijon mustard

2¹/₂ tablespoons tarragon vinegar or cider vinegar

10 ounces soft tofu

1 teaspoon freshly ground black pepper

¹/₄ cup water

*In a blender* or food processor, combine the shallots, mustard, vinegar, tofu, pepper, and water. Process for 2 to 3 minutes, until smooth. Transfer to a small bowl, cover, and refrigerate until ready to use.

## Herbed Silken Tofu Mayonnaise

Add ¹/₃ cup coarsely chopped fresh flat-leaf parsley, ¹/₄ cup coarsely chopped scallions, ¹/₄ cup coarsely chopped fresh basil, and 1 tablespoon chopped fresh tarragon. Stir well.

# Roasted Garlic

**A**LTHOUGH THIS GARLIC IS NOT ACTUALLY ROASTED, it tastes as though it is—and it's faster and easier to prepare than traditional roasted garlic.

2 teaspoons olive oil

2 bulbs garlic, cloves separated and peeled

¾ cup Vegetable Broth (page 280)

*In a small nonstick sauté pan,* heat the oil and sauté the garlic cloves for 2 to 3 minutes, until golden brown. Add half of the broth and simmer until it has evaporated and the garlic begins to stick to the pan.

*Add the remaining broth* and cook for about 5 minutes longer, until the garlic is soft. Cool, then mash with a fork. Cover and refrigerate for up to 3 days until ready to use.

# Nonfat Yogurt Cheese

**T**HIS IS A TEMPTING and satisfying replacement for cream cheese for bagels.

1 quart nonfat plain yogurt

¼ cup confectioners' sugar

2 teaspoons pure vanilla extract

*In a bowl,* combine the yogurt, sugar, and vanilla and whisk until smooth and the yogurt has thinned.

*Line a colander* or strainer with a double thickness of cheesecloth and set the colander over a bowl. Spoon the yogurt mixture into the colander and refrigerate for at least 8 hours, or overnight, so that the yogurt drains.

*Spoon the thickened yogurt mixture* into a bowl, cover, and refrigerate until ready to use.

# Fruit Butter

WHEN I MAKE FRUIT BUTTER, I use the fruit we have on hand at the end of the day. You can use pears or plums instead of the apples. Figs and very ripe bananas work nicely too. Use this on bagels or any hearty bread.

PER ¼ CUP:

*9 calories*

*0 g total fat (5% of calories)*

*0 g saturated fat*

*0 mg cholesterol*

*0 g protein (3% of calories)*

*2 g carbohydrates*

*(92% of calories)*

*0 g fiber*

*0 mg sodium*

MAKES ABOUT
2½ CUPS

NOTE: *Dried apricots are easier to find and often have more flavor than fresh, but if you prefer, use 3 fresh apricots (6 ounces) in place of the dried. You can replace the apple juice with peach or apricot nectar.*

3 apples, such as Jonathan Gold or Red or Golden Delicious, peeled, cored, and cut into wedges (12 ounces)

3 ounces berries, such as strawberries (if using strawberries, hull and halve them), blueberries, or raspberries (½ cup)

1 ounce dried apricots (see Note; ¼ cup)

⅔ cup apple juice (see Note)

2 tablespoons brown sugar (optional)

⅓ cup water

1 teaspoon fresh lemon juice

*In a nonreactive saucepan,* combine the apples, berries, apricots, apple juice, the brown sugar, if using, and water. Cover and cook over medium heat for about 15 minutes, or until the apples are fork-tender. Remove from the heat and set aside to cool for 15 to 20 minutes.

*Using a slotted spoon,* transfer the fruit to a food processor and process to a coarse consistency. Transfer to a bowl and stir in the lemon juice. This keeps in the refrigerator for up to 3 days.

# Index